Presidents from
Theodore Roosevelt through Coolidge,
1901–1929

PRESIDENTS FROM THEODORE ROOSEVELT THROUGH COOLIDGE, 1901–1929

Debating the Issues in Pro and Con Primary Documents

FRANCINE SANDERS ROMERO

The President's Position: Debating the Issues
Mark Byrnes, Series Editor

GREENWOOD PRESS
Westport, Connecticut • London

Library of Congress Cataloging-in-Publication Data

Presidents from Theodore Roosevelt through Coolidge, 1901–1929 : debating the issues in pro and con primary documents / [compiled by] Francine Sanders Romero.
    p. cm.—(The president's position—debating the issues)
    Includes bibliographical references and index.
    ISBN 0–313–31388–1 (alk. paper)
    1. Presidents—United States—History—20th century—Sources. 2. United States—Politics and government—1901–1953—Sources. 3. Roosevelt, Theodore, 1858–1919—Political and social views. 4. Taft, William H. (William Howard), 1857–1930—Political and social views. 5. Harding, Warren G. (Warren Gamaliel), 1865–1923—Political and social views. 6. Wilson, Woodrow, 1856–1924—Political and social views.
7. Coolidge, Calvin, 1872–1933—Political and social views. I. Romero, Francine Sanders. II. Series.
    E176.1.P9225   2002
    320′.6′097309041—dc21   2001023339

British Library Cataloguing in Publication Data is available.

Library of Congress Catalog Card Number: 2001023339
ISBN: 0–313–31388–1

First published in 2002

Greenwood Press, 88 Post Road West, Westport, CT 06881
An imprint of Greenwood Publishing Group, Inc.
www.greenwood.com

Printed in the United States of America

The paper used in this book complies with the
Permanent Paper Standard issued by the National
Information Standards Organization (Z39.48–1984).

10 9 8 7 6 5 4 3 2 1

Copyright Acknowledgment

The author and publisher are grateful to the following for granting permission to reprint from their materials:

R. G. Tugwell, "Reflections on Farm Relief," reprinted by permission of *Political Science Quarterly*, 43 (1928): 481–497.

To TR and FSR—
For inspiring the value of good work

CONTENTS

SERIES FOREWORD

When he was running for president in 1932, Franklin D. Roosevelt declared that America needed "bold, persistent experimentation" in its public policy. "It is common sense to take a method and try it," FDR said. "If it fails, admit it frankly and try another. But above all, try something." At President Roosevelt's instigation, the nation did indeed take a number of steps to combat the Great Depression. In the process, the president emerged as the clear leader of American public policy. Most scholars see FDR's administration as the birth of the "modern presidency," in which the president dominates both domestic and foreign policy.

Even before FDR, however, presidents played a vital role in the making of public policy. Policy changes advocated by the presidents—often great changes—have always influenced the course of events, and have always sparked debate from the presidents' opponents. The outcomes of this process have had tremendous effects on the lives of Americans. The President's Position: Debating the Issues examines the stands the presidents have taken on the major political, social, and economic issues of their times as well as the stands taken by their opponents. The series combines description and analysis of those issues with excerpts from primary documents that illustrate the position of the presidents and their opponents. The result is an informative, accessible, and comprehensive look at the crucial connection between presidents and policy. These volumes will assist students doing historical research, preparing for debates, or fulfilling critical thinking assignments. The general reader interested in American history and politics will also find the series interesting and helpful.

Several important themes about the president's role in policy making emerge from the series. First, and perhaps most important, is how greatly the president's involvement in policy has expanded over the years. This has happened because the range of areas in which the national government acts has grown dramatically and because modern presidents—unlike most of their predecessors—see taking the lead in policy making as part of their job. Second, certain issues have confronted most presidents over history; tax and tariff policy, for example, was important for both George Washington and Bill Clinton, and for most of the presidents in between. Third, the emergence of the United States as a world power around the beginning of the twentieth century made foreign policy issues more numerous and more pressing. Finally, in the American system, presidents cannot form policy through decrees; they must persuade members of Congress, other politicians, and the general public to follow their lead. This key fact makes the policy debates between presidents and their opponents vitally important.

This series comprises nine volumes, organized chronologically, each of which covers the presidents who governed during that particular time period. Volume one looks at the presidents from George Washington through James Monroe; volume two, John Quincy Adams through James K. Polk; volume three, Zachary Taylor through Ulysses Grant; volume four, Rutherford B. Hayes through William McKinley; volume five, Theodore Roosevelt through Calvin Coolidge; volume six, Herbert Hoover through Harry Truman; volume seven, Dwight Eisenhower through Lyndon Johnson; volume eight, Richard Nixon through Jimmy Carter; and volume nine, Ronald Reagan through Bill Clinton. Each president from Washington through Clinton is covered, although the number of issues discussed under each president varies according to how long they served in office and how actively they pursued policy goals. Volumes six through nine—which cover the modern presidency—examine three presidencies each, while the earlier volumes include between five and seven presidencies each.

Every volume begins with a general introduction to the period it covers, providing an overview of the presidents who served and the issues they confronted. The section on each president opens with a detailed overview of the president's position on the relevant issues he confronted and the initiatives he took, and closes with a list of suggested readings. Up to fifteen issues are covered per presidency. The discussion of each issue features an introduction, the positions taken by the president and his opponents, how the issue was resolved, and the long-term effects of the issue. This is followed by excerpts from two primary documents, one representing the president's position and the other representing his opponents' position. Also included in each volume is a timeline of significant events of the era and a general bibliography of sources for students and others interested in further research.

As the most prominent individual in American politics, the president receives enormous attention from the media and the public. The statements, actions, travels, and even the personal lives of presidents are constantly scrutinized. Yet it is the presidents' work on public policy that most directly affects American citizens—a fact that is sometimes overlooked. This series is presented, in part, as a reminder of the importance of the president's position.

Mark Byrnes

PREFACE

Trying to set a cohesive overview of the first quarter of the twentieth century on paper is like trying to get hold of a cat who does not want to be gotten hold of. Just when you think you have a handle on it, it pops out in some new and unexpected direction. But, in the end, it is this very complexity that is vital to understanding the period. This is not a far-off era full of one-dimensional people and issues irrelevant to our modern selves, as Americans too often view history. It is a vibrant and complicated time in which engaging characters grappled with much the same problems that confront us today. It is these qualities that are stressed here.

In the foreword to his autobiography, Theodore Roosevelt states (in regard to his vision for this nation), "what is most important is to insist on the vital need of combining certain sets of qualities, which separately are common enough, and, alas, useless enough."[1] I have borrowed his philosophy in writing this book, utilizing a balanced blend of materials and approaches to best produce a portrait of this period.

The choice of issues in particular was driven by this mix of strategies. In general, biographies of the presidents covered suggest key issues that of necessity are included. But I have also sought out somewhat lesser known controversies that provide insight into presidential character and philosophy, or the nature of the times. Certainly, some of the more well-known facets of these presidents clearly emerge—Roosevelt's trust-busting proclivities, William Howard Taft's overall conservatism, Woodrow Wilson's missionary-like zeal in foreign policy, and Warren G. Harding's and Calvin Coolidge's attempts to turn back the clock to more conservative times. But, I have also taken the opportunity to research and present some of the less publicized, but still significant, positions and qualities of each president. For example, I have tried to illustrate Roosevelt's subtle (and sometimes inconsistent) but deeply felt sympathy for the human condition, Taft's genuine respect for certain progressive reforms, Wilson's surprising reticence on policies he is often credited with achieving, Harding's unprecedented push for improvements in racial relations, and Coolidge's largely unsung level of energy in pushing economic reform. Additionally, where possible, I attempted to follow the path of certain issues throughout the period. Thus, an evolving (albeit frequently erratic) narrative of issues such as tariffs, taxes, trust regulation, and minority rights can be tracked over time and, sometimes, within a single presidency.

In regard to documents and general background material, I also sought out a variety of sources. In addition to the classic texts on these presidents and this period of history, contemporaneous works were utilized. The *Congressional Record*, the *New York Times*, and the massive collected letters and speeches of Roosevelt and Wilson were indispensable, as were autobiographies (Roosevelt's is particularly readable), and Mark Sullivan's illustrative chronicle of social history, *Our Times*. I also received valuable original source material on immigration, conscription, and veterans issues from a box of papers belonging to my grandfather, Francesco Saverio Riccio, that serendipitously came into my possession during the writing of this book.

Sometimes the choice of supporting document for an issue was obvious, but in other cases the search for the best one was difficult. In several cases, the so-called classic statement from a president or opponent was less educational than a more obscure one. Additionally, I have found that relying solely on official proclamations leaves out a good deal of the personal insights that are more readily apparent in letters, statements to newspapers, and autobiographical reminiscences. Thus, examples of a variety of presidential communications are included.

For some issues, while the president's position was clear from the historical record it was difficult to find evidence of this in his own words. Even in these years, presidents knew not to commit unpopular positions to paper. For example, Taft's reputed indifference to the natural resource conservation effort was only very subtly hinted at in his speeches and letters. Alternatively, another tendency was for presidential statements to quite clearly suggest a position that the president never really ascribed to, as with Wilson and the question of federal regulation of child labor.

I have also tried to seek out a mix of oppositional statements from Congress, the Supreme Court, editorials, and private citizens. As a result of institutional checks and balances, as well as the electoral system, U.S. presidents find that no venue is consistently supportive of their positions. Additionally, for some issues included here, presidents are caught in the middle and thus attacked from two sides and, where warranted, examples of this are included.

In producing this work, I have aspired to offer not a dry record of history, but a glimpse into the age itself, highlighting the vibrancy and complexity of these years and these presidents. Additionally, I have highlighted the many links to modern Americans.

I would like to thank Series Editor Mark Byrnes and Executive Editor Barbara Rader of Greenwood Press for the opportunity they granted me to write this book, as well as their continued assistance. Thanks also to my husband, who in addition to providing assistance on military issues, put up with over a year's worth of dinner table conversation on progressive reforms and the Coolidge tax plan.

NOTE

1. Theodore Roosevelt, *An Autobiography* (New York: Scribner's, 1913), vii.

TIMELINE

1901

September 6	President William McKinley shot by Leon Czolgosz
September 14	President McKinley dies; Theodore Roosevelt takes presidential oath of office in Buffalo, New York
October 16	Booker T. Washington dines at White House
December 16	Hay-Pauncefote Treaty approved by Senate

1902

March 10	Northern Securities Corporation suit filed
June 2	Anthracite coal strike begins
October 3	Roosevelt convenes coal strike conference
October 21	Coal miners return to work

1903

November 3	Panama liberated from Colombia

1904

February 23	Senate approves treaty authorizing construction of Panama Canal
March 14	Supreme Court finds Northern Securities Corporation in violation of Sherman Antitrust Act
November 8	Roosevelt reelected president over Democrat Alton B. Parker

1905

December 5	Roosevelt proposes several major reforms to Congress

1906

June 8	Antiquities Act passed by Congress
June 29	Hepburn Act passed by Congress
June 30	Pure Food and Drug Act passed by Congress
August 14	Brownsville, Texas raid occurs
August 27	Roosevelt directs public printer in use of simplified spelling

1907

March 2	Roosevelt proclaims twenty-one new forest reserves just before signing bill banning such actions
October 22	Currency panic of 1907 begins
November 4	Roosevelt approves U.S. Steel Corporation's acquisition of Tennessee Coal, Iron, and Railroad Company
December 16	World cruise by American battleships commences

1908

May 13	Roosevelt convenes Conference on the Conservation of Natural Resources
November 3	William Howard Taft elected president over Democrat William Jennings Bryan

1909

February 22	World cruise by American battleships ends
March 3	Taft inaugurated
March 4	Richard Ballinger appointed secretary of interior
March 23	Roosevelt leaves for African safari and European tour

1910

January 7	Chief Forester Gifford Pinchot fired by Taft
June 18	Roosevelt returns to United States
June 20	Ballinger cleared of fraud charges
November 4	Woodrow Wilson elected governor of New Jersey; Democrats win majority in House of Representatives

1911

March 23	Roosevelt makes "I took Panama" speech at University of California, Berkeley
June 15	Taft vetoes first Arizona and New Mexico statehood bill
October 26	U.S. Steel Corporation suit filed
December 5	Taft sends antitrust message to Congress

1912

February 24	Roosevelt announces he will run if offered Republican presidential nomination
June 22	Republican Party nominates President Taft

July 2	Democratic Party nominates Woodrow Wilson
August 7	National Progressive (Bull-Moose) Party nominates Roosevelt
October 14	Roosevelt shot by John Schrank in Milwaukee
November 5	Wilson elected president; Democrats take control of Congress, holding majority in House and winning majority in Senate

1913

February 3	Income Tax Amendment (Sixteenth Amendment) ratified
February 18	General Victoriano Huerta ascends to Mexican presidency
March 4	Wilson inaugurated
Spring/Summer	Segregation commences in federal agencies
October 3	Underwood Tariff bill signed into law by Wilson
December 23	Federal Reserve bill signed into law by Wilson

1914

April 9	American sailors briefly detained in Tampico, Mexico
April 19	Wilson asks Congress for authority to utilize armed forces in Mexico
April 21	Mexican port of Vera Cruz seized by U.S. Navy
June 28	Archduke Franz Ferdinand and his wife assassinated in Sarajevo, Bosnia
July 15	Huerta resigns Mexican presidency
August 6	First Lady Ellen Wilson dies
August 15	Panama Canal opens to commerce
August 19	Wilson makes neutrality statement to U.S. Senate
November 12	Black delegates visit Wilson to discuss segregation in federal agencies

1915

January 28	Wilson vetoes literacy test requirement for immigrants
March 4	Wilson signs Furuseth (Seaman's) bill into law
May 7	*Lusitania* sunk by German submarine, killing 128 Americans
June 8	William Jennings Bryan resigns as secretary of state, replaced by Robert Lansing
August 10	Civilian training camp opens in Plattsburg, Pennsylvania
October 6	Wilson announces his engagement to Edith Bolling Galt
October 15	American bankers loan $500 million to England and France
October 19	United States recognizes Venustiano Carranza as president of Mexico
November 4	Wilson requests increased military funding from Congress
December 18	Wilson marries Galt

1916

February 10	Lindley M. Garrison resigns as secretary of war, replaced by Newton D. Baker
March 9	Francisco "Pancho" Villa's forces attack Columbus, New Mexico, killing nine civilians and eight U.S. Cavalry Troopers
June 21	American and Mexican forces battle in Carrizal, Mexico
September 1	Wilson signs Own-Keating Child Labor bill into law
September 3	Wilson signs Adamson Act into law
November 7	Wilson reelected over Republican Charles Evans Hughes

1917

January 16	Zimmerman note sent
January 31	Germany informs United States of unlimited submarine warfare
February 5	General John Pershing's troops are withdrawn from Mexico; Congress overrides Wilson's second immigration literacy test veto
April 2	Wilson delivers war message to Congress
April 6	United States declares war on Germany
June 5	National draft registration day
November	First American casualties reported in France

1918

January 8	Wilson outlines Fourteen Points to Congress
April 24	First major engagement of American troops, in Seicheprey, France
May 26	Taft and Roosevelt reconcile during accidental meeting in Chicago
June 3	Supreme Court declares Child Labor Act unconstitutional
October 1	Apex of influenza epidemic; 202 deaths reported on this day
November 5	Republicans win majorities in House and Senate
November 11	Armistice signed
December 14	Wilson arrives in Paris for Versailles Peace Conference

1919

January 6	Roosevelt dies
January 16	Prohibition Amendment (Eighteenth Amendment) ratified
September	Wilson conducts speaking tour in support of League of Nations
September 26	Wilson suffers first attack, outside of Pueblo, Colorado
October 2	Wilson suffers massive stroke
November	Senate debates and rejects League of Nations provision

1920

January 16	Prohibition goes into effect
March 1	Supreme Court declares U.S. Steel Corporation is not in violation of Sherman Antitrust Act
March 19	Senate again rejects League of Nations provision
August 18	Woman Suffrage Amendment (Nineteenth Amendment) ratified
November 2	Warren G. Harding elected president over Democrat James M. Cox

1921

February 22	Congress approves temporary immigration restrictions
March 4	Harding inaugurated
April 20	Senate ratifies compensation treaty with Colombia
June 30	Taft nominated and confirmed as chief justice of the Supreme Court
July 2	Harding signs resolution of peace with Germany and Austria
Summer	National wave of violence attributed to Ku Klux Klan reported
October 26	Harding gives racial equality speech in Birmingham, Alabama
November 12	Harding convenes Conference on the Limitation of Armament in Washington, D.C.

1922

April	U.S. Senate gives final approval to all Washington Conference treaties
May 8	National Congress of Ku Klux Klan held in Atlanta
September 19	Harding vetoes Soldiers' Adjusted Compensation Act
September 21	Harding signs Fordney-McCumber Tariff bill into law
November 7	Republicans lose seats, but still retain majority in House and Senate

1923

August 2	Harding dies in San Francisco during speaking tour
August 3	Calvin Coolidge administered presidential oath of office by his father at their home in Vermont

1924

February 3	Wilson dies
May 15	Congress passes permanent restrictions on immigration
November 4	Coolidge reelected president over Democrat John W. Davis

1926

February 26   Revenue Act signed into law by Coolidge

1927

January–February   U.S. Marines sent to Nicaragua

February 25   Coolidge vetoes first McNary-Haugen bill

August 2   Coolidge announces he will not seek a second full term

1928

May 23   Coolidge vetoes second McNary-Haugen bill

1929

January 15   Senate ratifies Kellogg-Briand Peace Pact

INTRODUCTION

The first quarter of the twentieth century embodies perhaps the greatest period of transformation in U.S. history. Americans were favored by wondrous inventions such as the airplane, telephone, radio, automobile, and motion pictures. But they were also challenged by significant change in the established order. The rise of business and industry, group demands for rights, the use of frightening new weapons of war, and path-breaking theories that altered the way people thought about the origin of humanity, physics, and human psychology all contributed to a general social, political, and economic tumult in these years quite removed from the relative stability of most earlier eras.

Government at all levels was also forced to respond to this changing world. This book provides an overview of the key issues that confronted five U.S. presidents of these years—Theodore Roosevelt, William Howard Taft, Woodrow Wilson, Warren G. Harding, and Calvin Coolidge. The overall time frame addressed, from 1901 through early 1929, can be broken down into three broad categories—the Progressive Era, the war years, and the postwar "return to normalcy" years. Each is introduced below, with an emphasis on general conditions as well as the key economic, social, and foreign policy issues and controversies.

THE PROGRESSIVE ERA

The early years of the twentieth century, comprised of the presidencies of Roosevelt, Taft, and at least the first half of the Wilson administration, were dominated by the ideals and ideas of the progressive movement. If, in retrospect, there could be said to be a single moment when the

Progressive Era in America began, it might well be the death of President William McKinley from an assassin's bullet in September 1901. The act bestowed the presidency on Vice President Roosevelt, who invigorated the movement just as the movement energized him. And while the era in effect ended when the United States declared war on Germany in April 1917, the effects of the reform movement maintained a political force beyond this narrow time frame. For, despite the strong national backlash of the Harding and Coolidge years against the precepts of the movement, progressivism was distilled into a smaller and less powerful, but still potent, element. Overall, the progressive years stand out as an extraordinarily lively period in American politics, in which a struggle for control was waged between reformers seeking to ameliorate the effects of changing social and economic conditions, and conservatives opposed to the government growth these proposals entailed. Many of the policy accomplishments of this time remain in effect today and, on a more abstract level, the general philosophy of progressivism continues to inform at least some political discourse.

In general, the Progressive Era represents the rise and dominance of the belief that government could and should actively work to improve the lives of Americans. Up to this point, American government had been quite limited, particularly at the federal level. Few of the functions taken for granted today were even imagined throughout the first century or so of U.S. history. Another characteristic was the high degree of partisanship, patronage, and corruption at all levels, but particularly in the party "machine" dominated urban areas. To be sure, these tightly controlled and powerful organizations often provided essential goods to citizens such as jobs, support for widows and orphans, and capital improvements. But these necessities were doled out largely as political favors, and not in a systematic, needs-based manner. Furthermore, decisions tended to be made more in terms of what was good for the party and its leaders than what was good for the people overall. These features of government conflicted disastrously with the social and economic environment of the time by failing to meet the expanding needs of a rapidly changing nation. The economy was evolving from one based on small farms and businesses where citizens (in the best American tradition of individualism) provided for themselves, to one increasingly dominated by big business, characterized by a concomitant loss of self-sufficiency.

Throughout the late nineteenth century, the growing power of business and industry in general, and trusts in particular—that is, economic sectors tightly controlled by a single owner or small consortium—were challenging the ability of Americans to make meaningful choices. Those who earned their livelihood providing particular services or goods now dominated by trusts were finding it difficult to compete, and new entry into these areas was virtually impossible. Consumers purchasing goods and services from the powerful new industries were subject to high prices, low quality, and inconsistent availability. And workers in these industries (including many women and children) suffered long hours, low pay, dangerous working conditions, and the denial of the right to organize into protective unions or collectives. Additionally, given the move away from an economy comprised of self-sufficient units, financial swings had wide-ranging effects. The depression of 1893 was particularly painful, and had the effect of fostering the formation of more monopolies, which businesses turned to as a means to protect profits in the unstable fiscal climate.

The rise of populism in the late nineteenth century, emerging in response to these conditions and reaching its apex with the Democratic presidential nomination of populist William Jennings Bryan in 1896, was an important precursor to the progressive movement. In some ways, the movements were quite distinct. Populism, on the one hand, was an agrarian-based force conceived in the southern and midwestern states. It attracted its leadership and adherents largely from the Democratic Party. Progressivism, on the other hand, established roots mainly in the northeastern urban regions, and drew support mostly from the Republican Party. But the important link between these two movements is a shared origin—a dissatisfaction with an American democracy seemingly distorted by the rise of industry beginning in the latter half of the nineteenth century.

Progressivism, however, offered the more sophisticated and advanced theory of reform. Where populism was driven largely by dissatisfied farmers who wanted government to simply address their grievances, progressivism represented a broader and more expansive push by reformers to shape government into a mechanism that could be utilized as needed to improve national conditions. The idea was inspired by the rise of the social sciences, and an attendant faith in the ability of experts to devise rational and workable solutions to modern challenges.

Beginning in the late nineteenth and early twentieth centuries, progressive reformers such as Henry George, Herbert Croly, and Walter Lippmann (aided by muckraking journalists who offered detailed evidence of political and corporate corruption, dangerous workplace conditions, and urban poverty) began to offer an agenda by which this could be achieved. At the local level, they stressed means to ameliorate party-based corruption and to introduce professionalism and efficiency so that cities might tackle issues such as sanitation, employment, and public welfare more effectively. State-level reforms centered on expanding the franchise and removing corruption from elections, and at least limited regulation of business practices within the states—such as child labor, length of work days, and railroad rates. On the national level, their reforms were most ambitious, focusing on broad regulation of business and industry, and protection for large groups lacking in basic dignities of social, commercial, and political life. For example, they supported active enforcement of antitrust laws, extensive oversight of industry, and federal guarantees of woman suffrage.

Thus, in general, progressivism protested against both the laissez-faire and the overly politicized nature of government, asserting that a larger, more efficient, and professionalized system was needed to govern the newly industrialized and evolving nation. To at least some degree, the three presidents of this era reflect that sentiment. Yet, as will be apparent throughout this book, it is sometimes difficult to pin down *exactly* what policies progressivism stood for, or even who *was* a progressive, especially once the movement began to spread from a core group of reformers to the general public and politicians. While populists had united around well-defined policy goals, progressives did not. In fact, the strength and endurance of progressivism can perhaps be attributed to the fact that it *lacked* a clear agenda and widely accepted leadership. This meant it could be all things to all people. For example, when Taft, Roosevelt, and Wilson all competed in the 1912 presidential election, they each referred to themselves as a progressive, despite offering distinctly different platforms. But while progressivism could be vague and malleable, it was most articulate (and united adherents to the greatest degree) in its advocacy of the regulation of big business.

Economic Policies

The progressive movement offered a basically cohesive vision in the economic sector (as opposed to its lack of consistency on social and foreign policy issues) in which, to a far greater degree than ever before, government would attempt to ameliorate adverse conditions. Again, there is a populist history to this initiative, but where populists pushed largely for state responses designed to help farmers in particular, progressives offered the more expansive approach by focusing on broad federal solutions to help all affected citizens.

The overall economic accomplishment of the administrations of Roosevelt, Taft, and Wilson was to establish this more activist role for government. The effort was centered mainly on the federal oversight and regulation of trusts. Because of the extent of problems, the only real debate here was over how this goal should be accomplished, although there was some disagreement over whether trusts needed to be abolished outright or just closely monitored. Roosevelt utilized the Sherman Antitrust Act of 1896, which outlawed certain monopolies, but believed that the best way to oversee business and industry was through executive branch oversight agencies and commissions (e.g., the Interstate Commerce Commission and the Bureau of Corporations) and more detailed legislation. He sought to make the antitrust rules more clear, thus avoiding the effects of monopoly *before* the fact, and avoiding long and drawn out courtroom battles. Taft, on the other hand, pursued these matters almost entirely through the courts. In the Wilson administration, the strategy shifted in the direction Roosevelt had advocated, through the more detailed (although full of loopholes) Clayton Antitrust Act and the Federal Trade Commission, both of which functioned to more clearly define what *was* an illegal monopoly. Wilson also helped to push through passage of the currency regulating Federal Reserve Board in order to provide a stable lending and credit environment for business.

An economic issue of secondary importance in the Progressive Era was the question of tariffs. Most progressives fought them as an unnecessary boon to powerful industries (although some supported them for agricultural goods). But these mechanisms, which worked to protect domestic products by levying taxes on imported goods, were politically popular and difficult to dislodge. Roosevelt did not even tackle the issue as president, while Taft tried but failed to achieve any abatements. Wilson was able to push through dramatic reductions, but the impact was interrupted by a wartime disruption of imports and some tariff reinstatements. Thus, this issue remained unsettled and largely unfocused in these years. Finally, an achievement of at least symbolic importance at the time was authorization of a federal income tax through adoption of the Sixteenth Amendment in 1913. Its passage was key to providing at least a potential source of funding that would allow government programs to expand even further, thus helping to institutionalize the progressive legacy of governmental activism.

These attempts to establish a more competitive and open economy were meant to improve conditions for business owners, consumers, and workers. But progressivism also offered more direct attempts to better the lives of citizens. For along with, and largely as a result of, economic change came altered social conditions as well. As more Americans moved from farms to cities to seek new opportunities, the old structure and its rules began to crumble. And, as new groups took their place in the economy, they (or others on their behalf) also began to demand political and social equity.

Social Policies

The primary groups whose rights enjoyed increased scrutiny in this time frame were women, children, blacks, and immigrants. But here the imprecision of the progressive label is obvious, as the conventional image of progressives fighting for gains for these groups is substantially inaccurate. Although some of the more radical reformers, such as social worker Jane Addams and the writer Upton Sinclair, were committed to improvements for the victimized underclass, this was not necessarily a consistent component of the progressive agenda. In fact, many progressives believed that immigrants in particular (who were arriving in great numbers during these years) were actually part of the problem by creating a strain on city capacities and ultimately forming powerful and corrupt political machines. Overall, progressives were much more united in fighting for increased political power for white males (through direct primaries, direct election of U.S. senators, and so on) than they were for establishing even the most basic social and political rights for these other groups.

The three presidents of this era reflect this lack of agreement. None of them established a particularly notable record in the realm of social and political rights for the disadvantaged. As president at least (Roosevelt evolved somewhat in later years), each was at best only a tepid supporter of both women's suffrage and limitations on child labor, viewing such changes as largely outside the proper realm of federal power. Advances in these areas in these years largely occurred *despite* the lack of clear and consistent presidential support.

Roosevelt proved himself to be at least a symbolic advocate of the dignity and rights of immigrants in his professed sympathy for foreign-born miners in the 1902 strike against the anthracite coal mining industry, but neither he nor Taft had to deal with serious attempts to restrict immigration overall. Wilson, in his only steady position of support for one of these groups, fought a losing battle against the use of literacy tests to assess immigrant acceptability.

Finally, none of these presidents established a leadership role in the advancement of African American rights. Roosevelt did open a national dialogue on the race question by inviting the black educator Booker T. Washington to dinner at the White House, but he also drew criticism for dismissing an entire company of black soldiers for a crime that only a few had possibly committed. Taft said little on the issue, and Wilson actually took a step backwards by allowing and defending the practice of segregation in federal agencies.

Foreign Policy

It is even more difficult to offer a cohesive narrative of the decisions of the presidents of this era in regard to foreign policy. No dominant progressive position had emerged, as reformers were split between international activism and isolationism. Thus, the policy record is much more clearly attributable to each president's personal views than to an overarching agenda, although that did not stop Roosevelt and Wilson in particular from justifying their actions through a broad interpretation of progressive philosophies.

The most pressing foreign policy question in this prewar period was the role the United States should play in Latin America. Roosevelt was by far the most dominant actor here, actively involving American forces not only in the protection of neighbors in the Southern Hemisphere, but also in helping to foment a revolution in Panama so that the building of the Panama Canal could commence. In this policy realm, Roosevelt displayed a willingness to use government force to improve conditions not only in this country but others as well, thus allowing him to attribute an albeit somewhat shaky, progressive basis to his decisions. To be fair, Roosevelt did serve in a time characterized by more of an old style international balance of power that his successors were not faced with—one in which European powers played a meaningful and potentially threatening role in Latin America. Thus, his activism was not completely unjustified, although much of the criticism he drew was quite valid.

Foreign policy of any sort was minimal in the Taft administration, as Taft turned against the activism of his predecessor. Wilson, however, heated up the Latin American situation again through an almost obsessive intrusion into Mexican domestic disputes that he too justified through progressive principles. The apotheosis of U.S. activism in this part of the world (at least in these early years of the twentieth century) came when Wilson, twice, almost brought the United States into a war with Mexico. Once this situation was diffused, however, a significant scaling back of American aggression in Latin America ensued.

THE WAR YEARS

Wartime America (1917–1919), presided over by Wilson in his second term, was quite distinct from the years preceding and following it. U.S. entry into World War I (referred to then, and throughout this book, as the Great War) had a major impact on all policy realms that in some ways weakened, and in some cases enhanced, Progressive Era accomplishments.

Overall, this was a dark and difficult time for all Americans. The wartime economy brought some prosperity, but also a level of governmental authority never before experienced. A draft was initiated, federal agencies were granted jurisdiction over previously private realms, and Americans were beseeched to sacrifice on meatless, wheatless, gasless, and lightless days. Conditions in these years were worsened by the influenza epidemic that had first hit the East Coast in 1914. About one-quarter of the nation fell ill and, at the height of the crisis, 202 influenza deaths occurred on October 1, 1918. The optimism that largely characterized the earlier era was replaced by an increasingly stoic acceptance and determination.

Foreign Policy

Foreign policy of course ultimately defined this era, although there was no rush for America to join in the European war that began in the summer of 1914. Wilson, and the majority of Americans, remained staunch supporters of neutrality for as long as possible. But once the United States did declare war on Germany, the long history of relative isolationism (at least in regard to Europe) came to a rapid halt. Americans were now full participants in a global war and, for the most part, threw themselves into the fight.

Wartime policies carried the stamp of Wilson's personal vision. Throughout the war, both before and after U.S. entry, he sought to establish the United States (with himself in the lead) as an exemplary beacon of democracy and reason for European nations to emulate. Again, this reflected Wilson's own broad expansion of the progressive agenda to foreign relations. But while Americans were at least initially supportive of the war, they did not share Wilson's idealistic and spiritual optimism, as evidenced by the lack of enthusiasm for the League of Nations provision of the postarmistice Versailles Peace Conference. By that point, Americans simply wanted little more to do with Europe and the rest of the world.

Economic Policy

In response to the war, government expanded to unprecedented degrees—in fact, far beyond the progressive growth of the previous era. With little opposition, the federal government took over certain economic sectors and strictly regulated others. Boards were established to control foreign trade, oversee the granting of government contracts, and stabilize the price of various commodities. A food administration was formed to educate Americans on how to use less of the products needed for export to our allies in Europe, who were experiencing severe food shortages as a result of the war. High tariffs were reinstated, and extensive taxes (on corporate and personal incomes) were levied as well. Additionally, a propaganda effort was mounted to encourage sacrifice and keep morale high.

Yet, the economic impacts of the war were not all negative. Many sectors enjoyed greater profits as a result of the high level of exports. Additionally, because workers were in great demand with so many young men overseas, organized labor was the recipient of important concessions in these years, such as equal pay for women, eight-hour days, and guaranteed minimum wages on federal contract work.

Social Policy

Socially, any ongoing progressive efforts for inclusion and justice for minority groups were largely abandoned in the war years. Immigrants in particular became brutally discriminated against (both by federal policies and citizen volunteers targeting potentially seditious behavior) and a nativistic, anti-foreigner philosophy began to gain strength. Wilson's prediction, made just before asking Congress for the declaration of war, that "the spirit of ruthless brutality will enter into the very fibre of our national life"[1] was especially apt in this regard. Immigration largely ceased during these years, and the ideological groundwork was established for extensive postwar limits on new arrivals.

Any attempts to make gains for blacks were also largely halted in this conservative environment. Black soldiers faced segregated (and stunningly poor) accommodations in the military and were generally precluded from combat training. Clashes between black soldiers and local people in the towns where they were quartered worked to worsen racial relations. One social group that fared somewhat better was women. Suffragists were able to shame a worn-down Wilson into supporting the Nineteenth Amendment that granted women the right to vote. Additionally, many women were able to prove their abilities by filling in for servicemen in various business and governmental functions, although most were expected to return to their homes when the war ended.

POSTWAR—THE RETURN TO NORMALCY YEARS

The America of the Harding and Coolidge administrations was a complex nation. The Great War, although over, continued to exert effects, as Americans considered how best to avoid future aggression, and the economy strained to regain equilibrium. Socially, the nation was also struggling to find its way, while the burst of youthful, exuberant energy of the "roaring twenties" coexisted with a growing rural conservatism and a resurgence of religious fundamentalism. There was little evidence of pride in having won the war. Postwar literature on the experience focused on its horrors, and veterans returned home anxious to put those years behind them. The war seemed to leave Americans spent. Progressive ideals had lost their luster, and a mood of intolerance, selfishness, and cynicism appeared to overtake the nation.

Foreign Policy

Virtually the last thing people of the 1920s wanted was any sort of aggressive or activist foreign policy. There was broad consensus that avoidance of war must be the primary consideration, but disagreement on how to attain that goal. Some sought to actively promote international cooperation, and a vigorous peace movement emerged. Both Harding and Coolidge joined in the spirit of taking action to preserve peace, with Harding convening a naval arms limitation conference and Coolidge supporting the Kellogg-Briand Pact, a proposed multinational agreement to outlaw war. Critics tended to view these steps as at best naive and ineffectual and at worst dangerous. For many had returned to an earlier isolationist stance, in which even U.S. cooperation with other nations amounted to a potentially entangling and crippling weakness. While these steps probably meant little, and of course did not preclude the United States being drawn into a second world war just over twenty years later, they did provide a needed sense of optimism.

Economic Policy

Both presidents also struggled to reign in an explosive and turbulent economy. As an outgrowth of both the expectations fostered in the Progressive Era and the trying conditions many Americans now faced in dealing with inflation and unemployment, the federal government was entreated to provide remedies. These two presidents responded for the most part by attempting to remove and shrink government wherever possible, although existing progressive programs were largely kept in place. Their philosophy was that an unfettered business environment was needed to restore economic order. Thus, the chief policy focus was the drastic reduction of federal taxes.

In response to pleas for protection from certain economic sectors, permanent tariffs were reinstated, but other calls for government assistance were rejected. Legislation providing financial relief to farmers and veterans was vetoed as representing unwarranted class-based benefits. Overall, the strategies of the Harding and Coolidge years did have an immediate and stabilizing effect on the economy. However, the financial crises faced by particular groups were probably not heeded seriously enough, as they may have represented important warning signs of the looming Great Depression.

Social Policy

The important social changes of this period had little to do with government and more to do with evolutions and revolutions in private beliefs and behavior. The younger generation burst forth in these postwar years with a determination to break rules and push limits. Drinking (despite Prohibition), jazz music, smoking, and swearing were some of the favored new pastimes. Women, newly empowered to vote, also enjoyed the freedom of bobbed hair and shorter skirts.

At the same time, an ominous spirit of nativism and bigotry (which began during the pessimism and fear of the war years, and was encouraged by postwar economic anxieties) began to take hold in America's rural regions. The phrase "100% American" gained popularity as a means to signal intolerance of immigrants. This was also a period of ascendance for the Ku Klux Klan, united in opposition to basic rights for blacks and immigrants, which began a campaign of violence across the nation. Although Harding called on America to accept the political and economic rights of blacks, a federal antilynching bill failed to pass during his administration. Furthermore, many politicians of the period, including Coolidge, refused to condemn the Klan in public and were in fact supported by these groups. Sadly, while some blacks had hoped that their participation in the Great War would win them respect and acceptance, it did not. Tensions were if anything increased by the movement of many blacks into northern areas to work during the war; in 1919 ten black veterans were lynched while still in uniform.

This twenty-nine-year period encompasses a great many changes in American society and politics—some lasting and some less so. This book guides the reader through the key controversies of these times. Some of the policies addressed were constantly shifting—just as today, the status quo seemed to change depending on which party was in power. For example, questions of taxes, tariffs, and U.S. intervention abroad were not settled in that era or any other; rather, they remained influenced more by the particular party and personalities holding elective office. But many of the accomplishments of these years have proven enduring. The business regulations of the Progressive Era remain largely intact and guard against the dangers of monopolies, dangerous products, and exploitation of workers. The philosophy of challenging the existing power structure so that more Americans might participate in the nation's society and politics led to political reforms still in place today, and at least the recognition of the particular problems of minority groups as an issue to be addressed. Perhaps most importantly, this period of American history illustrates that government can be made effectively responsive to the needs of its citizens.

NOTE

1. Arthur S. Link, *Woodrow Wilson and the Progressive Era, 1910–1917* (New York: Harper and Row, 1954), 277.

THEODORE ROOSEVELT

(1901–1909)

INTRODUCTION

Upon acceding to the presidency as a result of President William Mc-Kinley's assassination in September 1901, Theodore Roosevelt, at only forty-three years of age, suddenly found himself in a role that as vice president he may have aspired to but, in the absence of a presidential campaign, was not fully prepared for. However, aided by the force of his bold personality, he flung himself into the job, utilizing the "bully pulpit" of the presidency to advance an agenda more vigorous than any of his predecessors that consisted of several progressive reforms as well as other innovations linked more directly to his personal visions.

Roosevelt and the Progressive Era in America are inextricably linked. The policies he advocated triggered increased acceptance of a greater role for the federal government in the economic realm in particular. Furthermore, the relationship worked in the other direction as well. This president's boldness, initiative, and willingness to expand presidential power were inspired by, and provided perhaps the perfect conduit for, the precepts of the progressive movement. Progressive optimism in the ability of government, particularly at the federal level, to take steps to ameliorate the negative impacts of economic and social change provided a message and an agenda that complemented Roosevelt's own enthusiasm and bluster. The greatest innovations, at least in terms of theories of governance, of the Roosevelt administration involved federal regulation of business and industry.

When Roosevelt took office on September 14, 1901, America's powerful business interests were unsure and somewhat wary of what the new president's position on antitrust regulation would be. On the one hand, Roosevelt's connection to the McKinley administration suggested the continuation of a governmental laissez-faire approach, a hallmark of the business friendly Republican Party of the late nineteenth century. On the other hand, the new president was perceived as unpredictable and generally somewhat of a loose cannon. Additionally, he had proposed or endorsed some vague regulations of business as the vice presidential candidate in 1900. Thus, corporate heads waited anxiously for his first pronouncement on the topic.

Although not declaring all out war, as he conceded the importance of a relatively unfettered business climate to the prosperity of the nation, Roosevelt did make it clear that he would strengthen existing polices against monopoly. The progressive and populist movements provided the basic concepts, but his interpretation and use invigorated the ideas.

While the Sherman Antitrust Act, an attempt to outlaw harmful monopolies, had been passed in 1890, it remained ineffective. But Roosevelt gave it another chance, by authorizing his attorney general to bring suit against certain monopolies under power of the act. The provisions were no different than they had been in the late nineteenth century, when the Supreme Court refused an interpretation that would allow for the actual destruction of monopolies. However, the new president's forceful insistence that the act should be used to its fullest potential likely had some impact on that hazy mixture of presidential initiative and public opinion that influences Court outcomes. Although Roosevelt did not pursue litigation with quite the vigor that his legacy might suggest, or even to the extent that his successor William Howard Taft did, he set the stage for meaningful implementation of federal trust regulations.

He would go on to advocate regulation of specific economic sectors as well. Again relying on existing law as a base, Roosevelt sought to bestow genuine power, for the first time, on the Interstate Commerce Commission. As constituted, this committee (created in 1887) had no meaningful control over the nation's railroad operators, who were free to set prices as high as they desired. The president successfully fought for passage of the Hepburn Act, allowing the ICC greater authority over rates. He also successfully advocated legislation authorizing the first federal food and drug regulation, as well as a Department of Corporations and Bureau of Commerce to provide information to the public on the previously mysterious inner workings of corporate finances.

Although somewhat of a stand-alone initiative, Roosevelt's celebrated advocacy of protection of the nation's unique land areas and natural resources was in some ways one more aspect of his economic agenda. While he did champion preservation for its own sake, he was also greatly disturbed by the injustice of the plundering of national resources for private economic gain, and sought to end generous federal lease agreements with forestry, mining, and ranching interests. The comprehensive policies he helped push to legislative success established a system for the protection of resources that remains in place today.

Although a progressive philosophy underlay Roosevelt's economic agenda from the start, his views continued to evolve and over time he became an increasingly avid advocate of government regulation of corporate and private property in the public interest. His positions became stronger and more defined in two stages: first after the 1904 elections, and second, when he sought his third term in 1912.

Understandably, given the means by which he had attained the presidency in 1901, Roosevelt remained somewhat insecure about his public mandate and his acceptance by party leaders until he was elected on his own merit. Invigorated by his landslide victory against Democrat Alton B. Parker in 1904 (which also established even larger Republican majorities in Congress), the president became much bolder and more creative, at least in his rhetoric, about the need to control the exploitative and destructive effects of capitalism. Thus, with the exception of the early Sherman Antitrust Act litigations, and his prounion stance in the anthracite coal miners' strike of 1902, most of the notable efforts occurred in the second term. Several of his most innovative policies were announced in his December 5, 1905, message to Congress.

By 1912, as a former president fighting for a third term, he emerged as a fairly radical reformer, advocating proposals that frightened away many Republicans, including some with progressive sympathies. During this period, through his New Nationalism platform, he began to support a nearly socialistic conception of broad federal regulation of property rights as a means to protect and advance the general welfare.

The major source of opposition to Roosevelt's economic policies in general was, not surprisingly, the nation's business and corporate interests, who felt increasingly threatened by the ever more activist agenda. However, there were subtleties to this issue that keep it from being quite so neatly pinned down. Roosevelt's continual efforts to achieve government oversight not through litigation (i.e., suits initiated after an illegal action had been committed), but through clarified legislation (which would make improper behavior more clearly defined before the fact, and thus more easily avoided) also won him some admirers from the business world, particularly during the 1912 campaign, when he and Taft clashed on the issue.

As president, Roosevelt was also challenged by government officials who resented not so much the content, but rather the form of his economic agenda that, it was argued, represented too much power in the hands of the president himself, at the expense of both Congress and state governments. The president's insistence that his actions were proper as long as the Constitution did not specifically forbid them was a continual source of friction with other governmental actors and, not incidentally, advanced a more vigorous view of the U.S. presidency that would be adopted by several of his successors.

Finally, a fairly minor but vocal source of opposition came from those adherents of progressivism (both in and outside government) who believed that Roosevelt was not fighting strongly enough, particularly in the early years of his administration, for increased federal regulation on behalf of the public good. Senator Robert La Follette of Wisconsin, one of the leaders of the Republican insurgents, noted in 1911 that "his strongest declarations in the public interest were invariably offset with something comforting for Privilege; every phrase denouncing 'bad' trusts was deftly balanced with praise for 'good' trusts."[1]

This criticism notwithstanding, Roosevelt's economic positions did reside solidly within the progressive tradition. Yet to characterize him as an all-around progressive president would be too simplistic. For one thing, the "progressive" position on certain issues—those involving social and foreign policies in particular—are difficult to pin down, as progressives themselves were split on them. Additionally (and perhaps as a result of this progressive disunity), the president's views in these policy areas were for the most part driven by his own vision of what was right.

In the social realm, where progressives in general seemed unable to reach consensus on the necessity of reform, Roosevelt was moderately forward thinking in his views, but certainly not in the vanguard in regard to the rights of women and African Americans, two high-profile social issues of the time. Although attracting public attention (both positive and negative) for inviting Booker T. Washington to dine at the White House, and generally advocating at least limited rights for blacks (such as public education and use of the railroads), Roosevelt also made the seemingly unjust decision to dismiss an entire company of black soldiers after several were accused of instigating a violent raid on Brownsville, Texas. Additionally, his tendency toward U.S. intervention in Latin America suggested that he did not consider other ethnic groups to be equally capable as Anglo-Americans.

Roosevelt also held complex views on the equality of women and the suffrage issue. He was sometimes praised for being progressive on this topic and sometimes criticized for being too conservative. To at least a certain extent, these views also evolved. Over time, Roosevelt became more accepting of social and political gains for both groups.

Linking Roosevelt's foreign policies to progressivism is similarly complicated by the fact that progressives were split between isolationist tendencies and a desire to export American democracy to other nations. What is clear, however, is that his foreign policies carry the stamp of his own sometimes imperious character and interventionist preferences.

Perhaps the most impressive symbolic act of his administration was sending U.S. battleships on an around-the-world cruise beginning on December 16, 1907, and ending on February 22, 1909. The two most notable foreign policy initiatives, the building of the Panama Canal and the Roosevelt corollary to the Monroe Doctrine, were also bold and unilateral. In the first, Roosevelt played an active role in gaining independence for Panama from Colombia, when the latter became recalcitrant over the price it would receive for the canal zone. The president's corollary to the Monroe Doctrine expanded upon that long-standing tenet by announcing that the United States would intervene not only when European nations moved toward territorial aggression in Latin America, but also when merely punitive actions were undertaken. These initiatives involved an energetic and interventionist American role in regard to Latin America that would never again be matched.

Here again, opposition was focused on both content and procedure. The view that the United States had a moral duty or right to intervene in the affairs of these nations was beginning to be sharply questioned, and Roosevelt's seemingly autocratic behavior in implementing these policies without congressional input was resented just as it was in regard to his economic policies. However, the strength of Roosevelt's preferences are illustrated by the impact they had beyond his term as president. Roosevelt, and his loyalists in Congress, remained an important force in favor of an activist American foreign policy well beyond his tenure in office.

His role in the Panama Canal episode led Roosevelt to successfully challenge several later attempts to provide compensation to Colombia—a step the former president felt would be an unwarranted and humiliating admission of guilt, and that his friends in Congress feared would undermine his legacy through the suggestion of wrongdoing. Additionally, during the years preceding America's entry into the Great War, Roosevelt was an early advocate for preparedness, while President Woodrow Wilson was still strongly urging strict neutrality. In one extreme example of his continued activism, Roosevelt tried to convince Wilson to allow him to lead a regiment. The offer, however, was rebuffed, and Roosevelt was reduced to home-front activities such as helping to organize a Girl Scout scrap metal drive.

In each of these key policy realms—economic, social, and foreign—Roosevelt's personality and style both helped and hindered his agenda. As he never really had a profession beyond public service broadly defined, Roosevelt is best considered a professional politician—a role in which he had great skills but also some notable limitations. His strength here was his power of persuasion. For example, his approach to the trust issue, in which he took care to note the vital and positive contributions of American business and industry, while advocating the destruction of dangerous monopolies, was a subtle yet effective strategy that worked to persuade the public as well as members of Congress of the wisdom of his views. Additionally, most Americans would not have known of the dangers to national lands and resources (and thus strongly supported federal initiatives to protect them) if it had not been for the president's many compelling speeches on the issue.

However, Roosevelt's sometimes uncontrollable ego and bluster also functioned as the destructive analog to his impressive political acumen. For example, he stubbornly pursued clearly unpopular policies such as simplified spelling and the Brownsville Texas, episode dismissals. He also tended to be uncompromising, harsh, and even cruel in his dealings with those who disagreed with him, as illustrated in his public feuds with Senator Joseph Foraker (R–Ohio) over the Brownsville issue, Justice Oliver Wendell Holmes over the trust question, and his successor and friend Taft over several components of the progressive agenda.

Sometimes, this pugnacious quality damaged his own policy achievements. The president once initiated a tenacious attack on a group of children's book authors ("nature-fakers") who annoyed Roosevelt with their portrayal of animals possessing human qualities such as bravery or altruism. When Roosevelt asserted, "I don't believe that some of these nature-writers know the heart of the wild things," his chief target, the Reverend William J. Long, responded that "every time Mr. Roosevelt gets near the heart of a wild thing he invariably puts a bullet through it,"[2] a comment gleefully reported by the press. Thus, the strength of his nature conservation record was unnecessarily (but purely by his own doing) belittled.

Yet this was all part of the Roosevelt legacy. Despite these occasional missteps, Roosevelt was a popular president well suited to the growing nation. He was blustery and insensitive at times, but brought genuinely novel and (sometimes) progressive ideas to the White House. His style and accomplishments fit a time that represented a maturing of America, from a nation coasting on the advances of the industrial revolution to one beginning to question the implications of these modern trends.

REGULATION OF TRUSTS

One of the most high-profile issues of the late nineteenth and early twentieth centuries was the regulation of business, especially restrictions on companies in similar commercial sectors who (by virtue of state enabling laws) combined together into large corporations, or "trusts," that had the potential to exert strong control over the provision of particular goods or services. There was growing sentiment that such monopolies were harmful to the general welfare by artificially keeping prices high and consumer choice low. These concerns led to passage of the Sherman Antitrust Act in 1890, which (on paper at least) provided for the dissolution of such corporations. But, while potentially a powerful tool, the law had been used sparingly and when given the chance the Supreme Court had refused to apply it to the sugar refining monopoly in 1895.

Roosevelt's initial pronouncement on this topic came in the first annual message to Congress in December 1901. The portion of his speech dealing with trusts certainly could not be portrayed as anything even close to an all-out assault. He repeatedly stressed the vital role of commerce to American prosperity and made clear that the rising fortunes of industry did not come at the expense of the average American. However, he also noted the "real and grave evils" attendant in overcapitalization and warned against the inadequacy of state-level regulation, stressing the need for federal law to control the negative aspects of trusts.

Business interests were relieved by the speech. They feared that harsher measures might have been proposed, although their concern was tempered by their knowledge that Congress would resist any new laws. But Roosevelt pressed on, becoming more strenuous in his public pronouncements against trusts. Although he believed legislation a more preferable tool than litigation, given the degree of congressional recalcitrance he decided to pursue the issue through the federal courts. Early in 1902, he authorized Attorney General Philander Knox to file a suit against the Northern Securities Corporation, asking the courts to utilize the Sherman Act to dissolve the corporation, thereby pitting the president against railroad magnates J. Pierpont Morgan, E.H. Harriman, and James J. Hill. In the autumn of 1901, these industrial giants had created the Northern Securities Corporation by combining several individual railroads through stock mergers, thus achieving monopoly control over all rail commerce and travel in the upper western portion of the country. Roosevelt feared this to be a first step toward controlling the rail system of the entire nation.

The case was decided in favor of the federal government on March 14, 1904, by a five to four majority, with Justice Holmes writing a strong dissent. The larger issue here was the propriety of federal regulation, but the more technical aspect of this case was whether the antitrust law applied to stock ownership as well as to actual interstate commerce. The majority saw little difference between the two activities in this case, stating that "those who were stockholders of the Great Northern and Northern Pacific and became stockholders in the holding company are now interested in preventing all competition between the two lines, and, as owner of stock . . . in the holding company, they will see to it that no competition is tolerated. No scheme or device could more certainly come within the words of the act,—'combination in the form of a trust or otherwise . . . in restraint of commerce.' "[3] They ruled that the Sherman Act was indeed relevant here, stating "if the antitrust act is held not to embrace a case such as is now before us, the plain intention of the legislative branch of the government will be defeated."[4] Holmes disagreed with the outcome and reasoning, writing that the administration had gone too far in pursuing this case. He believed that the mere transfer of stock ownership could not be seen as a violation of the Sherman Act and that, overall, the government's argument advanced a dangerously loose interpretation of that law.

Ironically, Roosevelt had appointed Holmes to the Court in part because he thought Holmes would be willing to interpret the Sherman Act as a broad grant of federal power to limit the trusts. The disagreement led to an irreparable rift between the president and his appointee. Roosevelt's immediate response to Holmes's dissent in this case was that he "could carve out of a banana a judge with more backbone."[5] Although they remained cordial, Holmes later stated that the case broke up their friendship largely because Roosevelt "could not forgive anyone who stood in his way."[6]

Roosevelt's victory here was an important first step in meaningful federal regulation of the trusts. Other successful court cases and, ultimately, legislation followed. Antitrust policies continued well past this era, and the conception of monopoly as a public harm that must be limited by federal regulation remains strong.

NOTES

1. Robert M. La Follette, *A Personal Narrative of Political Experiences* (Madison, Wisc.: La Follette, 1911), 484–485.

2. William Henry Harbaugh, *Power and Responsibility* (New York: Octagon Books, 1975), 295.

3. *Northern Securities Company v. United States*, 193 U.S. 197 (1904), 327.

4. Ibid., 360.

5. Harbaugh, *Power and Responsibility*, 161.

6. Ibid.

ROOSEVELT—REGULATION OF CORPORATIONS
(DECEMBER 3, 1901)

During the last five years business confidence has been restored, and the nation is to be congratulated because of its present abounding prosperity. Such prosperity can never be created by law alone, although it is easy enough to destroy it by mischievous laws. . . .

The captains of industry who have driven the railway systems across this continent, who have built up our commerce, who have developed our manufactures, have on the whole done great good to our people. Without them the material development of which we are so justly proud could never have taken place. Moreover, we should recognize the immense importance of this material development of leaving as unhampered as is compatible with the public good the strong and forceful men upon whom the success of business operations inevitably rests. The slightest study of business conditions will satisfy any one capable of forming a judgment that the personal equation is the most important factor in a business operation; that the business ability of the man at the head of any business concern, big or little, is usually the factor which fixes the gulf between striking success and hopeless failure.

. . .

All this is true; and yet it is also true that there are real and grave evils, one of the chief being overcapitalization because of its many baleful consequences; and a resolute and practical effort must be made to correct these evils.

There is a wide-spread conviction in the minds of the American people that the great corporations known as trusts are in certain of their features and tendencies hurtful to the general welfare. This springs from no spirit of envy or uncharitableness, nor lack of pride in the great industrial achievements that have placed this country at the head of the nations struggling for commercial supremacy. It does not rest upon a lack of intelligent appreciation of the necessity of meeting changing and changed conditions of trade with new methods, nor upon ignorance of the fact that combination of capital in the effort to accomplish great things is necessary when the world's progress demands that great things be done. It is based upon sincere conviction that combination and concentration should be, not prohibited, but supervised and within reasonable limits controlled; and in my judgment this conviction is right.

It is no limitation upon property rights or freedom of contract to require that when men receive from government the privilege of doing business under corporate form, which frees them from individual responsibility, and enables them to call into their enterprises the capital of the public, they shall do so upon absolutely truthful representations as to the value of the property in which the capital is to be invested. Corporations engaged in interstate commerce should be regulated if they are found to exercise a license working to the public injury. It should be as much the aim of those who seek for social betterment to rid the business world of crimes of cunning as to rid the entire body politic of crimes of violence. Great corporations exist only because they are created and safeguarded by our institutions; and it is therefore our right and our duty to see that they work in harmony with these institutions.

. . .

The large corporations, commonly called trusts, though organized in one State, always do business in many States, often doing very little business in the State where they are incorporated. There is utter lack of uniformity in the State laws about them; and as no State has any exclusive interest in or power over their acts, it has in practice proved impossible to get adequate regulation through State action. Therefore, in the interest of the whole people, the nation should, without interfering with the power of the States in the matter itself, also assume power of supervision and regulation over all corporations doing an interstate business. This is especially true where the corporation derives a portion of its wealth from the existence of some monopolistic element or tendency in its business. There would be no hardship in such supervision; banks are subject to it, and in their case it is now accepted as a simple matter of course. Indeed, it is probable that supervision of corporations by the National Government need not go so far as is now the case with the supervision exercised over them by so conservative a State as Massachusetts, in order to produce excellent results.

When the Constitution was adopted, at the end of the eighteenth century, no human wisdom could foretell the sweeping changes, alike in industrial and political conditions, which were to take place by the beginning of the twentieth century. At that time it was accepted as a matter of course that the several States were the proper authorities to regulate, so far as was then necessary, the comparatively insignificant and strictly localized corporate bodies of the day. The conditions are now wholly different and wholly different action is called for. I believe that a law can be framed which will enable the National Government to exercise control along the lines above indicated; profiting by the experience gained through the passage and administration of the Interstate Commerce Act. If, however, the judgment of the Congress is that it lacks the constitutional power to pass such an act, then a constitutional amendment should be submitted to confer the power.

Hagedorn, Hermann, ed. *The Works of Theodore Roosevelt*. Vol. 15. New York: Scribner's, 1925, 87–93.

JUSTICE OLIVER WENDELL HOLMES—NORTHERN SECURITIES DISSENT (MARCH 13, 1904)

Great cases, like hard cases, make bad law. For great cases are called great, not by reason of their real importance in shaping the law of the future, but because of some accident of immediate overwhelming interest which appeals to the feelings and distorts the judgment. These immediate interests exercise a kind of hydraulic pressure which makes what previously was clear seem doubtful, and before which even well settled principles of law will bend. What we have to do in this case is to find the meaning of some not very difficult words. . . .

The question to be decided is whether, under the act of July 2, 1890, it is unlawful, at any stage of the process, if several men unite to form a corporation for the purpose of buying more than half the stock of each of two competing interstate railroad companies, if they form the corporation, and the corporation buys the stock. I will suppose further that every step is taken, from the beginning, with the single intent of ending competition between the companies. I make this addition not because it may not be and is not disputed, but because, as I shall try to show, it is totally unimportant under any part of the statute with which we have to deal. . . .

This act is construed by the government to affect the purchasers of shares in two railroad companies because of the effect it may have, or, if you like, is certain to have, upon the competition of these roads. If such a remote result of the exercise of an ordinary incident of property and personal freedom is enough to make that exercise unlawful, there is hardly any transaction concerning commerce between the states that may not be made a crime by the finding of a jury or a court. . . .

It would seem to me impossible to say that the words "every contract in restraint of trade is a crime, punishable with imprisonment," would send the members of a partnership between, or a consolidation of, two trading corporations to prison,—still more impossible to say that it forbade one man or corporation to purchase as much stock as he liked in both. Yet those words would have that effect if this clause of section 1 applies to the defendants here. For it cannot be too carefully remembered that that clause applies to "every" contract of the forbidden kind. . . .

If the statute applies to this case it must be because the parties, or some of them, have formed, or because the Northern Securities Company is, a combination in restraint of trade among the states, or, what comes to the same thing, in my opinion, because the defendants, or some or one of them, are monopolizing, or attempting to monopolize, some part of the commerce between the states. But the mere reading of those words shows that they are used in a limited and accurate sense. According to popular speech, every concern monopolizes whatever business it does, and if that business is trade between two states it monopolizes a part of the trade among the states. Of course, the statute does not forbid that. It does not mean that all business must cease. A single railroad down a narrow valley or through a mountain gorge monopolizes all the railroad transportation through that valley or gorge. Indeed, every railroad monopolizes, in a popular sense, the trade of some area. Yet I suppose no one would say that the statute forbids a combination of men into a corporation to build and run such a railroad between the states. . . .

A partnership is not a contract or combination in restraint of trade between the partners unless the well known words are to be given a new meaning, invented for the purposes of this act. . . . The law, I repeat, says nothing about competition, and only prevents its suppression by contracts or combinations in restraint of trade, and such contracts or combinations derive their character as restraining trade from other features than the suppression of competition alone. To see whether I am wrong, the illustrations put in the argument are of use. If I am, then a partnership between two stage drivers who had been competitors in driving across a state line, or two merchants once engaged in rival commerce among the states, whether made after or before the act, if now continued, is a crime. For, again I repeat, if the restraint on the freedom of the members of a combination, caused by their entering into partnership, is a restraint of trade, every such combination, as well the small as the great, is within the act.

Northern Securities Company v. United States, 193 U.S. 197 (1904).

ANTHRACITE COAL STRIKE

Early in his presidency, Roosevelt became embroiled in an issue that encompassed the power of big business, labor union legitimacy, Republican Party politics, and the scope of presidential power. All of this was triggered by the Anthracite Coal Strike of 1902. In his arbitration attempt, Roosevelt came down squarely on the side of unions in general and the miners in particular, marginalized one of his potential Republican rivals, and set the stage for his activist view of the presidency.

The strike, centered in the anthracite fields of eastern Pennsylvania, began on June 2, 1902, when talks between mine operators and representatives of the United Mine Workers Union failed to produce an agreement. Specifically, the union demanded higher pay, shorter hours, safer working conditions, and a more precise method of weighing coal, which determined the wages of many miners. At its heart, however, this strike concerned the legitimacy of unions and their role in securing a higher standard of living for native-born and immigrant laborers. This union had, in 1897, won concessions and official recognition in the bituminous mines of western Pennsylvania, and its popular president, John Mitchell, hoped to extend that success to the anthracite regions as well.

Mitchell, however, was up against powerful interests who showed no signs of compromise. Several large railroad (80 percent of the anthracite fields were owned by the railroads that traversed them) and mining interests were involved, including Roosevelt's ever present antagonist J. P. Morgan. A previous dispute in the same region two years earlier had left the mine operators feeling hoodwinked by Mark Hanna, an Ohio senator and a Republican Party insider. In that earlier crisis, Hanna had pressured operators to raise wages, arguing that a strike would threaten President McKinley's reelection chances. While the miners looked once more to Hanna in 1902 to help press their demands, the operators were determined not to give in again.

Thus, in part, Roosevelt's involvement was triggered by his political need to supplant Hanna as the Republican Party's friend of labor since Hanna was a potential rival for the 1904 Republican presidential nomination. In addition, Roosevelt was spurred to action by increased public sympathy for the miners, which escalated over the summer of 1902 in response to the perceived insensitivity of the railroad and mine operators. In particular, George Baer, the president of the Reading Railroad, incited public wrath when he responded to a letter beseeching him to show Christian sympathy to the miners by arrogantly stating, "the rights and interests of the laboring man will be protected and cared for—not by the labor agitators, but by the Christian men to whom God in His infinite wisdom has given the control of the property interests of the country."[1] Additionally, although largely ungrounded, fears of a winter coal shortage had reached the verge of a public panic. Roosevelt, never one to avoid an exaggeration, later referred to the situation as a potential crisis, "only less serious than that of the Civil War."[2]

But in addition to these pragmatic reasons for entering the fray, the passage from Roosevelt's autobiography reflects the genuine sympathy he had felt for the plight of the miners. He asserts the importance of unions as a necessary counterweight to the growing power of big business that, contrary to many claims, represented *fewer* choices and freedoms for many poor Americans and immigrants. The response of William H. Truesdale (the president of the Delaware, Lackawanna, and Western Railroad Company) to Mitchell's demands is detached and cold in comparison, displaying no sympathy what so ever for the plight of the miners who, it is asserted rather bluntly, could choose another profession if they were unhappy.

On October 3, Roosevelt presided over a conference of the mine operators and Mitchell. It did not go well. Roosevelt, still in a wheelchair from a serious automobile accident, was unable to bring the two sides together. His sympathies were clearly with Mitchell who, he stated in a letter to Hanna, "did very well to keep his temper"[3] in response to the operators' belligerent behavior.

On October 21, a settlement was reached by the president's appointed Anthracite Coal Strike Commission, with a little help from Morgan, who encouraged the operators to abide by the commission's findings. Generally, the decision was favorable to the miners, granting them higher pay and fewer hours. However, the union did not receive the recognition it sought, largely because Morgan had earlier insisted that Mitchell be treated only as the miners' spokesman and not as the union leader. Thus, although making statements supportive of unions in general, the commission was unable to do more.

Although reaching fairly sympathetic conclusions, the contrast with the president's empathy with the miners' plight is noticeable in the commission report. It was especially insensitive in regard to the immigrant miners, stating (in regard to the question of their houses), "where they do not approach a proper standard, it is impossible to say how much choice and volition have had to do with their inferiority. The homes and surroundings of the English-speaking miners and mine workers are generally superior to those of the class just mentioned, and show an intelligent appreciation of the decencies of life and ability to realize them."[4]

The issue of presidential power was again triggered in this crisis, as Roosevelt was prepared to seize the mines if the appointment of the commission had not brought an end to the strike. As would become a pattern with this president, he claimed that the proposed action was proper since there was nothing in the Constitution specifically prohibiting it. Fifty years later, when President Harry S Truman attempted a similar action against the steel industry, a U.S. Federal District Court ruled such a course unconstitutional, noting that Roosevelt's views on this issue "do not comport with our recognized theory of government."[5]

NOTES

1. Henry F. Pringle, *Theodore Roosevelt, A Biography* (New York: Harcourt, Brace and World, 1956), 188.

2. Robert H. Wiebe, "The Anthracite Strike of 1902: A Record of Confusion," *Mississippi Valley Historical Review* 48 (1961): 243.

3. Joseph Bucklin Bishop, *Theodore Roosevelt and His Time*, vol. 1 (New York: Scribner's, 1920), 203.

4. Anthracite Coal Strike Commission, *Report to the President on the Anthracite Coal Strike* (Washington, D.C.: U.S. Government Printing Office, 1903), 42–43.

5. "Text of Ruling by Court Declaring Truman Steel Seizure Illegal," *New York Times*, April 30, 1952, 18.

ROOSEVELT—PASSAGE FROM AUTOBIOGRAPHY (1913)

The great Anthracite Strike of 1902 left an indelible impress upon the people of the United States. It showed clearly to all wise and far-seeing men that the labor problem in this country had entered upon a new phase. Industry had grown. Great financial corporations, doing a nationwide and even a world-wide business, had taken the place of the smaller concerns of an earlier time. The old familiar, intimate relations between employer and employee were passing. A few generations before, the boss had known every man in his shop; he called his men Bill, Tom, Dick, John; he inquired after their wives and babies; he swapped jokes and stories and perhaps a bit of tobacco with them. In the small establishment there had been a friendly human relationship between employer and employee.

There was no such relation between the great railway magnates, who controlled the anthracite industry, and the one hundred and fifty thousand men who worked in their mines, or the half million women and children who were dependent upon these miners for their daily bread. Very few of these mine workers had ever seen, for instance, the president of the Reading Railroad. Had they seen him many of them could not have spoken to him, for tens of thousands of the mine workers were recent immigrants who did not understand the language which he spoke and who spoke a language which he could not understand.

Again, a few generations ago an American workman could have saved money, gone West and taken up a homestead. Now the free lands were gone. In earlier days a man who began with pick and shovel might have come to own a mine. That outlet too was now closed, as regards the immense majority, and few, if any, of the one hundred and fifty thousand mine workers could ever aspire to enter the small circle of men who held in their grasp the great anthracite industry. The majority of the men who earned wages in the coal industry, if they wished to progress at all, were compelled to progress not by ceasing to be wage-earners, but by improving the conditions under which all the wage-earners in all the industries of the country lived and worked, as well of course, as improving their own individual efficiency.

Another change which had come about as a result of the foregoing was a crass inequality in the bargaining relation between the employer and the individual employee standing alone. The great coal-mining and coal-carrying companies, which employed their tens of thousands, could easily dispense with the services of any particular miner. The miner, on the other hand, however expert, could not dispense with the companies. He needed a job; his wife and children would starve if he did not get one. What the miner had to sell—his labor—was a perishable commodity; the labor of to-day—if not sold to-day—was lost forever. Moreover, his labor was not like most commodities—a mere thing; it was part of a living, breathing human being. The workman saw, and all citizens who gave earnest thought to the matter saw, that the labor problem was not only an economic, but also a moral, a human problem. Individually the miners were impotent when they sought to enter a wage-contract with the great companies; they could make fair terms only by uniting into trade unions to bargain collectively. The men were forced to coöperate to secure not only their economic, but their simple human rights. They, like other workmen, were compelled by the very conditions under which they lived to unite in unions of their industry or trade, and these unions were bound to grow in size, in strength, and in power for good and evil as the industries in which the men were employed grew larger and larger.

A democracy can be such in fact only if there is some rough approximation to similarity in stature among the men composing it. One of us can deal in our private lives with the grocer or the butcher or the carpenter or the chicken raiser, or if we are the grocer or carpenter or butcher or farmer, we can deal with our customers, because *we are all of about the same size*. Therefore a simple and poor society can exist as a democracy on a basis of sheer individualism. But a rich and complex industrial society cannot so exist; for some individuals, and especially those artificial individuals called corporations, become so very big that the ordinary individual is utterly dwarfed beside them, and cannot deal with them on terms of equality. It therefore becomes necessary for these ordinary individuals to combine in their turn, first in order to act in their collective capacity through that biggest of all combinations called the Government, and second, to act, also in their own self-defense, through private combinations, such as farmers' associations and trade unions.

This the great coal operators did not see. They did not see that their property rights, which they so stoutly defended, were of the same texture as were the human rights, which they so blindly and hotly denied. They did not see that the power which they exercised by representing their stockholders was of the same texture as the power which the union leaders demanded of representing the workmen, who had democratically elected them. They did not see that the right to use one's property as one will can be maintained only so long as it is consistent with the maintenance of certain fundamental human rights, of the rights to life, liberty and the pursuit of happiness, or, as we may restate them in these later days, of the rights of the worker to a living wage, to reasonable hours of labor, to decent working and living conditions, to freedom of thought and speech and industrial representation—in short, to a measure of industrial democracy and, in return for his arduous toil, to a worthy and decent life according to American standards. Still another thing these great business leaders did not see. They did not see that both their interests and the interests of the workers must be accommodated, and if need be, subordinated, to the fundamental permanent interests of the whole community. No man and no group of men may so exercise their rights as to deprive the nation of the things which are necessary and vital to the common life. A strike which ties up the coal supplies of a whole section is a strike invested with a public interest.

Roosevelt, Theodore. *An Autobiography.* New York: Scribner's, 1913, 470–473.

W. H. TRUESDALE—REPLY TO ANTHRACITE COAL STRIKE COMMISSION (NOVEMBER 1902)

This company denies that the average earnings of its employees engaged in mining coal are much less than the average annual earnings of other occupations requiring equal skill and training, and it asks that the petitioner be required to prove this allegation.

During the recent strike as also during the strike of 1900 many of its mine employees sought and secured employment in bituminous coal mines, others secured work in other than mining industries, but immediately after these strikes were over practically all these men returned to the employ of this company and none of consequence continued work in their new places. It submits that this would not have resulted had these employees been so inadequately paid as is claimed.

It submits furthermore that during the present period of unequaled prosperity throughout the country, if this company's mine employees had been so grossly underpaid as claimed they would have sought employment elsewhere and in other lines of work requiring similar and equal skill and training. It alleges the fact to be that its mine employees have not done this but have seemed anxious to continue in the employ of this company at the wages and under the conditions obtaining.

It admits that the work of a portion of its employees in the mines is of a hazardous character, rendering them liable to accidents, particularly if discipline is not maintained and they fail to live up to the company's rules, and the anthracite mining laws. It denies, however, that the work of this element of its mine employees is substantially more dangerous in character than that of many of its employees engaged in the transportation service of its railroad, who are paid no higher rates of wages and in some cases less than its mine workers. It denies that the work of the balance of its anthracite mine employees is of a dangerous character or renders them particularly liable to accident.

It denies that any of its mine employees are unduly liable to serious or permanent disease or that the death rate among them due to disease is high, or that incidental to their employment their lives are shortened, and asks for proof of this claim.

It is not informed and has no means of definitely ascertaining what is regarded as the "American standard of living" to the maintenance of which the annual earnings of its mine employees or any of them, are alleged to be insufficient. It asks that this claim be more accurately and definitely set forth.

It alleges however, that judging by the character of homes in which its mine employees live, the large percentage of whom own their own homes, the thrifty appearance of themselves and families as seen on Sundays and holidays when not at work, the infrequent cases where their wages in the hands of the company are held to satisfy legal process, the large aggregate of savings held in savings banks and building and loan associations, the large sums the foreign element of the mine employees monthly remit to their relatives in other countries, the mine workers in its employ are on an average as prosperous, comfortable and contented (or were, prior to the introduction of agitators and mischief-makers among them) as any body of workers in similar employment engaged in the promotion of any industry in this country.

It denies the truth of the allegation that the increased cost of living has made it impossible to maintain a fair standard of living upon the present basis of wages.

It alleges that the increase in the number of days worked by its mine employees in addition to previous increase in their rates of wages has not only fully covered the increase in cost of living but has enabled its frugal and careful employees to save a substantial amount per annum in addition thereto.

It admits that some of its anthracite mine employees force their children to work in the breakers and mills, but denies that this is the result of the low wages paid them, or that it is due to any but the common causes that influence parents engaged in other pursuits to force their children to work at an early age. As a rule in mining, as in all other industries, this action is largely due to either the incapacity, improvidence or cupidity of the parents. It denies that it employs any persons to work in its breaker or mines except those who are of sufficient age as prescribed by the acts of assembly in Pennsylvania in such cases made and provided.

. . .

This company alleges that the wonderful development of this country and the unequaled prosperity of its people, including the laboring element thereof, has been acquired as a result of the wonderful activity, industry and productiveness of the individual man; that this condition of prosperity has been reached under conditions where a ten-hour day for work has been regarded as a standard working day for men in many walks of life.

. . .

This company unequivocally asserts that it will under no condition recognize or enter into any agreement with the association known as the United Mine Workers of America or any branch thereof. Nor will it permit said association or its officers to dictate the terms and conditions under which it shall conduct its business. It charges that said association has been declared by the Federal courts to be unlawful, and that it is opposed to the vital principles of our Government. It is seeking to obtain an enforced enrollment on its membership list of all persons employed in or about coal mines in the United States. If it succeeds, it will have the power at any time, to paralyze the industries of our nation, and bring untold suffering upon our people. Its principles oppress the industrious and ambitious laborer down to the standard of the sluggard. It has not in the past, and there is no reason to believe that it will in the future, hesitate to sacrifice life, liberty and property, to gain its vicious and temporary end. It denies the right of man to sell his labor in a free market.

Anthracite Coal Strike Commission. *Report to the President*. Washington, D.C.: U.S. Government Printing Office, 1903, 103–105, 107–108.

PANAMA CANAL

Roosevelt's major legacy in regard to Latin America, the construction of the Panama Canal, was an epic one that perhaps more than any other highlights the peculiarities of his character. He referred to it as "by far the most important action I took in foreign affairs during the time I was President."[1] However, it is the issue in which Roosevelt's concurrent version of events seems to stray the farthest from the reality of the situation. Although the canal itself was widely viewed as necessary to American security and economic interests, the president's role in achieving it was highly controversial.

A canal linking the Atlantic and Pacific Oceans was aspired to since early Spanish explorers saw the potential of a waterway that could save a distance of eight thousand nautical miles on a route from the east to west coast of North America. Over the long period of plans and attempts to build a canal, there existed two key questions: Who would control the canal, and where would it be constructed?

In 1850, tensions between the United States and Great Britain led to the Clayton-Bulwer Treaty, which stipulated that the United States could not establish exclusive control over any canal it constructed. But this sharing of power with a European nation ran counter to the Monroe Doctrine (which established a protectorate role for America against European aggression in Latin America) and rankled many Americans. In 1901, it was superseded by the Hay-Pauncefote Treaty between the United States and Britain that established exclusive rights for the United States to build and control a canal. Although he was not instrumental to its passage, Roosevelt was proud that this document was negotiated very early in his administration.

The second issue, the location of the canal, was much more hardly fought. Because of a failed French attempt to construct a canal in the Colombian state of Panama (noted for its troublesome terrain and untamed rivers), popular and scientific opinion was leaning toward Nicaragua as the preferred location. However, due to the energetic lobbying efforts of French engineer Philippe-Jean Bunau-Varilla and American attorney William Nelson Cromwell, political opinion in the United States was finally swayed toward Panama.

By 1902, the U.S. Congress had passed the Spooner Act that called for a treaty to be drawn up with Colombia authorizing construction of the canal in the state of Panama. At this point, the real troubles began, as did a larger role for Roosevelt. Although the U.S. Senate confirmed the Hay-Herran Treaty in March 1903, Colombia became recalcitrant, and finally rejected the treaty in August. Colombian leaders complained that the agreement differed from what had initially been proposed, and feared that it represented too great a loss of their sovereignty. Roosevelt, who later referred to the leaders as "inefficient bandits,"[2] believed that they were attempting to extract a higher payment in return for ceding the canal zone. Three months after Colombia rejected the treaty, a brief and successful revolution ensued, establishing an independent nation of Panama and clearing the way for construction of the canal. But the role played by the United States, and Roosevelt in particular in this episode, was, and remains, somewhat hazy.

For Roosevelt, the answer to the dispute with Colombia was to be found in the 1846 treaty with New Grenada (the former name of Colombia). That document ceded to the United States a right to build the canal in Panama in return for a guarantee of Colombian sovereignty and free transit in the canal zone. Roosevelt believed that Colombia's rejection of the 1903 treaty was in essence an abrogation of this earlier document. Additionally, he asserted that Colombia's control over Panama had always been tenuous and that the state considered itself a separate entity. Despite these views that Panamanian independence was the proper and inevitable outcome, the president was careful (at least at the time) not to publicly advocate a revolution. The degree to which he privately encouraged it, however, is fairly well established. Bunau-Varilla and others were dispatched to Panama in the fall of 1903 with large sums of money and promises of American support. Additionally, the warship USS *Nashville* appeared off the coast of Colombia one day before the revolt. The United States was the first to recognize the newly independent nation.

Roosevelt explained and defended his actions in the 1903 message to Congress. At the time, many suspected that he had more to do with the revolution than he let on, but the brunt of opposition was not unleashed until, years later, the former president began to boast of his activist role. In a letter written in 1908, he made the first reference to "taking Panama." But it was in his speech in Berkeley, California, on March 23, 1911, where he fully acknowledged his part. He was excoriated for the speech in the press in the following days, with editorials blasting the perceived ethical lapse he now proudly acknowledged. For many interpreted the 1846 treaty in a different way, focusing more on the U.S. promise to protect Colombia's sovereignty, and the president's abrogation of this pact in the 1903 crisis. A *New York Times* editorial portrayed Roosevelt's earlier actions as perfidious and harmful to America's foreign relations.

Roosevelt toured the canal construction zone in 1906, a trip notable as the first time a sitting U.S. president traveled outside American borders. The canal opened to ships in the summer of 1914, and remained under U.S. control until the turn of the century. Lingering remorse over U.S. actions ultimately led to the ratification of a compensatory treaty with Colombia in 1921.

NOTES

1. Theodore Roosevelt, *An Autobiography* (New York: Scribner's, 1913), 512.

2. Joseph Bucklin Bishop, *Theodore Roosevelt and His Time*, vol. 1 (New York: Scribner's, 1920), 297.

ROOSEVELT—PANAMA CANAL (DECEMBER 7, 1903)

Last spring . . . a treaty concluded between the representatives of the republic of Colombia and of our government was ratified by the Senate. This treaty was entered into at the urgent solicitation of the people of Colombia and after a body of experts appointed by our government especially to go into the matter of the routes across the Isthmus had pronounced unanimously in favor of the Panama route. In drawing up this treaty every concession was made to the people and to the government of Colombia. We were more than just in dealing with them. Our generosity was such as to make it a serious question whether we had not gone too far in their interest at the expense of our own; for in our scrupulous desire to pay all possible heed, not merely to the real but even to the fancied rights of our weaker neighbor, who already owed so much to our protection and forbearance, we yielded in all possible ways to her desires in drawing up the treaty. Nevertheless, the government of Colombia not merely repudiated the treaty, but repudiated it in such manner as to make it evident by the time the Colombian Congress adjourned that not the scantiest hope remained of ever getting a satisfactory treaty from them. The government of Colombia made the treaty, and yet when the Colombian Congress was called to ratify it the vote against ratification was unanimous. It does not appear that the government made any real effort to secure ratification.

Immediately after the adjournment of the Congress a revolution broke out in Panama. The people of Panama had long been discontented with the republic of Colombia, and they had been kept quiet only by the prospect of the conclusion of the treaty, which was to them a matter of vital concern. When it became evident that the treaty was hopelessly lost, the people of Panama rose literally as one man. Not a shot was fired by a single man on the Isthmus in the interest of the Colombian Government. Not a life was lost in the accomplishment of the revolution. . . .

The control, in the interest of the commerce and traffic of the whole civilized world, of the means of undisturbed transit across the Isthmus of Panama has become of transcendent importance to the United States. We have repeatedly exercised this control by intervening in the course of domestic dissension, and by protecting the territory from foreign invasion. . . .

The above recital of facts establishes beyond question: First, that the United States has for over half a century patiently and in good faith carried out its obligations under the treaty of 1846; second, that when for the first time it became possible for Colombia to do anything in requital of the services thus repeatedly rendered to it for fifty-seven years by the United States, the Colombian Government peremptorily and offensively refused thus to do its part, even though to do so would have been to its advantage and immeasurably to the advantage of the State of Panama, at that time under its jurisdiction; third, that throughout this period revolutions, riots, and factional disturbances of every kind have occurred one after the other in almost uninterrupted succession, some of them lasting for months and even for years, while the central government was unable to put them down or to make peace with the rebels; fourth, that these disturbances instead of showing any sign of abating have tended to grow more numerous and more serious in the immediate past; fifth, that the control of Colombia over the Isthmus of Panama could not be maintained without the armed intervention and assistance of the United States. In other words, the government of Colombia, though wholly unable to maintain order on the Isthmus, has nevertheless declined to ratify a treaty the conclusion of which opened the only chance to secure its own stability and to guarantee permanent peace on, and the construction of a canal across, the Isthmus.

Under such circumstances the government of the United States would have been guilty of folly and weakness, amounting in their sum to a crime against the nation, had it acted otherwise than it did when the revolution of November 3 last took place in Panama. This great enterprise of building the interoceanic canal cannot be held up to gratify the whims, or out of respect to the governmental impotence, or to the even more sinister and evil political peculiarities, of people who, though they dwell afar off, yet, against the wish of the actual dwellers on the Isthmus, assert an unreal supremacy over the territory. The possession of a territory fraught with such peculiar capacities as the Isthmus in question carries with it obligations to mankind. The course of events has shown that this canal cannot be built by private enterprise, or by any other nation than our own; therefore it must be built by the United States.

Hagedorn, Hermann, ed. *The Works of Theodore Roosevelt.* Vol. 15. New York: Scribner's, 1925, 204–206, 210–212.

"A BELATED CONFESSION" (March 25, 1911)

Ex-President Roosevelt was uncommonly frank in his address at the Charter Day exercises of the University of California. He openly, and even boastfully, admitted that the despoiling of Colombia of her most precious province, Panama, was his own personal act. We quote Mr. Roosevelt's language:

I am interested in the Panama Canal because I started it. If I had followed traditional, conservative methods I would have submitted a dignified State paper of probably 200 pages to Congress and the debates on it would have been going on yet; but I took the Canal Zone and let Congress debate; and while the debate goes on the canal does also.

Quite so. "I took the Canal Zone." This is the opinion expressed by *The Times* when the deed was perpetrated, that Mr. Roosevelt took the Canal Zone. He speaks almost as though it were an act of condescension on his part to submit the matter to Congress at all. But he did "let Congress debate." This is the doctrine of the one man power, the man on horseback. Polk began the Mexican war, and he has been unsparingly denounced for it. But he made haste to let Congress assume the responsibility. We do not remember that he ever spoke of that transaction in quite the terms used by Mr. Roosevelt about the Canal Zone.

Doubtless Mr. Roosevelt's act hastened the beginning of work on the canal. He says nothing about the cost of this haste. It was very great. Leading authorities in international law have deplored this taking of the Canal Zone as an act of perfidy. In our treaty of 1846 with the Republic of New Granada, to all the covenants and benefits of which Colombia succeeded, it is declared that "the United States also guarantee in the same manner the rights of sovereignty and property which New Granada has and possesses over the said territory" of the Isthmus. It was the guarantor himself who trod upon this guarantee, violated it, and seized as his own spoil the estate which he had assured the owner that he would protect against all spoilers, including, of course, himself. We had advance knowledge of the breaking out of the revolution in Panama. Our warships were conveniently at hand. Without our support the rebels could never have withstood the forces of the parent Government. We forbade Colombia to send her forces into the Zone to suppress the uprising. It was in that way that Mr. Roosevelt took the Canal Zone.

Impartial men have considered it, as we have said, an act of perfidy. It has had a lasting effect in engendering in all the South American republics a sleepless suspicion of our motives, and alarm at our policies whenever we have had occasion to make a move in their direction. They were alarmed at our attitude toward Nicaragua. There has been fresh alarm in Mexico and Central America and throughout South America because of our dispatch of troops to Texas. They fear us where it would be immensely to our advantage to have their confidence.

Mr. Roosevelt seems to have been aware of these considerations when in his special message to Congress of Jan. 4, 1904, he attempted a laborious defense of his policy and his acts in the Canal Zone, and of his hasty recognition of a sovereignty that could never have been created, that could never have sustained itself, without our intervention and powerful support. Quite different is the tone of his address at Berkeley. "I took the Canal Zone." The act was characteristic. So is the boast.

New York Times, March 25, 1911.

MONROE DOCTRINE AND THE ROOSEVELT COROLLARY

In the words of Roosevelt, the Monroe Doctrine asserted that the Western Hemisphere was not "to be treated as subject to settlement and occupation by Old World powers."[1] This principle of U.S. foreign policy, first articulated in 1823, was advocated, enlarged, and realized to an unprecedented degree during the Roosevelt administration. Spurred by events in South America and the Caribbean, and by the president's own energetic reaction to them, an international debate over the true meaning and wisdom of the doctrine ensued.

Throughout his public life, Roosevelt was an ardent supporter of the Monroe Doctrine. As early as 1896, he had vigorously defended it in a letter to the *Harvard Crimson* (after that college newspaper urged President Grover Cleveland to keep out of a dispute between England and Venezuela), characterizing opponents as suffering from "spiritless submission."[2] However, his public positions developed over time, moving from vigilance only against hostile takeover attempts by European powers (the basic Monroe Doctrine) to the necessity of intervention in response to merely punitive actions (the Roosevelt Corollary). This evolution to the need for America to play the role of policeman in disputes between European and Latin American nations not involving territorial aggression was triggered by two events that occurred during his presidency.

In 1902, Germany, Great Britain, and Italy set up a naval blockade off the coast of Venezuela in order to force that nation to repay its debts. Although Roosevelt had no fondness for the Venezuelan leader Cipriano Castro, referring to him as an "unspeakably villainous little monkey,"[3] he was greatly disturbed by this turn of events. While he had stated in his first address to Congress that the United States would not protect any state against punishment for wrongdoing, this episode caused him to question whether there was any real difference between this sort of punishment and actual territorial expansion, noting that the debt-collection process could be a mere subterfuge for exercising control. The United States responded to the blockade by increasing naval strength in the area, and the episode was ultimately brought to an end through peaceful negotiation.

But the next case of a potential European punitive action against a Latin American state followed closely behind. Beginning in 1903, the Dominican Republic was in the throes of a revolution in which two rival governments (one of which was at sea in a small gunboat) were vying for power. As a result, customs fees could not be collected and this nation too began to default on the interest it owed on loans from European powers.

The president moved slowly, probably due to concerns over the 1904 elections. In 1904, he made a point of stating that he had no more desire to annex the Dominican Republic "than a gorged boa constrictor might have to swallow a porcupine wrong-end to."[4] Yet throughout 1904, he began to articulate a more expansive view of proper exercise of the Monroe Doctrine.

While he never did move to annex the Dominican Republic, Roosevelt ultimately intervened in 1905, establishing American control of the customshouses. After this point, he ardently embraced the so-called Roosevelt Corollary to the doctrine, stating in his December 5, 1905, message to Congress the necessity of a strong American role and the near impossibility of distinguishing between punitive actions taken to rectify the abrogation of contractual obligations and aggressive takeover attempts.

In typical Roosevelt fashion, he later exaggerated the degree of opposition to his actions in the Dominican Republic, stating sarcastically in his autobiography that "the friends of peace violently attacked me for averting war from, and bringing peace to the island,"[5] and attributing this to their "sheer, simple devotion to prattle and dislike of efficiency."[6] In fact, there was a great deal of support for both the specific action and the abstract principle, from the public at large and by financial interests who had holdings in the capital city of Santo Domingo. But there was concern as well, both internationally and at home. European nations objected to these new limitations on their ability to act to rectify wrongs committed against them. In Latin America, there was fear that the protection principle would be taken too far—meaning that the United States would simply replace the Europeans as the aggressors, although Roosevelt clearly tried to quell these concerns in the message to Congress.

Nationally, there were (by now commonplace in this administration) cries of outrage from Congress, particularly the Senate, that refused for several years to approve of the customshouse appropriation. Many members felt that the president had further overstepped his executive powers, while Roosevelt again asserted that nothing in the Constitution precluded his actions. Additionally, another debate ensued, this one concerned not so much with Roosevelt's specific decision as with the very wisdom of foreign policy by doctrine, particularly this one.

Pitfalls of doctrinal guidance were commonly recognized, but the conception of those dangers differed. For Roosevelt, the abstractness and vagueness of doctrines led governments who abided by them to appear potentially weak and indecisive—that is, they could use the flexibility of the doctrine to make blustering threats but then fail to follow up on them. His solution was to do the opposite, "speak softly and carry a big stick" (the phrase he used in conjunction with this controversy), and to clarify the doctrine by his own expansion of it.

But for others, the danger of vague doctrines was that they could accommodate too much action and discretion. As noted by Harvard sociologist William Graham Sumner, doctrines are potentially the source of unbridled and dangerous power. Both Roosevelt and Sumner sought to avoid war, but their philosophies on achieving this end were quite different. In Sumner's view, "if you want a war, nourish a doctrine,"[7] while Roosevelt (in the aforementional 1896 statement) asserted that "nothing will more certainly in the end produce war than to invite European aggressions of American states by abject surrender of our principles."[8]

Although exercised until the 1920s, over time both the Monroe Doctrine and the Roosevelt Corollary lost relevance. As Latin American nations began to more strenuously object to the paternalistic tone of these instruments of foreign policy, the necessity of the doctrine itself was weakened as European powers increasingly focused their attention and energies on other parts of the world.

NOTES

1. Theodore Roosevelt, *An Autobiography* (New York: Scribner's, 1913), 506.
2. Elton E. Morison, ed., *The Letters of Theodore Roosevelt* (Cambridge, Mass.: Harvard University Press, 1951), 504.

3. Henry F. Pringle, *Theodore Roosevelt, A Biography* (New York: Harcourt, Brace and World, 1956), 18.

4. Joseph Bucklin Bishop, *Theodore Roosevelt and His Time*, vol. 1 (New York: Scribner's, 1920), 431.

5. Roosevelt, *An Autobiography*, 509.

6. Ibid., 510.

7. William Graham Sumner, *War and Other Essays* (New York: AMS Press, 1970), 36.

8. Morison, *Letters of Theodore Roosevelt*, 505.

ROOSEVELT—THE MONROE DOCTRINE
(DECEMBER 5, 1905)

One of the most effective instruments for peace is the Monroe Doctrine as it has been and is being gradually developed by this nation and accepted by other nations. No other policy could have been as efficient in promoting peace in the western hemisphere and in giving to each nation thereon the chance to develop along its own lines. If we had refused to apply the doctrine to changing conditions it would now be completely outworn, would not meet any of the needs of the present day, and, indeed, would probably by this time have sunk into complete oblivion. It is useful at home, and is meeting with recognition abroad because we have adapted our application of it to meet the growing and changing needs of the hemisphere. When we announce a policy such as the Monroe Doctrine we thereby commit ourselves to the consequences of the policy, and those consequences from time to time alter. It is out of the question to claim a right and yet shirk the responsibility for its exercise. Not only we, but all American republics who are benefited by the existence of the doctrine, must recognize the obligations each nation is under as regards foreign peoples no less than its duty to insist upon its own rights.

. . .

There are certain essential points which must never be forgotten as regards the Monroe Doctrine. In the first place we must as a nation make it evident that we do not intend to treat it in any shape or way as an excuse for aggrandizement on our part at the expense of the republics to the south. We must recognize the fact that in some South American countries there has been much suspicion lest we should interpret the Monroe Doctrine as in some way inimical to their interests, and we must try to convince all the other nations of this continent once and for all that no just and orderly government has anything to fear from us. There are certain republics to the south of us which have already reached such a point of stability, order, and prosperity that they themselves, though as yet hardly consciously, are among the guarantors of this doctrine. These republics we now meet not only on a basis of entire equality, but in a spirit of frank and respectful friendship, which we hope is mutual. If all of the republics to the south of us will only grow as those to which I allude have already grown, all need for us to be the especial champion of the doctrine will disappear, for no stable and growing American republic wishes to see some great non-American military power acquire territory in its neighborhood. All that this country desires is that the other republics on this continent shall be happy and prosperous; and they cannot be happy and prosperous unless they maintain order within their boundaries and behave with a just regard for their obligations toward outsiders. It must be understood that under no circumstances will the United States use the Monroe Doctrine as a cloak for territorial aggression. We desire peace with all the world, but perhaps most of all with the other peoples of the American continent. There are, of course, limits to the wrongs which any self-respecting nation can endure. It is always possible that wrong actions toward this nation, or toward citizens of this nation, in some state unable to keep order among its own people, unable to secure justice from outsiders, and unwilling to do justice to those outsiders who treat it well, may result in our having to take action to protect our rights; but such action will not be taken with a view to territorial aggression, and it will be taken at all only with extreme reluctance and when it has become evident that every other resource has been exhausted.

Moreover, we must make it evident that we do not intend to permit the Monroe Doctrine to be used by any nation on this continent as a shield to protect it from the consequences of its own misdeeds against foreign nations. If a republic to the south of us commits a tort against a foreign nation, such as an outrage against a citizen of that nation, then the Monroe Doctrine does not force us to interfere to prevent punishment of the tort, save to see that the punishment does not assume the form of territorial occupation in any shape. The case is more difficult when it refers to a contractual obligation. Our own government has always refused to enforce such contractual obligations on behalf of its citizens by an appeal to arms. It is much to be wished that all foreign governments would take the same view. But they do not; and in consequence we are liable at any time to be brought face to face with disagreeable alternatives. On the one hand, this country would certainly decline to go to war to prevent a foreign government from collecting a just debt; on the other hand, it is very inadvisable to permit any foreign power to take possession, even temporarily, of the custom-houses of an American republic in order to enforce the payment of its obligations; for such temporary occupation might turn into a permanent occupation. The only escape from these alternatives may at any time be that we must ourselves undertake to bring about some arrangement by which so much as possible of a just obligation shall be paid. It is far better that this country should put through such an arrangement, rather than allow any foreign country to undertake it. To do so insures the defaulting republic from having to pay debt of an improper character under duress, while it also insures honest creditors of the republic from being passed by in the interest of dishonest or grasping creditors. Moreover, for the United States to take such a position offers the only possible way of insuring us against a clash with some foreign power. The position is, therefore, in the interest of peace as well as in the interest of justice. It is of benefit to our people; it is of benefit to foreign peoples; and most of all it is really of benefit to the people of the country concerned.

Hagedorn, Hermann, ed. *The Works of Theodore Roosevelt*. Vol. 15. New York: Scribner's, 1925, 300–303.

WILLIAM GRAHAM SUMNER—"WAR" (1903)

If you want war, nourish a doctrine. Doctrines are the most frightful tyrants to which men ever are subject, because doctrines get inside of a man's own reason and betray him against himself. Civilized men have done their fiercest fighting for doctrines. . . . What are they all? Nothing but rhetoric and phantasms. Doctrines are always vague; it would ruin a doctrine to define it, because then it could be analyzed, tested, criticized, and verified; but nothing ought to be tolerated which cannot be so tested. Somebody asks you with astonishment and horror whether you do not believe in the Monroe Doctrine. You do not know whether you do or not, because you do not know what it is; but you do not dare to say that you do not, because you understand that it is one of the things which every good American is bound to believe in. Now when any doctrine arrives at that degree of authority, the name of it is a club which any demagogue may swing over you at any time and apropos of anything. . . .

[J]ust think what an abomination in statecraft an abstract doctrine must be. Any politician or editor can, at any moment, put a new extension on it. The people acquiesce in the doctrine and applaud it because they hear the politicians and editors repeat it, and the politicians and editors repeat it because they think it is popular. So it grows. During the recent difficulty between England and Germany on one side and Venezuela on the other, some newspapers here began to promulgate a new doctrine that no country ought to be allowed to use its naval force to collect private debts. This doctrine would have given us standing-ground for interference in that quarrel. That is what it was invented for. Of course it was absurd and ridiculous, and it fell dead unnoticed, but it well showed the danger of having a doctrine lying loose about the house, and one which carries with it big consequences It may mean anything or nothing, at any moment, and no one knows how it will be. You accede to it now, within the vague limits of what you suppose it to be; therefore you will have to accede to it to-morrow when the same name is made to cover something which you never have heard or thought of. If you allow a political catchword to go on and grow, you will awaken some day to find it standing over you, the arbiter of your destiny, against which you are powerless, as men are powerless against delusions.

The process by which such catchwords grow is the old popular mythologizing. Your Monroe Doctrine becomes an entity, a being, a lesser kind of divinity, entitled to reverence and possessed of prestige, so that it allows of no discussion or deliberation. . . . The Monroe Doctrine is an exercise of authority by the United States over a controversy between two foreign states, if one of them is in America, combined with a refusal of the United States to accept any responsibility in connection with the controversy. That is a position which is sure to bring us into collision with other States, especially because it will touch their vanity, or what they call their honor—or it will touch our vanity, or what we call our honor, if we should ever find ourselves called upon to "back down" from it. Therefore it is very true that we must expect to need a big navy if we adhere to the doctrine. What can be more contrary to sound statesmanship and common sense than to put forth an abstract assertion which has no definite relation to any interest of ours now at stake, but which has in it any number of possibilities of producing complications which we cannot foresee, but which are sure to be embarrassing when they arise!

What has just been said suggests a consideration of the popular saying, "In time of peace prepare for war." If you prepare a big army and navy and are all ready for war, it will be easy to go to war; the military and naval men will have a lot of new machines and they will be eager to see what they can do with them. There is no such thing nowadays as a state of readiness for war. It is a chimera, and the nations which pursue it are falling into an abyss of wasted energy and wealth.

Sumner, William Graham. *War and Other Essays*. New York: AMS Press, 1970, 36–39.

RAILROAD REGULATION

Railroads, since their inception, have played a complex role in America's political economy. In particular, the question of the degree to which they could or should be regulated by government remained unsettled from the late nineteenth century through much of the Progressive Era. But growing public opposition to the railroads' power could not be ignored, and the push for change reached its culmination with passage of the Hepburn Act in 1906, a railroad rate regulation law advocated by Roosevelt early in his second term. In supporting this reform, he staked out a middle ground that drew opposition from both sides—those who wanted to preserve the status quo and those who favored more radical change.

As the railroad concerns grew large and powerful, throughout the late nineteenth and early twentieth centuries, they (like all private businesses) remained virtually free from government regulation. Although railroads, as public conveyances, did have some nominal common law responsibilities (such as at least attempting to provide service wherever it was needed), they were unencumbered in regard to the rates they charged to transport passengers and cargo. Furthermore, railroads enjoyed a governmentally granted *privilege*—the power of eminent domain. This meant these private companies had the right to enlist judicial intervention when landowners refused to sell property for the purpose of railroad expansion.

Given this advantageous position that the railroads held, an increasing number of citizens and politicians believed that, in return, states should have the right to regulate rates, which many found unreasonably high as well as inconsistent, with the largest corporate clients granted the lowest rates. This notion of governmental control, predating progressivism and advanced by the populist movement in particular, had resulted in the passage of some state regulations. Additionally, the Interstate Commerce Commission (ICC) was created by the U.S. Congress in 1887 for the purpose of overseeing pricing and other practices on a nationwide basis.

But neither of these reforms had any meaningful effect. State statutes were struck down by the U.S. Supreme Court in 1897, which declared that in the absence of legislation by the U.S. Congress, interstate rail transportation (and virtually all companies did interstate as opposed to solely intrastate business) could not be regulated. The railroads also fought at the national level, and the ICC was effectively weakened to the point where it could recommend but not enforce reasonable pricing guidelines.

In his first message to Congress, Roosevelt had proposed one limited action—eradication of rate rebates that railroads offered to favored shippers (or that powerful shippers demanded and received). In response, the Elkins Act was passed in 1903, leading to at least more consistent pricing practices. Thus, one of the abuses was eliminated (although the railroads themselves were at that point relieved to abandon these discounts), but the overall rate issue remained. After gaining new confidence as a result of his 1904 reelection, the president began to stress the need for rate regulation. He broached the topic in speeches made in late 1904 and 1905, but set out his most detailed proposal in his December 5, 1905, message to Congress. As in the earlier antitrust message, Roosevelt was careful not to vilify the railroads, and he called for a moderate approach. However, he clearly articulated the need to restore meaningful regulatory power to the ICC by giving it the authority both to mandate reasonable rate guidelines and to exact penalties on companies who ignored these directives. These provisions formed the basis of the Hepburn bill.

Naturally, the railroads reacted strongly. While taking care to note the positive aspects of the ICC, David Wilcox, the president of the Delaware and Hudson Railroad, testified to a House committee in early 1905 (when Roosevelt's position was clear, if not yet completely detailed) that increased regulatory oversight was unnecessary and burdensome. He based his argument on the assertion that rates were not unreasonable, and that government intervention into railroad practices was unprecedented and would threaten the health of the U.S. economy as well as the freedom of American business.

Others felt Roosevelt's proposal did not go far enough. Senator Robert La Follette, a progressive Republican who had fought the railroad interests while serving as the governor of Wisconsin, unsuccessfully attempted to strengthen the bill in the Senate. His complaint was that the legislation allowed the ICC to determine whether rates were relatively reasonable but not if they were reasonable per se. That is, La Follette believed that the issue of whether the railroads in general were making too much profit needed to be addressed. In his statements to the American Political Science Association, William F. Folwell went one step farther and suggested that railroad profits should be completely done away with so that the public could no longer be exploited in its use of this necessary utility.

The Hepburn Act passed easily in the House as a result of a deal Roosevelt had worked out with Speaker of the House Joe Cannon. The fight was much more intense in the Senate as a large number of Republicans loyal to the railroad interests refused to support the president's bill. It ultimately was pushed to passage in 1906 through an alliance of Democrats and progressive Republicans. Approval of this act represented a definitive weakening of the ability of business and industry to resist government control. In particular, the Hepburn Act showed that the administration could infuse an agency with meaningful administrative power, and would not have to address all such abuses through lengthy litigation processes. It remains a hallmark of progressivism.

ROOSEVELT—RAILROAD LEGISLATION
(DECEMBER 5, 1905)

... This power to regulate rates, like all similar powers over the business world, should be exercised with moderation, caution, and self-restraint; but it should exist, so that it can be effectively exercised when the need arises.

The first consideration to be kept in mind is that the power should be affirmative and should be given to some administrative body created by the Congress. If given to the present Interstate Commerce Commission, or to a reorganized Interstate Commerce Commission, such commission should be made unequivocally administrative. I do not believe in the government interfering with private business more than is necessary. I do not believe in the government undertaking any work which can with propriety be left in private hands. But neither do I believe in the government flinching from overseeing any work when it becomes evident that abuses are sure to obtain therein unless there is governmental supervision. It is not my province to indicate the exact terms of the law which should be enacted; but I call the attention of the Congress to certain existing conditions with which it is desirable to deal. In my judgment the most important provision which such law should contain is that conferring upon some competent administrative body the power to decide, upon the case being brought before it, whether a given rate prescribed by a railroad is reasonable and just, and if it is found to be unreasonable and unjust, then, after full investigation of the complaint, to prescribe the limit of rate beyond which it shall not be lawful to go—the maximum reasonable rate, as it is commonly called—this decision to go into effect within a reasonable time and to obtain from thence onward, subject to review by the courts. ...

Let me most earnestly say that these recommendations are not made in any spirit of hostility to the railroads. On ethical grounds, on grounds of right, such hostility would be intolerable; and on grounds of mere national self-interest we must remember that such hostility would tell against the welfare not merely of some few rich men, but of a multitude of small investors, a multitude of railway employees, wage-workers, and most severely against the interest of the public as a whole. I believe that on the whole our railroads have done well and not ill; but the railroad men who wish to do well should not be exposed to competition with those who have no such desire, and the only way to secure this end is to give to some government tribunal the power to see that justice is done by the unwilling exactly as it is gladly done by the willing. Moreover, if some government body is given increased power the effect will be to furnish authoritative answer on behalf of the railroad whenever irrational clamor against it is raised, or whenever charges made against it are disproved. I ask this legislation not only in the interest of the public but in the interest of the honest railroad man and the honest shipper alike, for it is they who are chiefly jeoparded by the practices of their dishonest competitors. This legislation should be enacted in a spirit as remote as possible from hysteria and rancor. If we of the American body politic are true to the traditions we have inherited we shall always scorn any effort to make us hate any man because he is rich, just as much as we should scorn any effort to make us look down upon or treat contemptuously any man because he is poor. We judge a man by his conduct—that is, by his character—and not by his wealth or intellect. If he makes his fortune honestly, there is no just cause of quarrel with him. . . .

The question of transportation lies at the root of all industrial success, and the revolution in transportation which has taken place during the last half-century has been the most important factor in the growth of the new industrial conditions. Most emphatically we do not wish to see the man of great talents refused the reward for his talents. Still less do we wish to see him penalized; but we do desire to see the system of railroad transportation so handled that the strong man shall be given no advantage over the weak man. We wish to insure as fair treatment for the small town as for the big city; for the small shipper as for the big shipper. In the old days the highway of commerce, whether by water or by a road on land, was open to all; it belonged to the public and the traffic along it was free. At present the railway is this highway, and we must do our best to see that it is kept open to all on equal terms. Unlike the old highway it is a very difficult and complex thing to manage, and it is far better that it should be managed by private individuals than by the government. But it can only be so managed on condition that justice is done the public. It is because, in my judgment, public ownership of railroads is highly undesirable and would probably in this country entail far-reaching disaster, that I wish to see such supervision and regulation of them in the interest of the public as will make it evident that there is no need for public ownership. The opponents of government regulation dwell upon the difficulties to be encountered and the intricate and involved nature of the problem. Their contention is true. It is a complicated and delicate problem, and all kinds of difficulties are sure to arise in connection with any plan of solution, while no plan will bring all the benefits hoped for by its more optimistic adherents. Moreover, under any healthy plan the benefits will develop gradually and not rapidly. Finally, we must clearly understand that the public servants who are to do this peculiarly responsible and delicate work must themselves be of the highest type both as regards integrity and efficiency.

Hagedorn, Hermann, ed. *The Works of Theodore Roosevelt.* Vol 15. New York: Scriber's 1925, 275–276, 278–281.

DAVID WILCOX—TESTIMONY TO HOUSE COMMITTEE ON INTERSTATE AND FOREIGN COMMERCE (JANUARY 21, 1905)

When I applied to the chairman of this committee for a hearing, I did not apply on behalf of the Delaware and Hudson Company but on behalf of its employees and security holders and on behalf of those who are dependent upon them. My constituency, I may say, is perhaps 100,000; probably that.

What has been the cause of the prosperity of this property and upon what depend its 100,000 people? Upon nothing else in the world but the income of the property. Without the income the property is of no value. Without the income there would be no incentive to operate it; and, therefore, necessarily, any proposition which tends to place in the hands of the government, however ably administered, the question as to whether or not this substantial mass of property shall earn anything, which tends to qualify or limit its earning capacity, affects not the company for these companies, gentlemen, are of very little importance. They are artificial persons. They are the means by which the property of the owners is held together and is made productive. That is all there is of it.

If the American people so wish, the corporations may die. But what is to become of the people who are interested in them? What is to become of this enormous mass of property, upon which rests the prosperity not merely of the class whom I have named but also of those who sell supplies to them, and of the communities through which they pass, and of the communities which will be built up by their extension? It seems to me that that is the serious question—What effect is what you may do here going to have upon the future welfare, productiveness, and value of the greatest single industrial interest of the country . . . ?

What I say, gentlemen, is that it is a very, very serious moment when an Anglo-Saxon government undertakes the charge of people's money and says how much they shall earn by the exercise of their constitutional rights of liberty and property. And it should be recognized that possibly we are at the parting of the ways, and that if this be done it will go on until those constitutional guarantees have but little value, and the only profession worth exercising in the country will be that of holding office in some administrative board.

The Annals of America. Vol. 13. Chicago: Encyclopaedia Britannica, 1968, 4–5.

WILLIAM F. FOLWELL—REMARKS ON RAILROAD PROFITS (1904)

. . . I feel disposed to use a minute or two in what I am sure many of you will think an unnecessarily radical and revolutionary proposition; but when I hear discussions upon rates of this kind, interesting as they are and valuable as they are, I still think there is a deeper question in regard to rates which ought to be had in mind. We have been discussing rates from the standpoint of railway ownership. We have not discussed them from the standpoint of the general public. All the speakers, I think, have agreed, and all others will agree, that the railway has become a public carrier; it is a servant of the public through and through. It cannot be regarded any more as a private common carrier. Now, I wish to make this revolutionary proposition, that transportation has become absolutely necessary to every individual. I cannot live unless the railroad brings to my door the means of subsistence; it is absolutely impossible. I submit this proposition, and I will take the risk of being called socialistic, that there should be no more chance to make money out of transportation than there is in carrying the mails. What do you think of that? I think that is a proposition you ought to consider. There should be no opportunity of exploiting the public by means of this absolutely necessary function, and I am going so far in my teaching as to say this. I am not in favor of government ownership, but I am in favor of an arrangement by which railroads shall be constructed and operated in such a manner as to pay the wages and salaries, all the salaries necessary to secure the very best talent; to pay a fair interest on all the capital or all the wealth that is actually in the road and no more; to maintain a fund for maintaining the road, and for such extensions as may be necessary; and for paying a fair, ordinary tax; and then when all these expenses have been paid any excess of income should go into the public treasury.

"Discussion." *Proceedings of the American Political Science Association* 1 (1904): 221.

SIMPLIFIED SPELLING

Although not one of the most substantial issues of this administration, the simplified spelling episode did cause quite a stir at the time, and it provides an illustrative glimpse into Roosevelt's blustery character and the sometimes maddening or humorous effect it could have on others. The president's efforts to endorse a phonetically based spelling system (and to have it represent the official language of the executive branch) elicited nationwide merriment, as well as reasoned responses and angry denunciations triggered by perceptions of this issue as one more example of the president's excesses.

The simplified spelling movement predated Roosevelt's interest by over thirty years. Scholars first began to advocate spelling words as they were pronounced and dropping unnecessary letters in the 1870s. This was not quite the break with tradition that it might seem to modern readers. In fact, the American spelling rules in place at that time only dated back to about 1806, when the first dictionary was published in this country. Prior to that time, writers tended to follow their own idiosyncratic preferences. The simplified spelling advocates did not wish to return to this chaotic state—they wanted standardization, but with logical and consistent rules. Their arguments for moving to this system revolved primarily around the greater ease with which children could be taught to spell and adults could remember how to spell properly. Second, they noted that the new rules would result in shorter and less costlier books. For example, they claimed the *Encyclopaedia Britannica* would consist of twenty volumes instead of twenty-four, and its cost would drop by $24.

In August 1906, Roosevelt endorsed a recommendation made by the Spelling Reform Association, headed at that time by his friend, Professor Brander Matthews of Columbia University. This recommendation called for changing the spelling of three hundred words, such as replacing "thru" for "through," "dropt" for "dropped," and "check" for "cheque." (Actually, 90 percent of these were already recognized at the time by *Webster's Dictionary* as alternate spellings.) The president directed Charles Stillings, the U.S. printer, that all documents emanating from executive departments, agencies, and so on were to be printed using these rules. In his letter to Stillings (using simplified spelling), the president provided an explanation for the decision, arguing it was not a revolutionary change, but simply a common sense evolution. He also noted that its ultimate fate would rest on its reception by the American public.

But, by taking the curious step of justifying an executive order to the public printer, Roosevelt clearly implied that he knew the action would be controversial. And indeed this order provided fodder for Roosevelt critics of various sorts for the remainder of that year. The media had a field day with the issue. The *New York Times* stated that it (and hopefully other newspapers) would assume these "heterographical freaks"[1] were misprints and correct them to proper spellings. Other newspapers humorously considered how the president would now spell his own name (although the proposed rules would not in fact affect proper names). The *Louisville Courier-Journal* suggested "Rucevelt," noting that the first syllable would rhyme with "goose," while the *Baltimore Sun* asked, "Will he make it Rusevelt, or will he get down to the fact and spell it Butt-in-sky?"[2]

More serious objections came from some academics and various sources in Great Britain, aghast at the "President's American" usurping the "King's English." Additionally, a great deal of opposition was recorded in Congress, which debated the issue in December 1906. It is clear from the congressional discussions that this matter represented more than just a question of spelling. It reflected the consistent, and growing, opposition to Roosevelt's general activism, seen as a usurpation of legislative power and discretion.

Some members of Congress simply took this opportunity to attack the plan and the president on a fairly nonsensical basis. For example, one representative asked whether the Supreme Court could adequately respond to a claim of denial of "dew" process of law. But others offered more reasoned criticisms of both simplified spelling and Roosevelt's role. Representative James "Champ" Clark (D–Missouri), while acknowledging some potential benefits to phonetic spelling, pointed out that the association's rules were really not so simple after all, as some of the changes were inconsistent. He also questioned how phonetic spelling makes sense in a nation with so many regional dialects, and thus different ways of pronouncing the same word. Clark moderately but firmly asserted that not just here but in other areas as well the president had continually overstepped his constitutional powers.

At the end of this lengthy debate, Congress approved a provision effectively negating Roosevelt's order, and the president quickly backed down, noting in a letter to Matthews that it was "worse than useless to go into an undignified contest when I was beaten."[3] However, he promised to continue using simplified spelling in his personal correspondences.

Overall, the episode illustrates how Roosevelt threw himself into controversies, even fairly insubstantial ones, without a second thought if he believed himself to be in the right. The side Roosevelt championed in this particular episode is typical, as this president prided himself on challenging the accepted order of things and advocating innovation. Although simplified spelling was never claimed as a progressive reform, it fits with Progressive Era attempts to move toward greater efficiency in all things. Interestingly, many of the association's proposed changes have since come to be the accepted spellings of words, such as "theater" instead of "theatre." Even "thru," which Roosevelt himself believed was the most resisted of the changes and the trigger to overall opposition to the new rules, is now accepted as proper by dictionaries.

NOTES

1. Mark Sullivan, *Our Times, 1900–1925*, vol. 3 (New York: Scribner's, 1939), 178.
2. Ibid., 181.
3. Ibid., 190.

ROOSEVELT—LETTER TO THE PUBLIC PRINTER (AUGUST 27, 1906)

I inclose herewith copies of certain circulars of the Simplified Spelling Board, which can be obtained free from the board at No. 1 Madison avenue, New York City. Please hereafter direct that in all Government publications of the Executive Departments the 300 words enumerated in circular No. 5 shall be spelled as therein set forth. If anyone asks the reason for the action, refer him to circulars 3, 4, and 6, as issued by the Simplified Spelling Board. Most of the criticism of the proposed step is evidently made in entire ignorance of what the step is, no less than in entire ignorance of the very moderate and common-sense views as to the purposes to be achieved, which views are so excellently set forth in the circulars to which I have referred. There is not the slightest intention to do anything revolutionary or initiate any far-reaching policy. The purpose simply is for the Government, instead of lagging behind popular sentiment, to advance abreast of it and at the same time abreast of the views of the ablest and most practical educators of our time, as well as of the most profound scholars.

If the slight changes in the spelling of the 300 words proposed wholly or partially meet popular approval, then the changes will become permanent without any reference to what public officials or individual private citizens may feel; if they do not ultimately meet with popular approval they will be dropt; and that is all there is about it. They represent nothing in the world but a very slight extension of the unconscious movement which has made agricultural implement makers and farmers write "plow" instead of "plough"; which has made most Americans write "honor" without the somewhat absurd, superfluous "u"; and which is even now making people write "program" without the "me"— just as all people who speak English now write "bat," "set," "dim," "sum," and "fish," instead of the Elizabethan "batte," "sette," "dimme," "summe," and "fysshe": which makes us write "public," "almanac," "era," "fantasy," and "wagon," instead of the "publick," "almanack," "aera," "phantasy," and "waggon" of our great-grandfathers. It is not an attack on the language of Shakespeare and Milton, because it is in some instances a going back to the forms they used, and in others merely the extension of changes which, as regards other words, have taken place since their time. It is not an attempt to do anything far-reaching or sudden or violent; or indeed anything very great at all. It is merely an attempt to cast what slight weight can properly be cast on the side of the popular forces which are endeavoring to make our spelling a little less foolish and fantastic.

Congressional Record. 59th Congress, 2nd sess., 1906. Vol. 41, 214.

REPRESENTATIVE JAMES B. CLARK—REMARKS ON SIMPLIFIED SPELLING (DECEMBER 10, 1906)

Mr. Chairman, this matter is not so much of a joke as it might seem at first blush. I most heartily indorse what the Committee on Appropriations did in this matter when they say:

Hereafter, in printing documents authorized by law or ordered by Congress or either branch thereof the Government Printing Office shall follow the rules of orthography established by Webster's or other generally accepted dictionaries of the English language.

Before the President issued his remarkable ukase there was no trouble in this country about spelling. Everybody either tried to conform his spelling to the generally accepted authorities or he paid no attention to the authorities at all and spelled to suit himself.

I will not go as far as the gentlemen from Georgia [Mr. (Leonadis F.) Livingston] went in saying that this order of the President makes "confusion worse confounded." I think that is an extravagant statement, too. But I do think that it makes a muddle where there was no sense in having any muddle. Some time before very long the people of the United States are going to insist on having a President who will attend strictly to his own constitutional functions and expend his energies only on subjects of great pith and moment. . . .

In the shape in which this question now arises it is a practical problem. A gentleman asked me if I am in favor of phonetic spelling. I am not certain whether we could adopt it, but if we could there is no question that if we had the phonetic system of spelling which has forty-four letters in it we would absolutely save two years of the time that a child is learning to spell. . . .

There is something practical about that, but there are three arguments against that. All the etymologists will be against it. The men who want to learn the derivation of words will be against it. Every printed book in the English language is an argument against it, and every human being who has learned to spell in the usual way is a living, moving argument against it. They do not want to take the trouble to learn to spell any other way. . . .

As to this order of the President, it is absolutely pitiable. It produces confusion without doing any good. I undertake to say that if you take the scholars of the House, such as my learned friend from Massachusetts [Mr. (Frederick H.) Gillett], and ask them to pick 300 words for the experiment in simplified spelling no two would pick the same words and no two would agree on the spelling of the 300 words. The President says "thru"; but the gentleman from Massachusetts objects to spelling the word "through," in the way that the President spelled it all through his message—"thru"—because in certain places the letter "u" has a different sound from what it has in the word "through." The gentleman from Massachusetts would spell it "throo," because, so he thinks, "u" never has the sound of "oo." Now, that is all a question of geography. It depends on the section of country you are in as to whether certain sounds prevail. For instance, the word "calf" is as much entitled, under Webster's Standard Dictionary, to be pronounced "c-a-w-f" as palm is entitled to be pronounced "p-a-w-m"; yet let a man go into an agricultural section of the country, where they raise calves, and go around through the country talking about a c-a-w-f, and he will run good risk of having a writ de lunatico inquirendo sworn out for him.

The changing of the spelling of these 300 words does not do any good. It simply muddles things.

Congressional Record. 59th Congress, 2nd sess., December 10, 1906. Vol. 41, 222–223.

THE BROWNSVILLE EPISODE

The Brownsville episode illustrates how emotionally charged the issue of race had become by the early twentieth century. Additionally, it shows that the national debate on the topic was complex and subtle—it was not simply a matter of whether blacks did or did not deserve civil rights. This incident was complicated even further by questions of equal justice as well as party politics and, as usual, the impact of Roosevelt's personality.

The only agreed upon facts are that on August 14, 1906, in Brownsville, Texas, a mob raid occurred in which a white bartender was killed and a policeman was wounded. No suspects were apprehended at the time, but townspeople alleged that the crimes were perpetuated by about a dozen soldiers from nearby Fort Brown, members of an all black battalion of the Twenty-fifth U.S. Infantry. From the moment of their arrival six weeks earlier, tensions had been high, as the soldiers resented the town's segregation codes, and local whites took offense at the soldiers' presence. Several scuffles between Brownsville citizens and soldiers preceded the raid.

By late August, military investigators concluded that the raid had been perpetuated by men from this battalion, but because of a putative conspiracy of silence it was impossible to tell who the specific criminals were. A recommendation was thus made that the entire three companies (167 men) be dishonorably discharged. President Roosevelt concurred, the men were dismissed, and a national debate ensued.

There were two themes of opposition to the president's decision. The first was that the alleged proof of any soldiers' guilt was tenuous at best. Senator Joseph Foraker (R–Ohio; nicknamed "Fire Alarm" for his aggressive style), who was the leader of this charge, called for a congressional investigation of the episode. Foraker pointed out that the morning following the raid all of the soldiers' guns were inspected and none appeared to have been recently fired. He believed that the spent cartridges found in the area of the raid and that were traceable to the guns used by these troops had in fact been planted there to cover up the fact that the crime was committed by one or more Brownsville citizens.

Foraker and Roosevelt had clashed before, on the railroad regulation issue, and the president assumed the senator was using this episode to advance his own aspirations to the presidency in 1908. The two men exchanged angry comments in public over the Brownsville incident at the annual Gridiron Dinner early in 1907. Losing his temper completely at the senator's admonition, Roosevelt declared angrily, "The only reason I didn't have them hung was because I couldn't find out which ones . . . did the shooting."[1]

The second major source of opposition to the president's decision came from those who believed that one or more soldiers had committed the crime, but that the blanket dishonorable discharge for all was extremely unjust and discriminatory. Newspapers across the nation, and the black press in particular, asserted that Roosevelt had violated basic principles of justice in punishing all for a crime only a few could have committed. The prominent black writer W.E.B. Du Bois described the decision as a "wretched judicial lynching."[2]

One of the more unusual criticisms of Roosevelt came in a congressional speech given by Senator "Pitchfork" Ben Tillman of South Carolina. Tillman, one of a growing new breed of very conservative southern Democrats who drew support largely from poor and uneducated whites, was possibly the most openly racist member of the U.S. Congress at the time. He managed to use this incident both to attack Roosevelt and to air his harsh prejudices. For Tillman, there was no doubt that the crime had been committed by one or more of the soldiers, as he believed blacks to be fully untrustworthy and lacking in moral character. However, he blamed the president for sending the troops to Brownsville in the first place, where they were so clearly unwanted, and argued that the results of the inevitable violent outcome should not be borne by those who had not participated in any crime. He feared that the dismissed soldiers had become martyrs to other blacks.

Roosevelt at first reacted to the storm of criticism with his usual disbelief and stubbornness. He viewed himself as the friend of blacks in America, and was stung that he was accused of being unjust and prejudicial. Like many Americans of this era, Roosevelt did not fully believe in the equality of the races. This was evidenced, for example, by his Latin American policies that stressed the need for white men to educate and "elevate" the other races. However, in general, Roosevelt was broadminded on racial issues, at least for his time. He had hosted Booker T. Washington, the black president of the Tuskegee Institute, for dinner at the White House (as Tillman sarcastically alludes to in his speech), stressed the importance of education for all races, and in 1908 threatened a railroad line with legal action if they continued to deny service to blacks. His message to Congress on the Brownsville episode stresses that the race of the soldiers had nothing to do with his decision and that each man must be judged by his conduct and not his color. Later, somewhat abashed by the storm of criticism, he agreed that soldiers who could retrospectively prove their innocence should not be punished. Fourteen soldiers were ultimately reinstated, although the real story of what happened in Brownsville has never been completely clarified.

Overall, the episode did not cause serious harm to Roosevelt's reputation of progressivism on the racial issue. Washington reminded blacks that, while the Brownsville decision was regrettable, the president had "favored them in nine out of ten cases."[3] With few exceptions, blacks did not abandon his chosen successor, Taft, in the 1908 elections, viewing the openly racist Democratic candidate William Jennings Bryan as the far less appealing choice. (Foraker never became a viable candidate; by 1908 his political career was ruined by evidence of long-term payments to him from the Standard Oil Company.) Even Du Bois, in his 1919 obituary of Roosevelt, noted that "even in our hot bitterness over the Brownsville Affair we knew that he *believed* he was right, and he of all men had to act in accordance with his beliefs."[4]

NOTES

1. William Henry Harbaugh, *Power and Responsibility* (New York: Octagon Books, 1975), 292.

2. Henry Lee Moon, ed., *The Emerging Thought of W.E.B. Du Bois* (New York: Simon and Schuster, 1972), 96.

3. James A. Tinsley, "Roosevelt, Foraker, and the Brownsville Affray," *Journal of Negro History* 41 (1956): 49.

4. Moon, *Emerging Thought*, 335.

ROOSEVELT—MESSAGE TO CONGRESS ON
BROWNSVILLE EPISODE (DECEMBER 19, 1906)

Any assertion that these men were dealt with harshly because they were colored men is utterly without foundation. Officers or enlisted men, white men or colored men, who were guilty of such conduct would have been treated in precisely the same way, for there can be nothing more important than for the United States army, in all its membership, to understand that its arms cannot be turned with impunity against the peace and order of the civil community. . . . In my message at the opening of the Congress I discussed the matter of lynching. In it I gave utterance to the abhorrence which all decent citizens should feel for the deeds of the men (in almost all cases white men) who take part in lynchings, and at the same time I condemned, as all decent men of any color should condemn, the action of those colored men who actively or passively shield the colored criminal from the law. In the case of these companies we had to deal with men who in the first place were guilty of what was practically the worst possible form of lynching—for a lynching is in its essence lawless and murderous vengeance taken by an armed mob for real or fancied wrongs—and who in the second place covered up the crime of lynching by standing with a vicious solidarity to protect the criminals.

It is of the utmost importance to all our people that we shall deal with each man on his merits as a man, and not deal with him merely as a member of a given race; that we shall judge each man by his conduct and not his color. This is important for the white man, and it is far more important for the colored man. More evil and sinister counsel never was given to any people than that given to colored men by those advisers, whether black or white, who, by apology and condonation, encourage conduct such as that of the three companies in question. If the colored men elect to stand by criminals of their own race because they are of their own race, they assuredly lay up for themselves the most dreadful day of reckoning. Every far-sighted friend of the colored race in its efforts to strive onward and upward should teach first, as the most important lesson alike to the white man and the black, the duty of treating the individual man strictly on his worth as he shows it. Any conduct by colored people which tends to substitute for this rule the rule of standing by and shielding an evildoer because he is a member of their race, means the inevitable degradation of the colored race. It may and probably does mean damage to the white race, but it means ruin to the black race.

Throughout my term of service in the Presidency I have acted on the principle thus advocated. In the North as in the South I have appointed colored men of high character to office, utterly disregarding the protests of those who would have kept them out of office because they were colored men. So far as was in my power, I have sought to secure for the colored people all their rights under the law. I have done all I could to secure them equal school training when young, equal opportunity to earn their livelihood and achieve their happiness when old. I have striven to break up peonage; I have upheld the hands of those who, like Judge Jones and Judge Speer, have warred against this peonage, because I would hold myself unfit to be President if I did not feel the same revolt at wrong done a colored man as I feel at wrong done a white man. I have condemned in unstinted terms the crime of lynching perpetrated by white men, and I should take instant advantage of any opportunity whereby I could bring to justice a mob of lynchers. In precisely the same spirit I have now acted with reference to these colored men who have been guilty of a black and dastardly crime. In one policy, as in the other, I do not claim as a favor, but I challenge as a right, the support of every citizen of this country, whatever his color, provided only he has in him the spirit of genuine and far-sighted patriotism.

Roosevelt, Theodore. *Addresses and Papers.* New York: Sun Dial Classics, 1908, 346–348.

SENATOR BEN TILLMAN—REMARKS ON THE BROWNSVILLE DISMISSALS (JANUARY 12, 1907)

Of course, being nothing more than a cornfield lawyer, my contribution to the legal discussion of this question will be very limited and comparatively worthless. . . .

But the ridiculousness of the situation is made apparent when one considers that a Senator from the North, who, by reason of his radical and aggressive utterances and, probably, actions in the past once gave him the name of "Fire Alarm"—I say that Senator finds himself aligned with that Senator from the South who is supposed to have a broiled negro for breakfast, who is known to justify lynching for rape, and whose attitude is one of not hatred toward the negroes, but of a feeling akin to it, in the belief that white men are made of better clay than negroes and that white men alone are entitled to participate in government—I say this alliance is an odd one.

I want to say, Mr. President, that I appear here in this connection, and

I shall present the views which I shall give to the Senate upon the broad and general proposition, although coming from South Carolina and known as probably the most ultra of my brethren in this Chamber on the subject of the race questions—that even I, while I may be alone, and, as I am informed, am already alone in my attitude—even I want to see the negroes treated fairly and justly.

The President of the United States has, in my opinion, dealt with certain men of the Twenty-fifth Infantry very unjustly. He has gone entirely too far in dealing with some of them, while he has stopped very, very far short of meting out proper punishment and justice to others of them. My proposition in discussing this question will be to try to prove that even he has no right nor any authority to punish an innocent man because some men are guilty. . . .

I do not imagine that any evidence will ever be produced or can be produced to show that this crime was not committed by some of the Twenty-fifth Infantry stationed at Fort Brown. I am thoroughly satisfied of it myself. I am convinced by the negative rather than the positive testimony, and from my knowledge of negro character after fifty-nine years contact with them. I claim to know as much about the characteristics of the American negro as any man living, and I have no more doubt the negro soldiers did these infamous things than that I am alive and standing here. . . .

In this District [Washington, D.C.] we have thought it necessary to have separate schools for the races, and we have found it necessary to prevent the negroes from voting. . . . It is well understood that no negro would any more dare to go to the Willard Hotel or the Raleigh and expect to be served at the bar or in the restaurant than if he were to go to the White House—no; not as easily. But why ignore a great fact, which is that caste feeling is universal; that it pulsates in the bosom of the Senator from Minnesota, though he may not be aware of it, and that you can not ignore caste feeling. . . .

These troops, having been taught that their uniform was a badge of nobility, entitling them to every consideration that every other man should get, are sent to this southern city, where class prejudice, if you want to designate it as such, exists. . . . But let us not forget that this feeling is not peculiarly southern. It is well nigh universal. When these men went there and soon discovered that the people of the town did not recognize the President's idea and were not ready to subscribe to it, that they were unwilling to grant them the privileges that they thought they had the right to expect, they immediately set about to bring on an excuse or to provoke condition which would make them feel justified in doing what they did. . . .

I want to be just to the negro if I know how. Probably I do not know how. But I would be sufficiently just not to lynch 167 of them because twenty odd had been guilty of something. No southern mob has ever gone that far in the way of taking life without due process of law. . . .

To sever the connection of these men with the Army is entirely too much punishment for those who have done nothing, it is entirely too little punishment for those who shot up Brownsville. So one would wish that Major Penrose's recommendation had been followed, and that the detectives had been given an opportunity to try to ferret out the culprits.

But it was not done; and then in great haste, without waiting to see if something might not turn up which would disclose the culprits, the connection with the Army of the whole lot is severed, and they are roaming up and down the world now discredited. "Discredited," did I say? Why, Senators, they are the heroes of the hour among the 10,000,000 negroes in the United States. They are martyrs in the cause of social equality. They have been driven out of the Army by the act of their good friend Theodore Roosevelt—I mean the man they thought once was their apostle of equal rights. The negroes of the North have been passing resolutions of censure and condemnation and protest in conventions and in churches for the last several months. But if anyone can imagine that these 167 men are not to-day looked upon by the negroes in this country with admiration, then Senators here know nothing of the negro character.

Congressional Record. 59th Congress, 2nd sess., January 12, 1907. Vol. 41, 1030–1033.

CONSERVATION OF NATURAL RESOURCES

One of the greatest legacies of the Roosevelt administration is the protection of the nation's resources. Two particular aspects of this policy focus are notable. First, Roosevelt's conservation initiative represented a visionary policy in terms of the comprehensive approach it took to various resource issues. No previous president, and arguably none since, has committed himself to such a broad conservation effort. Second, the initiative was inextricably tied to progressive principles. For Roosevelt, this was one more round in the fight for economic justice and efficiency. However, because of the very boldness of this agenda, it was inevitably seen as excessive by congressional, state, and private-sector critics. Although narrower questions on the best way to achieve conservation goals were debated later, the initial controversy centered on the necessity or desirability of any major conservation effort.

While Roosevelt certainly did not discover the loss and degradation of resources such as unique land formations, mineral reserves, forests, and animal species (and was not the first president to advocate a federal response), he did commit himself fully to the cause. Significantly, his program moved beyond the stopgap preservation of particular sites to a more holistic and systematic approach. For example, instead of simply working to protect additional land parcels, Roosevelt changed the very system by which forests were acquired and administered by the federal government. When he took office, control of national forests was assigned to the Land Office of the Department of the Interior. However, the employees who were proficient in forest management were housed in the separate Bureau of Forestry and had little authority. Roosevelt convinced Congress to grant all decision-making power to experts in a newly created Forestry Service, headed by the ardent conservationist Gifford Pinchot, within the Department of Agriculture. Thus, an informed and strategic approach to expansive land and forest protection could be more easily pursued.

As Roosevelt became more aggressive in his attempts to protect land and resources from private exploitation after his 1904 reelection, he faced growing resistance from Congress. But this did not slow his efforts. For example, after setting aside several sites as national parks, Congress refused to authorize more. Roosevelt got around the hurdle by utilizing the Antiquities Act of 1906, which allows the president to preserve areas of historic or scientific interest as national monuments without congressional approval. Similarly, when Roosevelt discovered there was no law forbidding him from establishing wildlife preserves, he set about creating many of them, including the fifty-one bird sanctuaries of which he was most proud.

To his critics, the president's most maddening and imperious action came in response to a 1907 agriculture spending bill provision that explicitly forbade the executive branch from granting protected status to any additional forests in six western states. He responded by (at the urging of Pinchot) setting aside sixteen million acres in the ten-day window he had to sign or veto the bill. Roosevelt later noted that in response to his ploy, "the opponents of the forest service turned handsprings in their wrath."[1]

For this president, however, the destruction of resources was only part of the problem. His legacy of conservation was a key component of his general progressive agenda of restoring economic justice to the nation and removing the grip of concentrated wealth and monopoly from the American economy. The fact that private interests were profiting from the utilization and sale of in-common resources such as coal, timber, oil, and water was intolerable. In some cases, these interests were illegally accessing these goods (sometimes with the complicity of corrupt government officials); in others, they were the beneficiaries of generous federal lease programs that granted usage rights for fees far below market value. This represented an inequity to the president—the use of public goods for private profit with little real compensation to the American people was unjust. Thus, he fought for more vigorous enforcement of laws protecting resources and for the rescission of several out-of-date leasing policies.

Another progressive principle relevant to this issue is the quest for greater efficiency. Roosevelt was not a strict preservationist but a conservationist. That is, he believed that at least some resources should be exploited, but with greater efficiency. This explains some policies that do not seem to fit with modern principles of environmentalism. For example, Roosevelt's reclamation initiative—the irrigation of lands previously unsuitable for farming or human habitation—was designed to fundamentally alter ecosystems and bring more people into previously uninhabitable areas. But he felt it was government's responsibility to achieve this goal because it would make life less difficult for Americans settling the western regions.

By 1908, Roosevelt had come to believe that the fight for conservation must spread to the state level, and as such he organized the Governors Conservation Conference. His opening speech to this White House assembly outlined his general devotion to the cause and stressed its significance to the nation's future. Yet, although the accolades for the conference illustrated the broad public approval of the conservation agenda, Roosevelt's philosophy was not universally welcomed. The remarks of Representative Sylvester C. Smith (D–Calif.) two years later sum up the opposition views—that conservation policies critically ignored the needs (and property rights) of the people as well as the authority of states to determine the use of their own resources, while granting far too much decision-making power to the executive branch.

NOTE

1. Theodore Roosevelt, *An Autobiography* (New York: Scribner's, 1913), 404–405.

ROOSEVELT—"THE NATURAL RESOURCES—THEIR WISE USE OR THEIR WASTE" (MAY 13, 1908)

This conference on the conservation of natural resources is in effect a meeting of the representatives of all the people of the United States called to consider the weightiest problem now before the nation; and the occasion for the meeting lies in the fact that the natural resources of our country are in danger of exhaustion if we permit the old wasteful methods of exploiting them longer to continue.

With the rise of people from savagery to civilization, and with the consequent growth in the extent and variety of the needs of the average man, there comes a steadily increasing growth of the amount demanded by this average man from the actual resources of the country. Yet, rather curiously, at the same time the average man is apt to lose his realization of this dependence upon nature.

. . .

... It is almost impossible for us in this day to realize how little our Revolutionary ancestors knew of the great store of natural resources whose discovery and use have been such vital factors in the growth and greatness of this nation, and how little they required to take from this store in order to satisfy their needs.

Since then our knowledge and use of the resources of the present territory of the United States have increased a hundredfold. Indeed, the growth of this nation by leaps and bounds makes one of the most striking and important chapters in the history of the world. Its growth has been due to the rapid development, and alas! that it should be said, to the rapid destruction of our natural resources. Nature has supplied to us in the United States, and still supplies to us, more kinds of resources in a more lavish degree than has ever been the case at any other time or with any other people. Our position in the world has been attained by the extent and thoroughness of the control we have achieved over nature; but we are more, and not less, dependent upon what she furnishes than at any previous time of history since the days of primitive man.

. . .

The steadily increasing drain on these natural resources has promoted to an extraordinary degree the complexity of our industrial and social life. Moreover, this unexampled development has had a determining effect upon the character and opinions of our people. The demand for efficiency in the great task has given us vigor, effectiveness, decision, and power, and a capacity for achievement which in its own lines has never yet been matched. So great and so rapid has been our material growth that there has been a tendency to lag behind in spiritual and moral growth; but that is not the subject upon which I speak to you today. Disregarding for the moment the question of moral purpose, it is safe to say that the prosperity of our people depends directly on the energy and intelligence with which our natural resources are used. It is equally clear that these resources are the final basis of national power and perpetuity. Finally, it is ominously evident that these resources are in the course of rapid exhaustion.

This nation began with the belief that its landed possessions were illimitable and capable of supporting all the people who might care to make our country their home; but already the limit of unsettled land is in sight, and indeed but little land fitted for agriculture now remains unoccupied save what can be reclaimed by irrigation and drainage. We began with an unapproached heritage of forests; more than half of the timber is gone. We began with coal-fields more extensive than those of any other nation and with iron ores regarded as inexhaustible, and many experts now declare that the end of both iron and coal is in sight.

The mere increase in our consumption of coal during 1907 over 1906 exceeded the total consumption in 1876, the Centennial year. The enormous stores of mineral oil and gas are largely gone. Our natural waterways are not gone, but they have been so injured by neglect, and by the division of responsibility and utter lack of system in dealing with them, that there is less navigation on them now than there was fifty years ago. Finally, we began with soils of unexampled fertility and we have so impoverished them by injudicious use and by failing to check erosion that their crop-producing power is diminishing instead of increasing. In a word, we have thoughtlessly, and to a large degree unnecessarily, diminished the resources upon which not only our prosperity but the prosperity of our children must always depend.

We have become great because of the lavish use of our resources and we have just reason to be proud of our growth. But the time has come to inquire seriously what will happen when our forests are gone, when the coal, the iron, the oil, and the gas are exhausted, when the soils shall have been still further impoverished and washed into the streams, polluting the rivers, denuding the fields, and obstructing navigation. These questions do not relate only to the next century or to the next generation. It is time for us now as a nation to exercise the same reasonable foresight in dealing with our great natural resources that would be shown by any prudent man in conserving and widely using the property which contains the assurance of well-being for himself and his children.

. . .

. . . But all these various uses of our natural resources are so closely connected that they should be co-ordinated and should be treated as part of one coherent plan and not in haphazard and piecemeal fashion.

Hagedorn, Hermann, ed. *The Works of Theodore Roosevelt*. Vol. 16. New York: Scribner's, 1926, 119–124, 126.

REPRESENTATIVE SYLVESTER C. SMITH—REMARKS ON CONSERVATION (APRIL 20, 1910)

If this House should remain in session two or three days and devote itself to the discovery of what is the meaning of this word "conservation" and get that meaning fixed in the mind of the House and of the country, the time would be well spent. I think I have never known in the history of this country, or of any other of which I have read, a case where a word has been injected into the administrative and political life of the country and used again and again and again and again by everybody without anyone attempting to give it the peculiar or technical meaning which they all seem to think it possesses. I have begged with tears in my eyes of my distinguished friend from New York [Mr. (Herbert) Parsons] and my distinguished friend from Oklahoma [Mr. (Scott) Ferris] and my distinguished friends from other parts of the country to endeavor to give us the definition which they have in mind for the word "conservation." Now I am going to give you something of what I think the western notion of the word is. I am not authorized to speak for other people, but I will speak for Smith, and I think he speaks for his constituents and the West. The word "conservation" means to conserve, and the word "conserve" means to save, preserve, and it does not mean to preserve a thing in idleness. Nor does it mean a federal tax on the products or the natural resources of the West. I think the definition which the gentleman from Oklahoma would give, and those we may call the orthodox school of conservationists would give, come to two things: First, a federal tax on the remaining resources of the country in the ownership of the Nation. I am dead against it. Second, I think it means some kind of federal supervision, or guardianship over the people who are endeavoring to make use of the land and the mines and the water rights of the West, and I am dead against that also. We are not imbeciles in the West. We are capable of taking care of ourselves. We are capable of managing our farms, our mines, our water rights, and our forests without any federal wet nursing throughout every day in the year. . . .

A year or two ago . . . I came across this very extraordinary situation. It was labeled "conservation" on both sides, and blown in the bottle. A man who applies for a homestead in a forest reserve was told that he could have a lease only, and that he could probably keep the land as long as he paid the rent. That is conservation, too, according to this orthodox notion of things. It led to a tax payable to the Federal Government, and was the beginning of a system of national tenancies, than which there is nothing more damnable than can be conceived.

I never was so angry in my life as I was when the information of that practice came to my knowledge. . . . I was thoroughly angry to think that, under the guise of this word "conservation," they had undertaken to fasten upon this country the most despisable system of land ownership that ever existed on the face of the earth—national tenancies—and to make the American farmer the chattel of the man controlling the affairs of the Forest Service. . . .

I might go on and instance these things for a long time as to what is considered conservation, and it all leads to two things, namely, a federal tax and a federal guardian to supervise and to tell you how to run your business, which the American people have been running for themselves since this was a Nation. Why should you undertake to foist any such foreign, new-fangled system upon the people of the West? The East, the South, and the Middle West went forth and possessed themselves of all that was good and glorious that lay before them. They took the soil as homesteads, they took the forests, and they took the mines. What did they do with them? They devoted them to the beneficial uses of mankind. We had gentlemen come before our committee and almost weep as they pointed out to us with mathematical precision how soon we would consume all the coal there was in the country. And when we asked them what part of the consumption of coal they thought we had better shut off first, of course they were at the end of their tether. There has not been any coal mined except what this country needed.

Congressional Record, 61st Congress, 2nd sess., April 20, 1910. Vol. 45, 5062–5063.

WOMAN SUFFRAGE

As with many of his public positions, Roosevelt's views on woman suffrage were subtle. The strong opposition that some suffragists accused him of is not an accurate portrayal. Rather, the key characteristic of his opinion is that he simply did not believe the political rights of women to be of major import. This, and not an ingrained assumption of the inferiority of women, is what contrasted his ideas on the subject with suffrage advocates.

Actually, Roosevelt's beliefs on the role of women in society, while somewhat complex and evolving and thus difficult to clearly pin down, were rather advanced for his time. One telling piece of evidence is that his senior dissertation at Harvard University was entitled, "The Practicability of Equalizing Men and Women before the Law." In that paper, written in 1880, he stated, "The man should have no more right over the person or property of his wife than she has over the person or property of her husband. I would have the word 'obey' used not more by the wife than the husband."[1]

As president, his views on women avoided extremes. He asserted neither that women should inhabit the same societal roles as men, nor that women were simply unequipped and thus unfit for such activities. Instead, he described an ideal nation in which men used their talents in public matters and women used their talents in the home. Thus, the genders were equal but had different functions to perform. In particular, he stressed the need for women to bear children as a patriotic duty, stating his belief that all women who were able should have at least four children, in order to make up for those who were less fertile or never married.

It is clear in retrospect that one of the flaws in Roosevelt's concept of separate but equal spheres for men and women was his failure to understand that the so-called woman's role might be unfulfilling, and that not all women came naturally to domestic life. One indication of this is a letter he proudly included in his autobiography from a woman who, at age forty-five and after raising nine children, wrote the president that she was so out of touch with the world that she could no longer have an intelligent conversation with her husband about current events. Roosevelt's response, basically that her husband needed to show her the respect that any mother of nine deserved, tellingly seems to miss the point.

But, to be fair, such concerns were not really addressed even by the suffrage advocates. Their issues focused on the basic injustice of denying women the right to vote, as well as the beneficial policies (e.g., temperance, child labor prohibitions, and so on) that could result if women were granted political rights. In arguing for this cause, social worker and progressive activist Jane Addams turned Roosevelt's own arguments against him, writing that in order for women to fulfill their domestic functions (which she defined in a much broader and more modern way than Roosevelt) in industrialized America they needed to utilize the power of the ballot. In contrast, in his 1908 letter to Harriet Taylor Upton, a suffragist who demanded to know why he did not publicly advocate the cause, as well as in his February 1912 editorial in *The Outlook*, Roosevelt stated that while he supported suffrage for women who wanted it, he simply did not see it as a pressing need either for the women themselves or for society as a whole, again stressing the contributions women made in the realm of home and family.

Roosevelt's position on the issue shifted during the 1912 presidential campaign, when he adopted a woman suffrage plank in his platform. By the time of the writing of his autobiography in 1913, Roosevelt claims to have been transformed "from a zealous instead of a lukewarm adherent to the cause"[2] by women like Addams, whose devotion to progressive issues he admired. The Nineteenth Amendment granted the right to vote to all American women in 1920.

NOTES

1. Henry F. Pringle, *Theodore Roosevelt, A Biography* (New York: Harcourt, Brace and World, 1956), 331.

2. Theodore Roosevelt, *An Autobiography* (New York: Scribner's, 1913), 163.

ROOSEVELT—LETTER TO HARRIET TAYLOR UPTON
(NOVEMBER 10, 1908)

I will give you exactly my feeling about your request that I speak a word for woman suffrage in my annual message. I do not think it would be wise to do so; not in the least because of any consideration about myself, but because I think that it is not in any shape or way a live issue at this time, and because I do not see what good would come of my mentioning it.

Personally I believe in woman suffrage, but I am not an enthusiastic advocate of it because I do not regard it as a very important matter. I am unable to see that there has been any special improvement in the position of women in those States in the West that have adopted woman suffrage, as compared with those States adjoining them that have not adopted it. I do not think that giving the women suffrage will produce any marked improvement in the condition of women. I do not believe that it will produce any of the evils feared, and I am very certain that when women as a whole take any special interest in the matter they will have the suffrage if they desire it. But at present I think most of them are lukewarm; I find some actively for it and some actively against it.

I am, for the reasons above given, rather what you would regard as lukewarm or tepid in my support of it because, while I believe in it, I do not regard it as of very much importance. I believe that man and woman should stand on an equality of right, but I do not believe that equality of right means identity of function; and I am more and more convinced that the great field, the indispensable field, for the usefulness of the woman is as the mother of the family. It is her work in the household, in the home, her work in bearing and rearing the children, which is more important than any man's work, and it is that work which should be normally the woman's special work, just as normally the man's work should be that of the breadwinner, the supporter of the home, and if necessary the soldier who will fight for the home. There are exceptions as regards both man and woman; but the full and perfect life, the life of highest happiness and of highest usefulness to the State, is the life of the man and the woman who are husband and wife, who live in the partnership of love and duty, the one earning enough to keep the home, the other managing the home and the children.

Bishop, Joseph Bucklin. *Theodore Roosevelt and His Time*. Vol. 2. New York: Scribner's, 1920, 127–128.

ROOSEVELT—"WOMEN'S RIGHTS; AND THE DUTIES OF BOTH MEN AND WOMEN" (FEBRUARY 3, 1912)

I believe in woman's suffrage wherever the women want it. Where they do not want it, the suffrage should not be forced upon them. I think that it would be well to let the women themselves, and only the women, vote at some special election as to whether they do or do not wish the vote as a permanent possession. . . . Though I do not think that the damage prophesied from women's voting would come, or has come where it has been tried, I also think that very much less effect would be produced, one way or the other, than the enthusiasts believe. In other words, I do not regard the movement as anything like as important as either its extreme friends or extreme opponents think. It is so much less important than many other reforms that I have never been able to take a very heated interest in it. . . .

I feel that, instead of having to develop in the future, as something hitherto unknown, the highest and most useful type of woman, we already have that type with us now. The all-important thing is to endeavor in every way to raise as many other individuals as possible to the serene level of this type. In the same way, the important thing to work for in marriage is to raise the average marriage relations to the level of those that already obtain in the finest type of existing marriage. No woman will ever be developed who will stand above the highest and finest of the wives and mothers of to-day and of the yesterdays. The exercise of the suffrage can never be the most important of women's rights or women's duties. The vital need for women, as for men, is to war against vice, and frivolity, and cold selfishness, and timid shrinking from necessary risk and effort.

Hagedorn, Hermann, ed. *The Works of Theodore Roosevelt*. Vol. 16. New York: Scribner's, 1926, 208, 209, 218.

JANE ADDAMS—"WHY WOMEN SHOULD VOTE" (1915)

For many generations it has been believed that woman's place is within the walls of her own home, and it is indeed impossible to imagine the time when her duty there shall be ended or to forecast any social change which shall release her from that paramount obligation.

This paper is an attempt to show that many women to-day are failing to discharge their duties to their own households properly simply because they do not perceive that as society grows more complicated, it is necessary that woman shall extend her sense of responsibility to many things outside of her own home if she would continue to preserve the home in its entirety. One could illustrate in many ways. A woman's simplest duty, one would say, is to keep her house clean and wholesome and to feed her children properly. Yet if she lives in a tenement house, as so many of my neighbors do, she cannot fulfill these simple obligations by her own efforts because she is utterly dependent upon the city administration for the conditions which render decent living possible. Her basement will not be dry, her stairways will not be fireproof, her house will not be provided with sufficient windows to give light and air, nor will it be equipped with sanitary plumbing, unless the Public Works Department sends inspectors who constantly insist that these elementary decencies be provided. Women who live in the country sweep their own dooryards and may either feed the refuse of the table to a flock of chickens or allow it innocently to decay in the open air and sunshine. In a crowded city quarter, however, if the street is not cleaned by the city authorities—no amount of private sweeping will keep the tenement free from grime; if the garbage is not properly collected and destroyed a tenement house mother may see her children sicken and die of diseases from which she alone is powerless to shield them, although her tenderness and devotion are unbounded. She cannot even secure untainted meat for her household, she cannot provide fresh fruit, unless the meat has been inspected by city officials, and the decayed fruit, which is so often placed upon sale in the tenement districts, has been destroyed in the interests of public health. In short, if woman would keep on with her old business of caring for her house and rearing her children she will have to have some conscience in regard to public affairs lying quite outside of her immediate household. The individual conscience and devotion are no longer effective. . . .

Ever since steam power has been applied to the processes of weaving and spinning woman's traditional work has been carried on largely outside of the home. The clothing and household linen are not only spun and woven, but also usually sewed by machinery; the preparation of many foods has also passed into the factory and necessarily a certain number of women have been obliged to follow their work there. . . . Because many thousands of those working in factories and shops are girls between the ages of fourteen and twenty-two, there is a necessity that older women should be interested in the conditions of industry. . . .

If woman's sense of obligation had enlarged as the industrial conditions changed she might naturally and almost imperceptibly have inaugurated movements for social amelioration in the line of factory legislation and shop sanitation. That she has not done so is doubtless due to the fact that her conscience is slow to recognize any obligation outside of her own family circle, and because she was so absorbed in her own household that she failed to see what the conditions outside actually were. It would be interesting to know how far the consciousness that she had no vote and could not change matters operated in this direction. After all, we see only those things to which our attention has been drawn, we feel responsibility for those things which are brought to us as matters of responsibility. If conscientious women were convinced that it was a civic duty to be informed in regard to these grave industrial affairs, and then to express the conclusions which they had reached by depositing a piece of paper in a ballot-box, one cannot imagine that they would shirk simply because the action ran counter to old traditions. . . .

Public-spirited women who wish to use the ballot, as I know them, do not wish to do the work of men nor to take over men's affairs. They simply want an opportunity to do their own work and to take care of those affairs which naturally and historically belong to women, but which are constantly being overlooked and slighted in our political institutions. In a complex community like the modern city all points of view need to be represented; the resultants of diverse experiences need to be pooled if the community would make for sane and balanced progress. If it would meet fairly each problem as it arises, whether it be connected with a freight tunnel having to do largely with business men, or with the increasing death rate among children under five years of age, a problem in which women are vitally concerned, or with the question of more adequate streetcar transfers, in which both men and women might be said to be equally interested, it must not ignore the judgments of its entire adult population. To turn the administration of our civic affairs wholly over to men may mean that the American city will continue to push forward in its commercial and industrial development, and continue to lag behind in those things which make a City healthful and beautiful. After all, woman's traditional function has been to make her dwelling-place both clean and fair. . . . If women have in any sense been responsible for the gentler side of life which softens and blurs some of its harsher conditions, may they not have a duty to perform in our American cities? In closing, may I recapitulate that if woman would fulfill her traditional responsibility to her own children; if she would educate and protect from danger factory children who must find their recreation on the street; if she would bring the cultural forces to bear upon our materialistic civilization; and if she would do it all with the dignity and directness fitting one who carries on her immemorial duties, then she must bring herself to the use of the ballot—that latest implement for self-government. May we not fairly say that American women need this implement in order to preserve the home?

"Douglass Archives of American Public Addresses." http://douglass.speech. nwu.edu/adda_a03.htm, accessed May 31, 2000.

RECOMMENDED READINGS

Bates, J. Leonard. "Fulfilling American Democracy: The Conservation Movement, 1907 to 1921." *The Mississippi Valley Historical Review* 44 (1957): 29–57.

Bishop, Joseph Bucklin. *Theodore Roosevelt and His Time*. 2 vols. New York: Scribner's, 1920.

Beale, Howard K. *Theodore Roosevelt and the Rise of America to World Power*. Baltimore: Johns Hopkins University Press, 1934.

Brands, H.W. *T.R., The Last Romantic*. New York: Basic Books, 1997.

Harbaugh, William Henry. *Power and Responsibility*. New York: Octagon Books, 1975.

Mowry, George E. *The Era of Theodore Roosevelt, 1900–1912*. New York: Harper and Row, 1958.

Pringle, Henry F. *Theodore Roosevelt, A Biography*. New York: Harcourt, Brace and World, 1956.

Roosevelt, Theodore. *American Ideals*. New York: AMS Press, 1969.

———. *An Autobiography*. New York: Scribner's, 1913.

Theodore Roosevelt (video recording). The American Experience Series, 1997.

Theodore Roosevelt Association. www.theodoreroosevelt.org. Accessed November 28, 2000.

Tinsley, James A. "Roosevelt, Foraker, and the Brownsville Affray." *Journal of Negro History* 41 (1956): 43–65.

Weaver, John D. *The Senator and the Sharecropper's Son: Exoneration of the Brownsville Soldiers*. College Station: Texas A&M Press, 1997.

Wiebe, Robert H. "The Anthracite Strike of 1902: A Record of Confusion." *The Mississippi Valley Historical Review* 48 (1961): 229–251.

2

WILLIAM HOWARD TAFT

(1909–1913)

INTRODUCTION

William Howard Taft attained the presidency, as Theodore Roosevelt had, by having the position virtually thrust upon him. In Taft's case, this was a result of Roosevelt deciding that Secretary of War Taft was the perfect man to succeed him, virtually ordering him to run in the 1908 election. However, where (with far less notice) Roosevelt quickly adapted and seemed to bask and blossom in the role, Taft never achieved a similar level of comfort. This Republican president's principal legacy was not so much one of issue agendas and accomplishments but of a philosophy of the limited nature of executive authority, and the importance of retaining stability in governmental policies and institutions. This outcome followed from two distinct but related tensions faced by Taft upon becoming president—his disagreements with his predecessor on procedure, if not necessarily outcomes, and the increasingly contentious nature of his own party.

First, while Taft liked and admired Theodore Roosevelt and genuinely approved of most of his policy goals, he seriously questioned the means by which they had been achieved. For Taft, presidents were granted very narrowly defined powers by the Constitution, and had no license to move beyond that framework. Roosevelt's attempts to bypass congressional and state opposition by acting unilaterally and without consultation was simply not a strategy the new president could emulate. For, above all, Taft was an attorney who was guided first and foremost by the law and the Constitution in all political matters. Where he did agree with the progressive agenda, he generally pursued it through slower and less imperious means—that is, by turning decisions over to Congress or the states. Additionally, his focus on the law highlights a key difference between Taft and the majority of progressives that was largely glossed over in the 1908 election. When reforms sought to strengthen laxly enforced laws, Taft welcomed them; but when they sought to fundamentally change the laws (or the processes by which laws were created), he was strongly opposed.

While he accepted that laws could and did slowly evolve in response to thoughtful and enduring public opinion shifts, he did not believe that potentially ephemeral popular preferences should override long-standing legal and constitutional principles. This philosophy was illustrated by his views on the growing movement for greater public control over judges and judicial decisions—a cause championed by Roosevelt. For Taft, this movement was anathema. Not only were established traditions challenged, but this also occurred in his cherished legal arena. This view led to his initial veto of the Arizona–New Mexico statehood bills in June 1911. More importantly, the overall result of his frequently opposing the means, and sometimes the goals, of reform was a general slowing of the progressive agenda begun by Roosevelt.

The second trigger to the deceleration of reforms was that, upon being elected president, Taft became at least the symbolic head of a deeply divided Republican Party, which lost its majority in the House of Representatives during the 1910 midterm elections. The conservative and progressive elements of the party had for some time been growing increasingly distinct from one another, particularly in regard to the propriety of extensive governmental regulations. Roosevelt had been able to hold things together to a degree—sometimes through the force of his persuasive gifts and ability to deal with both sides in an issue, and sometimes by his schemes of simply ignoring Congress altogether. Taft, lacking in the first talent and unwilling to utilize the second strategy, was forced to take sides. Given his disinclination to rapid change, it is not surprising that he stood for the most part with the conservatives in his party, beginning with his early decision not to support the progressives in their attempt to remove conservative Speaker Joe Cannon.

Thus, his personal ideology and the Republican split largely explain Taft's overall record as president, best characterized as one in which the greatest efforts were expended not on change, but on preserving the status quo (or, sometimes, wresting it back to where it was before the Roosevelt administration). However, it would be incorrect to fully characterize Taft as simply a reactionary conservative. Although in many instances he drastically scaled back the Roosevelt agenda, in some ways (although with his own distinctive approach) he extended it.

The economic realm provides the best illustration of Taft's rather subtle achievements. He actually pursued the antitrust agenda quite vigorously, initiating more suits in four years than the Roosevelt administration had in seven. But where Roosevelt had advocated moving away from the litigation method (a blunt tool with which trusts were usually either left intact or completely broken up) to congressionally created oversight boards and more specific legislation (which could elicit broader and more rapid change), Taft was content to continue to pursue the matter in the courts through utilization of the Sherman Antitrust Act. This meant that change came more slowly, on a case-by-case basis.

Similarly, in regard to the protection of natural resources, while Taft was annoyed with the fervor that had come to accompany the term "conservation" and believed that Roosevelt had greatly exceeded executive authority on this matter, more acres were actually granted protected status during Taft's term. But, again, he allowed this goal to be achieved more slowly, through the legislative process as opposed to presidential decree. In addition to this procedural distinction, another significant Taft-Roosevelt difference was apparent in both issues. Taft pursued monopolies and the abuse of natural resources because these practices violated existing laws; Roosevelt sought reform because the practices were simply, to his thinking, wrong.

Yet, perhaps because of his lesser degree of political acumen, Taft was willing to fight some battles that Roosevelt had avoided. He achieved even greater empowerment for the Interstate Commerce Commission (ICC) by successfully advocating a policy that precluded the railroads' use of court-granted injunctions as a means to delay ICC orders to lower rates. Another achievement was approval of a corporate income tax. Additionally, he supported, although did not actively fight for, the Sixteenth Amendment to the Constitution that authorized the personal income tax. Taft also pursued tariff reductions, but was opposed by the conservative element in his party and ultimately failed in the effort. He was, in the end, forced to justify the continued high rates to the American people. Thus, Taft did support several less visible but genuinely progressive economic reforms, but as a result of the tariff concessions became even more closely bound to the party conservatives.

While establishing a limited but not insubstantial record in the economic realm, Taft had little to say on social issues. The only real controversy came in regard to his policy of (unlike Roosevelt) refusing to appoint African Americans to federal positions in the southern states. However, he justified this as an attempt to avoid racial tensions, and made up for the decision by granting more federal posts to blacks in the North.

Similarly, Taft established only a limited foreign policy agenda. The major initiative he did support, an effort to spread American influence abroad through strategic investments, was largely ineffectual. In China in particular, Taft's attempt to secure U.S. backing of several large projects was resented by all relevant parties—the Chinese, the other nations that had already staked a claim to the projects, and the American bankers who were asked to provide the funds. There were no grand visions to the Taft foreign policy agenda, and even the lesser visions were flawed.

Thus, while making some modest progressive contributions of his own, the overall impact of Taft's administration was to establish a model of restraint, and of contrast to the Rooseveltian and progressive agenda. This all became most apparent in 1912 when Taft first faced Roosevelt as a challenger for the Republican nomination, and then Roosevelt and Wilson (the Progressive and Democratic Party nominees, respectively) in the presidential campaign.

Taft was increasingly seen as (and became) a very conservative candidate. With no real changes of his own to advocate, he was forced to provide challenges to the innovations suggested by his opponents. The campaign highlighted Taft's limitations as a politician—he was simply unwilling to make incendiary speeches promising to give the people what they wanted, although the conservative stance did please party leaders. The campaign accentuated and publicized Taft's and Roosevelt's diverging views on an active versus passive presidency, and the necessity and propriety of various progressive reforms. The election went to Wilson, who in many ways offered a compromise between Taft's growing conservatism and Roosevelt's ever more radical brand of progressivism.

It is difficult to fault Taft for the limited agenda he left behind. He never wanted to become president, aspiring instead to the role of chief justice of the U.S. Supreme Court, a position he finally attained in 1921. Additionally, he was thrust into an untenable situation—following a president whose basic philosophy of the office was diametrically opposed to his own, and trying to manage a party in which progressive ideas were becoming increasingly marginalized. In retrospect, it is clear that Roosevelt's activist agenda simply could not have been sustained in the Taft administration. But despite leaving only a moderate record of reforms (that are often unduly ignored in the shadow of his predecessor), Taft did provide an important legacy—a philosophy of a passive and legally governed presidency that, albeit not particularly exhilarating, represents one viable view of what the writers of the Constitution envisioned for this office.

CONTINUING THE CONSERVATION AGENDA

As with many issues, Taft's record on conservation appears to pale in comparison with that of his predecessor. While supportive of policies designed to protect and conserve the nation's resources, he pursued this end less zealously than Roosevelt had. Taft, always concerned with legal proprieties, worried that various conservation policies might be unconstitutional or of dubious legality. His apprehension of the potential federal trampling of states' rights or executive usurpation of congressional power led him to act cautiously on this issue. But, while his divergence from Roosevelt's policies was more a matter of degree than substance, it still led to an embarrassing split with Chief Forester Gifford Pinchot (who was a Roosevelt loyalist) as well as a major administration scandal.

Perhaps the most notable characteristic of the Taft presidency was his rejection of the general Roosevelt philosophy that a president could do anything as long as there was no obvious law against it. Taft preferred the more conservative approach of acting only under clear authorization, and his predecessor's policies in regard to natural resources in particular seemed to him to border on illegality. This accusation had also been made by state governments, citizens, and members of Congress who believed that various actions had been taken without appropriate authority.

One of Taft's first actions as president, contrary to an earlier assurance he made to Roosevelt, was to replace Secretary of the Interior James R. Garfield. This son of former president James A. Garfield had been one of Roosevelt's faithful supporters and was an advocate of the activist approach to conservation. He was replaced by Richard A. Ballinger, a former Land Office commissioner who was generally believed to have close ties to western groups opposed to Roosevelt's policies. Taft ordered Ballinger to rescind many of the Roosevelt-Garfield orders conferring protected status on public lands until Congress (the proper authority in these matters) could act on them. In particular, lands that had been designated as national monuments or as potential sites of water-based power sources (which Roosevelt did not believe any private citizen should control) were reopened to public use. Additionally, several irrigation projects were halted because the funds had never been properly appropriated by Congress. While Taft did not object to the substance of these policies, he simply could not accept the means by which they had been achieved. His orders resulted in a slowing down or reversal of many of the Roosevelt administration's conservation accomplishments.

These actions might not have led to so much controversy were it not for the role played by Pinchot who, even more than Garfield, was a Roosevelt disciple and a driving force behind the earlier conservation policies. He was so loyal to Roosevelt that he referred to Taft's inauguration as a "dreadful day,"[1] and the replacement of his good friend Garfield convinced him that the new president was not to be trusted on the conservation issue. It is not completely clear why Taft initially retained Pinchot in his administration, since he, like Garfield, represented the more drastic approach the president opposed, but it was probably because Pinchot's expertise in forestry was so widely respected. In a June 1909, letter to his brother, Taft wrote, "I do regard Gifford as a good deal of a radical and a good deal of a crank, but I am glad to have him in the government."[2] Ultimately, Pinchot forced his own dismissal as a result of a scandal involving Ballinger.

The Ballinger-Pinchot controversy arose in 1909. It involved an extremely complicated story of possibly illegal Alaskan coal mining permits authorized during Ballinger's tenure as the Land Office commissioner. Assertions were made by federal inspector Louis R. Glavis that Ballinger had legal ties to parties who acted improperly in the matter. Although the president urged Pinchot "do not make Glavis's cause yours,"[3] Pinchot helped to bring the matter to public attention. He saw it as a means to more broadly implicate the entire conservation policy of the administration. Taft fully supported Ballinger, yet did not want to lose his chief forester over the dispute. In the end, however, the president was forced to dismiss Pinchot after he publicly questioned Taft's scruples.

Ballinger demanded a congressional hearing to clear his name and the charges against him were found to be without merit. However, the administration was embarrassed when the hearings revealed that the president had purposely postdated a letter he wrote dismissing Glavis, to make it appear as though the firing did not take place until a report on the matter had been delivered, when in fact the decision was made earlier.

While the rift between Taft and Pinchot became mired in politics, personalities, and scandal, it was, at its core, a disagreement over the means by which to achieve conservation goals. Although their differences remained subtle in their respective public pronouncements, they are significant and are reflected in Taft's address to the National Conservation Commission (the state governor's group earlier organized by Roosevelt), as well as the earlier letter to William Kent (a conservation advocate and future member of House of Representatives), versus Pinchot's December 4, 1909, essay in *The Outlook*. Although both men profess support for preservation and the wise use of resources, Taft stresses the need to remain within the bounds of constitutional and legal authority. Pinchot, however, focuses on the more abstract necessity for conservation in general, stressing the progressive-tinged economic justice aspects. He may even be seen as advocating the broad sort of "eloquent and entertaining," yet unrealistic, proposals that Taft warns against. This argument as to the necessity and propriety of broad federal (especially executive) action in regard to the conservation of natural resources as opposed to state and/or congressional authority continues to the present day.

NOTES

1. Gifford Pinchot, *Breaking New Ground* (Seattle: University of Washington Press, 1947), 382.
2. Henry F. Pringle, *The Life and Times of William Howard Taft*, vol. 1 (Hamden, Conn.: Archon Books, 1964), 480.
3. Ibid., 491.

TAFT—LETTER TO WILLIAM KENT (JUNE 29, 1909)

It is not impossible, of course, after such an administration as Roosevelt's, and after the change of method that I could not but adopt in view of my different way of looking at things, that questions should arise as to whether I was going back on the principles of the Roosevelt administration. . . . We have a government of limited power under the Constitution, and we have got to work out our problems on the basis of law. Now, if that is reactionary, then I am a reactionary. I get very impatient at criticism by men who do not know what the law is, who have not looked it up and yet ascribe all sorts of motives to those who live within it. . . . Pinchot is not a lawyer and I am afraid he is quite willing to camp outside the law to accomplish his beneficent purposes. I have told him so to his face. . . . I do not undervalue the great benefit that he has worked out, but I do find it necessary to look into the legality of his plans.

Pringle, Henry F. *The Life and Times of William Howard Taft*. Vol. 1. Hamden, Conn.: Archon Books, 1964, 480.

TAFT—ADDRESS TO THE NATIONAL CONSERVATION CONGRESS (SEPTEMBER 5, 1910)

Conservation as an economic and political term has come to mean the preservation of our natural resources for economical use, so as to secure the greatest good to the greatest number. . . . Today we desire to restrict and retain under public control the acquisition and use by the capitalist of our natural resources. . . . As President of the United States I have, as it were, inherited this policy, and I rejoice in my heritage. . . .

I think it of the utmost importance that after the public attention has been roused to the necessity of a change in our general policy to prevent waste and a selfish appropriation to private and corporate purposes of what should be controlled for the public benefit, those who urge conservation shall feel the necessity of making clear how conservation can be practically carried out, and shall propose specific methods and legal provisions and regulations to remedy actual adverse conditions. I am bound to say that the time has come for a halt in general rhapsodies over conservation, making the word mean every known good in the world, for after the public attention has been roused such appeals are of doubtful utility and do not direct the public to the specific course that the people should take, or have their legislators take, in order to promote the cause of conservation. The rousing of emotions on a subject like this, which has only dim outlines in the minds of the people affected, after a while ceases to be useful, and the whole movement will, if promoted on these lines, die for want of practical direction and of demonstration to the people that practical reforms are intended.

Real conservation involves wise, non-wasteful use in the present generation, with every possible means of preservation for succeeding generations; and though the problem to secure this end may be difficult, the burden is on the present generation promptly to solve it and not to run away from it as cowards, lest in the attempt to meet it we may make some mistake. As I have said elsewhere, the problem is how to save and how to utilize, how to conserve and still develop; for no sane person can contend that it is for the common good that nature's blessings should be stored only for unborn generations.

I beg of you, therefore, in your deliberations and in your informal discussions, when men come forward to suggest evils that the promotion of conservation is to remedy, that you invite them to point out the specific evils and the specific remedies; that you invite them to come down to details in order that their discussions may flow into channels that shall be useful rather than into periods that shall be eloquent and entertaining, without shedding real light on the subject. The people should be shown exactly what is needed in order that they make their representatives in Congress and the State legislature do their intelligent bidding.

Congressional Record. 61st Congress, 3rd sess., 1910. Vol. 46, 34–39.

GIFFORD PINCHOT—"THE ABC OF CONSERVATION" (DECEMBER 4, 1909)

The central thing for which Conservation stands is to make this country the best possible place to live in, both for us and for our descendants. It stands against the waste of the natural resources which cannot be renewed, such as coal and iron; it stands for the perpetuation of the resources which can be renewed, like the food-producing soils and the forests; and, most of all it stands for an equal opportunity for every

American citizen to get his fair share of benefit from these resources, both now and hereafter.

Conservation stands for the same kind of practical common-sense management of this country by the people that every business man stands for in the handling of his own business. It believes in prudence and foresight instead of reckless blindness; it holds that resources now public property should not become the basis for oppressive private monopoly; and it demands the complete and orderly development of all our resources for the benefit of all the people, instead of the partial exploitation of them for the benefit of a few. . . .

Conservation has much to do with the welfare of the average man to-day. It proposes to secure a continuous and abundant supply of the necessaries of life, which means a reasonable cost of living and business stability. It advocates fairness in the distribution of the benefits which flow from the natural resources. It will matter very little to the average citizen when scarcity comes and prices rise, whether he cannot get what he needs because there is none left or because he cannot afford to pay for it. In both cases the essential fact is that he cannot get what he needs. Conservation holds that it is about as important to see that the people in general get the benefit of our natural resources as to see that there shall be natural resources left.

Conservation is the most democratic movement this country has known for a generation. Its holds that the people have not only the right but the duty to control the use of the natural resources, which are the great sources of prosperity. And it regards the absorption of these resources by the special interests, unless their operations are under effective public control, as a moral wrong. . . .

It is of the first importance to prevent our water powers from passing into private ownership as they have been doing, because the greatest source of power we know is falling water. Furthermore, it is the only great unfailing source of power. Our coal, the experts say, is likely to be exhausted during the next century, our natural gas and oil in this. Our rivers, if the forests on the watersheds are properly handled, will never cease to deliver power. Under our form of civilization, if a few men ever succeed in controlling the sources of power, they will eventually control all industry as well. If they succeed in controlling all industry, they will necessarily control the country. This country has achieved political freedom; what our people are fighting for now is industrial freedom. And unless we win our industrial liberty we cannot keep our political liberty. I see no reason why we should deliberately keep on helping to fasten the handcuffs of corporate control upon ourselves for all time merely because the few men who would profit by it most have heretofore the power to compel it. . . .

It must be clear to any man who has followed the development of the

Conservation idea that no other policy now before the American people is so thoroughly democratic in its essence and in its tendencies as the Conservation policy. It asserts that the people have the right and the duty, and that it is their duty no less than their right, to protect themselves against the uncontrolled monopoly of the natural resources which yield the necessaries of life. We are beginning to realize that the Conservation question is a question of right and wrong, as any question must be which may involve the difference between prosperity and poverty, health and sickness, ignorance and education, well-being and misery, to hundreds and thousands of families. Seen from the point of view of human welfare and human progress, questions which begin as purely economic often end as moral issues. Conservation is a moral issue because it involves the rights and the duties of our people—their rights to prosperity and happiness, and their duties to themselves, to their descendants, and to the whole future progress and welfare of this Nation.

The Outlook. December 4, 1909, 770–772.

DOLLAR DIPLOMACY

President Taft's foreign policy initiatives centered on guiding and enabling private investment in regions he believed were key to America's strategic interests. This so-called Dollar Diplomacy was focused mainly on Latin America and China. Although the doctrine was largely unsuccessful in both areas, it was particularly controversial in China where it embroiled the United States in a political situation far beyond Taft's capacity to control. The policy was rescinded by Wilson early in his administration.

Taft's actions in China were a combination of two previously established doctrines. The concept of Dollar Diplomacy was actually pioneered by Roosevelt during the crisis in the Dominican Republic. In establishing U.S. control over the customshouse and stabilizing a situation that threatened American investments, he put into practice the notion that a strong economic presence could result in strategic and diplomatic rewards. Private and public goals were thus intertwined.

It was easy for Taft and his Secretary of State Philander Knox to continue this practice in Latin America unimpeded by foreign investment competition, as other nations had begun to lose interest in the region. However, the policy led to increased resentment from Central and South American nations, who came to see the initiative as imperialistic and patronizing, and to believe they were being treated as virtual subsidiaries of U.S. corporations.

Despite this lack of success, Taft and Knox attempted to extend the policy to China, inspired by the long-standing Open Door Doctrine. This referred to a nineteenth-century American statement of support for continued Chinese independence as well as open trade with all interested nations (although, having no role in China at the time, the United States was not really in any position to have made such a unilateral statement). However, by the turn of the century there were some fears that the open door was closing, at least to the United States, as Russia, Germany, France, Great Britain, and Japan all seemed to be carving out their own exclusive spheres of influence. This was disturbing for strategic reasons as well as economic, as American industries needed large foreign markets as an outlet for their increasing supply.

Taft's first attempt to establish a role for American dollars in China came in the form of negotiations of the Hukuang Loan, beginning in 1909. Basically, this represented the United States insinuating itself into a British and French consortium helping to finance a railroad through the Yangtze River Valley. In response to Taft's plea that their role represented an "indispensable instrumentality" for a "practical and real application of the open door policy,"[1] a group of U.S. bankers including J.P. Morgan and E.H. Harriman provided capital for the project. This was followed by other railroad projects, and a loan to aid China in a currency reform project.

In his final address to Congress, Taft portrayed the positives of this overall initiative, asserting that it would lead to greater U.S. political influence in China as well as increased trade opportunities. He stressed its potential role in establishing a solid relationship with the newly emerging republican government in China. But in many ways, the project was a failure. As in Latin America, Chinese leaders were also treated as pawns in American profit making and power aggrandizing schemes, and they came to resent the intrusions. Additionally, very little profit actually accrued to the American investors. They were reluctant to participate in the first place due to their concerns over returns on these projects, and their fears were realized. Exports to China also decreased notably during the Taft administration.

But the biggest problem in trying to exercise Dollar Diplomacy in China was the complicated political situation the United States attempted to barge into. All of the major nations that had established a presence felt resentment toward the U.S. overtures and wanted Americans to play by their rules or (preferably) not at all. Even the British government, America's closest ally, was not able to lend support due to its own fear of upsetting the delicate balance of power. At home, Taft was criticized for naively failing to understand the political complexity of China.

Although not attacking Taft's decision directly, Wilson's statement that the U.S. government would no longer impose on the banking consortium to finance Chinese loans clearly repudiates the Dollar Diplomacy Doctrine to the extent that it linked private investment with U.S. strategic and diplomatic interests. While stressing the positive aspect of keeping trade relations open, Wilson states that this would be kept completely separate from foreign policy initiatives, thus restoring the true Open Door policy, in which the United States was to remain unentangled in China's internal politics. The United States rapidly removed itself from Chinese affairs, a move lauded at the time by an editorial in the *American Journal of International Law* as a "restoration and reaffirmation of policies which in the past have made the American name known and respected in the uttermost parts of the earth."[2] The United States maintained this open trade relationship until the revolution of 1949 established the People's Republic of China.

NOTES

1. Fred L. Israel, ed., *The State of the Union Messages of the Presidents*, vol. 3 (New York: Chelsea House, 1967), 2347–2348.

2. "The Passing of Dollar Diplomacy," *American Journal of International Law* 7 (1913): 339.

TAFT—COMMENTS FROM FOREIGN POLICY MESSAGE TO CONGRESS (DECEMBER 3, 1912)

The diplomacy of the present administration has sought to respond to modern ideas of commercial intercourse. This policy has been characterized as substituting dollars for bullets. It is one that appeals alike to idealistic humanitarian sentiments, to the dictates of sound policy and strategy, and to legitimate commercial aims. It is an effort frankly directed to the increase of American trade upon the axiomatic principle that the Government of the United States shall extend all proper support to every legitimate and beneficial American enterprise abroad. How great have been the results of this diplomacy, coupled with the maximum and minimum provision of the tariff law, will be seen by some consideration of the wonderful increase in the export trade of the United States. Because modern diplomacy is commercial, there has been a disposition in some quarters to attribute to it none but materialistic aims. How strikingly erroneous is such an impression may be seen from a study of the results by which the diplomacy of the United States can be judged.

. . .

In China the policy of encouraging financial investment to enable that country to help itself has had the result of giving new life and practical application to the open-door policy. The consistent purpose of the present administration has been to encourage the use of American capital in the development of China by the promotion of those essential reforms to which China is pledged by treaties with the United States and other powers. The hypothecation to foreign bankers in connection with certain industrial enterprise, such as the Hukuang railways, of the national revenues upon which these reforms depended, led the Department of State early in the administration to demand for American citizens participation in such enterprises, in order that the United States might have equal rights and an equal voice in all questions pertaining to the disposition of the public revenues concerned. The same policy of promoting international accord among the powers having similar treaty rights as ourselves in the matters of reform, which could not be put into practical effect without the common consent of all, was likewise adopted in the case of the loan desired by China for the reform of its currency. The principle of international cooperation in matters of common interest upon which our policy had already been based in all of the above instances has admittedly been a great factor in that concert of the powers which has been so happily conspicuous during the perilous period of transition through which the great Chinese nation has been passing.

. . .

Congress should fully realize the conditions which obtain in the world as we find ourselves at the threshold of our middle age as a Nation. We have emerged full grown as a peer in the great concourse of nations. We have passed through various formative periods. We have been self-centered in the struggle to develop our domestic resources and deal with our domestic questions. The Nation is now too matured to continue in its foreign relations those temporary expedients natural to a people to whom domestic affairs are the sole concern. In the past our diplomacy has often consisted, in normal times, in a mere assertion of the right to international existence. We are now in a larger relation with broader rights of our own and obligations to others than ourselves. A number of great guiding principles were laid down early in the history of this Government. The recent task of our diplomacy has been to adjust those principles to the conditions of to-day, to develop their corollaries, to find practical applications of the old principles expanded to meet new situations. Thus are being evolved bases upon which can rest the superstructure of policies which must grow with the destined progress of this Nation. The successful conduct of our foreign relations demands a broad and a modern view. We can not meet new questions nor build for the future if we confine ourselves to outworn dogmas of the past and to the perspective appropriate at our emergence from colonial times and conditions.

Israel, Fred L., ed. *The State of the Union Messages of the Presidents.* Vol. 3. New York: Chelsea House, 1967, 2490, 2491, 2492, 2510.

WOODROW WILSON—MESSAGE TO AMERICAN BANKERS ON DOLLAR DIPLOMACY (MARCH 19, 1913)

We are informed that at the request of the last administration a certain group of American bankers undertook to participate in the loan now desired by the Government of China (approximately $125,000,000). Our Government wished American bankers to participate along with the bankers of other nations, because it desired that the good will of the United States toward China should be exhibited in this practical way, that American capital should have access to that great country, and that the United States should be in a position to share with the other powers any political responsibilities that might be associated with the development of the foreign relations of China in connection with her industrial and commercial enterprises. The present administration has been asked by this group of bankers whether it would also request them to participate in the loan. The representatives of the bankers through whom the administration was approached declared that they would continue to seek their share of the loan under the proposed agreements only if expressly requested to do so by the Government. The administration has declined to make such request, because it did not approve the conditions of the loan or the implications of responsibility on its own part which it was plainly told would be involved in the request.

The conditions of the loan seem to us to touch very nearly the administrative independence of China itself, and this administration does not feel that it ought, even by implication, to be a party to those conditions. The responsibility on its part which would be implied in requesting the bankers to undertake the loan might conceivably go to length in some unhappy contingency of forcible interference in the financial, and even the political, affairs of that great oriental State, just now awakening to a consciousness of its power and of its obligations to its people. The conditions include not only the pledging of particular taxes, some of them antiquated and burdensome, to secure the loan, but also the administration of those taxes by foreign agents. The responsibility on the part of our Government implied in the encouragement of a loan thus secured and administered is plain enough and is obnoxious to the principles upon which the government of our people rests.

The Government of the United States is not only willing, but earnestly desirous, of aiding the great Chinese people in every way that is consistent with their untrammeled development and its own immemorial principles. The awakening of the people of China to a consciousness of their responsibilities under free government is the most significant, if not the most momentous, event of our generation. With this movement and aspiration the American people are in profound sympathy. They certainly wish to participate, and participate very generously, in the opening to the Chinese and to the use of the world the almost untouched and perhaps unrivaled resources of China.

The Government of the United States is earnestly desirous of promoting the most extended and intimate trade relationship between this country and the Chinese Republic. The present administration will urge and support the legislative measures necessary to give American merchants, manufacturers, contractors, and engineers the banking and other financial facilities which they now lack and without which they are at a serious disadvantage as compared with their industrial and commercial rivals. This is its duty. This is the main material interest of its citizens in the development of China. Our interests are those of the open door—a door of friendship and mutual advantage. This is the only door we care to enter.

Papers Relating to the Foreign Relations of the United States, 1913. Washington, D.C.: U.S. Government Printing Office, 1920, 170–171.

JUDICIAL RECALL

One of the long-standing ideals of American government—the necessity of an independent judiciary—became a topic of disagreement between President Taft and Roosevelt over the course of the 1912 campaign. Although the specific target varied somewhat, from popular recall of judges to popular recall of decisions, the basic issue was whether the general public and majority rule should wield power over the judiciary, as Roosevelt advocated, or whether courts should remain strictly insulated from such pressures, the position Taft supported.

Revived during the Progressive Era, this basic controversy had its roots in the debates surrounding the passage of the U.S. Constitution. At that time, Alexander Hamilton argued in a series of essays for the importance of an insulated judiciary, while opponents voiced their fears of any branch of government being too independent from public preferences. This gets to a conundrum at the very core of the American form of government. Due to a fear of a potential tyranny of the majority, there are several provisions designed to make public input indirect, such as an independent judiciary, where judges do not face election and in which judicial decisions are secure from legislative interference. This is the model advocated by Hamilton and adopted into the U.S. Constitution for federal courts (and copied by some but not all state court systems). But fears remained that instead of protecting powerless minorities, such insulated courts would repeatedly eschew public opinion in order to protect privileged interests.

Many progressives believed that this fear had in fact been realized. Of particular concern was a series of judicial decisions at both the federal and state level in which reform statutes (usually targeting unsafe or exploitative working conditions, and largely opposed by wealthy businessmen) were struck down by courts. Although many states already had one provision to attempt to insure greater judicial responsiveness—the selection of judges by direct election—the view was that greater enforcement mechanisms were necessary to rein in out-of-touch jurists. The most commonly advocated were judicial recall elections and mechanisms for the overturning of unpopular judicial decisions.

For Taft, the debate was triggered by the 1911 bill granting statehood to New Mexico and Arizona. The Arizona constitution in particular included several features designed to enhance popular participation. For example, initiative and referendum clauses allowed the public to vote directly on policy issues, thus bypassing the legislature. But the most controversial aspect was the judicial recall provision, by which voters could remove justices from office outside of the normal election period. On the basis of this clause, Taft vetoed the enabling bill, stating in his message to Congress that it represented a dangerous move toward a tyranny of the majority that threatened minority and individual freedoms. He noted that judicial decisions do ultimately reflect changing social mores, but that an insulated system allows this process to occur slowly and thoughtfully.

For Roosevelt, the controversy was activated by the aforementioned judicial decisions striking down popular legislation. He believed such outcomes showed that judges were sympathetic only to the claims of fellow elites or, at best, were simply ignorant of the conditions affecting the majority of Americans. His solution was not the recall of justices, but a mechanism that Taft found equally frightening: allowing the people (through ballot measures) to make the final determination on the constitutionality of statutes struck down by state courts. Roosevelt stated in several 1912 campaign speeches that the cause of social justice would be advanced by this reform, and that at least the people could not do a worse job of judging constitutionality than the courts had.

Roosevelt's views on this topic and other democratic reforms had a deleterious effect on his chances to become the Republican presidential nominee. The conservative wing of the party was uncomfortable with these fairly radical proposals, and as a result were increasingly drawn to the seemingly more pragmatic Taft. It is fitting that this issue split the progressives, for it gets to the heart of one of the nebulous legacies of this movement. Was the progressive movement an attempt to improve government *for* the masses by lifting it from the vagaries of mere politics (which would support judicial independence) or was it meant to give government back *to* the masses (which would support the recall provisions)?

Taft won the immediate battle on the Arizona question, forcing the recall provision to be expunged from the state constitution. But that was merely a ruse, as the state restored the procedure by amendment after being granted statehood, although in the 1970s Arizona did move to a nominating selection mechanism. While the push for recall of either judges or judicial decisions eventually lost steam, it still occasionally resurfaces. More importantly, the broad controversy over whether it is best for courts to be independent or responsive remains relevant and still somewhat unsettled today.

TAFT—VETO OF NEW MEXICO–ARIZONA ENABLING ACT (AUGUST 15, 1911)

I return herewith, without my approval, House Join Resolution No. 14, "To admit the territories of New Mexico and Arizona as states into the Union on an equal footing with the original states."

. . .

Under the Arizona constitution all elective officers, and this includes county and state judges, six months after their election, are subject to the recall. It is initiated by a petition signed by electors equal to 25 percent of the total number of votes cast for all the candidates for the office at the previous general election. Within five days after the petition is filed the officer may resign. Whether he does or not, an election ensues in which his name, if he does not resign, is placed on the ballot with that of all other candidates.

. . .

This provision of the Arizona constitution, in its application to county and state judges, seems to me so pernicious in its effect, so destructive of independence in the judiciary, so likely to subject the rights of the individual to the possible tyranny of a popular majority, and, therefore, to be so injurious to the cause of free government that I must disapprove a constitution containing it.

. . .

Of course, a mere difference of opinion as to the wisdom of details in a state constitution ought not to lead me to set up my opinion against that of the people of the territory. It is to be their government, and while the power of Congress to withhold or grant statehood is absolute, the people about to constitute a state should generally know better the kind of government and constitution suited to their needs than Congress or the executive. But when such a constitution contains something so destructive of free government as the judicial recall, it should be disapproved.

. . .

A popular government is not a government of a majority, by a majority, for a majority of the people. It is a government of the whole people by a majority of the whole people under such rules and checks as will secure a wise, just, and beneficent government for all the people. It is said you can always trust the people to do justice. If that means all the people and they all agree, you can. But ordinarily they do not all agree, and the maxim is interpreted to mean that you can always trust a majority of the people. This is not invariably true; and every limitation imposed by the people upon the power of the majority in their constitutions is an admission that it is not always true. No honest, clearheaded man, however great a lover of popular government, can deny that the unbridled expression of the majority of a community converted hastily into law or action would sometimes make a government tyrannical and cruel.

. . .

What I have said has been to little purpose if it has not shown that judges to fulfill their functions properly in our popular government must be more independent than in any other form of government, and that need of independence is greatest where the individual is one litigant and the state, guided by the successful and governing majority, is the other. In order to maintain the rights of the minority and the individual and to preserve our constitutional balance, we must have judges with courage to decide against the majority when justice and law require.

By the recall in the Arizona constitution, it is proposed to give to the majority power to remove arbitrarily and without delay any judge who may have the courage to render an unpopular decision. . . . Other candidates are permitted to present themselves and have their names printed on the ballot, so that the recall is not based solely on the record or the acts of the judge but also on the question whether some other and more popular candidate has been found to unseat him. Could there be a system more ingeniously devised to subject judges to momentary gusts of popular passion than this?

. . .

Think of the opportunity such a system would give to unscrupulous political bosses in control, as they have been in control not only of conventions but elections! Think of the enormous power for evil given to the sensational, muckraking portion of the press in rousing prejudice against a just judge by false charges and insinuations, the effect of which in the short period of an election by recall it would be impossible for him to meet and offset! Supporters of such a system seem to think that it will work only in the interest of the poor, the humble, the weak, and the oppressed; that it will strike down only the judge who is supposed to favor corporations and be affected by the corrupting influence of the rich. Nothing could be further from the ultimate result. The motive it would offer to unscrupulous combinations to seek to control politics in order to control the judges is clear.

. . .

Again, judicial recall is advocated on the ground that it will bring the judges more into sympathy with the popular will and the progress of ideas among the people. It is said that now judges are out of touch with the movement toward a wider democracy and a greater control of governmental agencies in the interest and for the benefit of the people. The righteous and just course for a judge to pursue is ordinarily fixed by statute or clear principles of law, and the cases in which his judgment may be affected by his political, economic, or social views are infrequent. But even in such cases judges are not removed from the people's influence. Surround the judiciary with all the safeguards possible, create judges by appointment, make their tenure for life, forbid diminution of salary during their term, and still it is impossible to prevent the influence of popular opinion from coloring judgments in the long run.

Congressional Record. 62nd Congress, 1st sess., 1911. Vol. 47, 3964–3966.

THEODORE ROOSEVELT—"THE RECALL OF JUDICIAL DECISIONS" (APRIL 10, 1912)

In the New York *World* of Thursday appears a detailed statement that some very eminent lawyers of New York have undertaken the formation of what they style the "Independent Judiciary Association." They propose, to use their own words, "to combat the spread of two ideas," namely, the recall of judges, and the referendum to the people of a certain class of cases of judicial decisions; and they assert, in President Taft's words, that these ideas "lay the axe at the root of the tree of well-ordered freedom." Many of the signers are distinguished men, standing high in their community; but we can gain a clew as to just what kind of well-ordered freedom they have in mind, the kind of "freedom" to the defense of which they are rushing, when we see among the signers of this call the names of attorneys for a number of corporations not distinguished for a high-keyed sense of civic duty, or for their disinterested conduct toward the public. . . .

I hold absolutely to my conviction that some basis of accommodation must be found between the declared policy of the States on matters of social justice within the proper scope of regulation in the interest of health, of decent living and working conditions, and of morals, and the attempt of the courts to substitute their own ideas on these subjects for the declarations of the people, made through their elected representatives in the several States. . . .

My proposal is for the exercise of the referendum by the people themselves in a certain class of decisions of constitutional questions in which the courts decide against the power of the people to do elementary justice. When men of trained intelligence call this "putting the axe to the tree of well-ordered freedom," it is quite impossible to reconcile their statements both with good faith and with even reasonably full knowledge of the facts.

. . .

. . . If in any case the legislature has passed a law under the police power for the purpose of promoting social and industrial justice and the courts declare it in conflict with the fundamental law of the State, the constitution as laid down by the people, then I propose that after due deliberation—for a period which could not be for less than two years after the passage of the original law—the people shall themselves have the right to declare whether or not the proposed law is to be treated as constitutional.

. . .

Some of my opponents say that under my proposal there would be conflicting interpretations by the people of the Constitution. In the first place, this is mere guesswork on the part of our opponents. In the next place, the people could not decide in more conflicting fashion, could not possibly make their decisions conflict with one another to a greater degree, than has actually been the case with the courts. . . .

. . .

When the legislature of New York passed a law limiting the hours of labor of women in factories to ten hours a day for six days a week, and forbade their being employed after nine in the evening and before six in the morning, the New York court of appeals declared it unconstitutional, and a malign inspiration induced them to state in their opinion that the time had come for courts "fearlessly" to interpose a barrier against such legislation. Fearlessly! The court fearlessly condemned helpless women to be worked at inhuman toil for hours so long as to make it impossible that they should retain health or strength; and "fearlessly" upheld the right of big factory owners and small sweat-shop owners to coin money out of the blood of the wretched women and girls whom they worked haggard for their own profit. To protect such wrong-doers was of course an outrage upon the decent and high-minded factory owners who did not wish to work the women and girls to an excessive degree, but who were forced to do so by the competition of the callous factory owners whom the court, by this decision, deliberately aided and abetted in their wrong-doing. . . .

It would be an absolute physical impossibility for the people of the State, voting at the polls, to have interpreted the constitution more mischievously than the court of appeals has repeatedly interpreted it during the last quarter of a century, as regards the class of cases which I am now considering.

My proposal is merely to give the people an effective constitutional weapon for use against wrong and injustice. . . .

I shall protest against the tyranny of the majority whenever it arises, just as I shall protest against every other form of tyranny. But at present we are not suffering in any way from the tyranny of the majority. We suffer from the tyranny of the bosses and of the special interests, that is, from the tyranny of minorities.

Hagedorn, Hermann, ed. *The Works of Theodore Roosevelt*. Vol. 17. New York: Scribner's, 1926, 190–191, 193, 195–196, 198–202.

TRUSTS AND THE SHERMAN ANTITRUST ACT

Given his predecessor's trust-busting reputation, it was not surprising that Taft kept up the fight against illegal corporate combinations. However, in the course of his administration, Taft put his own stamp on this issue, placing his full faith in litigation based on the Sherman Antitrust Act, the 1890 law designed to restrict dangerous monopolies. In contrast, while Roosevelt had pursued a similar strategy out of necessity, he had continuously pushed for a more flexible and less litigious approach— one that utilized an oversight commission and a more detailed set of regulations regarding what specific practices were forbidden under the Sherman Act. These dissimilar philosophies are illustrated by the fact that Taft pursued seventy suits in four years, while Roosevelt only initiated forty suits in seven years. Although these differences at first appeared to represent merely a fairly subtle disagreement over the means to reach similar ends, this erupted into a battle between Taft and Roosevelt in late 1911, and helped set the stage for the 1912 presidential campaign.

By this point, late in the Taft administration, the issue had moved beyond the question of whether trusts could or should be restrained by the U.S. government. Roosevelt had successfully fought that battle early on, and not only the current and previous presidents but most Americans now accepted the necessity of regulation. Taft and Roosevelt also agreed on more subtle points, such as the need to emphasize monopolistic practices over mere size alone (i.e., a large corporation did not necessarily amount to an illegal trust), and the importance of dealing fairly with companies that made an honest effort to abide by the Sherman Act, even if they happened to violate some of its technicalities. But their distinct positions on achieving these goals were clearly revealed in the late autumn of 1911, triggered by the Taft administration's antitrust suit against the U.S. Steel Corporation, filed on October 26.

The charge that U.S. Steel had violated the Sherman Act when it acquired the struggling Tennessee Coal, Iron, and Railroad Company perturbed Roosevelt on both an ideological and personal level. In 1907, he had given the merger his presidential stamp of approval, viewing the acquisition as necessary to stave off the collapse of several other corporations that had invested heavily in the Tennessee company. He firmly believed that U.S. Steel was making the purchase not for profit or monopoly building motives but simply to stabilize the business economy. The 1911 suit implied that Roosevelt had been hoodwinked by this story, and he greatly resented that, having faith in his own ability to differentiate between a "good" and "bad" trust.

This prompted his November 18, 1911, editorial in *The Outlook*, where he set out his philosophy that the Sherman Act, while an important baseline, needed to be supplemented by clearer laws and/or an oversight body to ensure compliance. He believed that this approach would be a substantial improvement over the current method of implementing the Sherman Act on a case-by-case basis in which corporations would either be left alone or completely dissolved. For Roosevelt, this was much too blunt of a method in which important details were not duly considered. For example, the Supreme Court could potentially punish companies simply for being too large or alternatively (as in the tobacco trust case) break up trusts in theory but not in reality, leaving the market monopoly relatively intact. Roosevelt and others also felt that the so-called rule of reason—a standard allowing a great deal of flexibility in determining what was illegal—granted the Court far too much discretion.

Taft's message to Congress on December 5 was clearly influenced by the Roosevelt article, as illustrated by his reference to "glittering generalities . . . brought out in recent days." Here, Taft (while acknowledging that some additional legislation would be helpful) proclaimed his faith in the Sherman Act as the definitive antitrust document, and in the Supreme Court's ability to use it to maximum effect. One of the hallmarks of this administration, the president's faith in the sanctity of courts and the "majesty of the law," is clearly displayed.

Ultimately, despite representing a fairly narrow and technical dispute over the means to reach an agreed upon goal, this became a major issue in the 1912 campaign. Both Taft and Woodrow Wilson opposed Roosevelt's call for additional legislation or an antitrust oversight body and attracted corporate support for their positions. However, although Roosevelt referred disparagingly to the "Wall Street crowd" in his editorial, some historians believe that his strategy may have been designed to win their approval. Although the business community in general opposed regulations, there was also a widespread apprehension of becoming the target of a federal lawsuit. By working to more clearly define what practices were disallowed, additional regulations could actually make it easier for some corporations to avoid such litigation in the first place.

Ironically, it was during the Wilson administration that at least some of Roosevelt's recommendations came to fruition, with passage of the Clayton Act (defining antitrust violations in greater detail) and the creation of the Federal Trade Commission, an antitrust oversight board. Roosevelt's philosophy also triumphed when the U.S. Steel case was decided against the government on March 1, 1920.

TAFT—MESSAGE TO CONGRESS ON THE SHERMAN ACT AND TRUSTS (DECEMBER 5, 1911)

In May last the Supreme Court handed down decisions in the suits in equity brought by the United States to enjoin the further maintenance of the Standard Oil Trust and of the American Tobacco Trust, and to secure their dissolution. The decisions are epoch-making and serve to advise the business world authoritatively of the scope and operation of the antitrust act of 1890. . . .

But now that the anti-trust act is seen to be effective for the accomplishment of the purpose of its enactment, we are met by a cry from many different quarters for its repeal. It is said to be obstructive of business progress, to be an attempt to restore old-fashioned methods of destructive competition between small units, and to make impossible those useful combinations of capital and the reduction of the cost of production that are essential to continued prosperity and normal growth.

In the recent decisions the Supreme Court makes clear that there is nothing in the statute which condemns combinations of capital or mere bigness of plant organized to secure economy in production and a reduction of its cost. It is only when the purpose or necessary effect of the organization and maintenance of the combination or the aggregation of immense size are the stifling of competition, actual and potential, and the enhancing of prices and establishing a monopoly, that the statute is violated. Mere size is no sin against the law. The merging of two or more business plants necessarily eliminates competition between the units thus combined, but this elimination is in contravention of the statute only when the combination is made for purpose of ending this particular competition in order to secure control of, and enhance, prices and create a monopoly.

The complaint is made of the statute that it is not sufficiently definite in its description of that which is forbidden, to enable business men to avoid its violation. The suggestion is, that we may have a combination of two corporations, which may run on for years, and that subsequently the Attorney General may conclude that it was a violation of the statute, and that which was supposed by the combiners to be innocent then turns out to be a combination in violation of the statute. The answer to this hypothetical case is that when men attempt to amass such stupendous capital as will enable them to supress competition, control prices and establish a monopoly, they know the purpose of their acts. Men do not do such a thing without having it clearly in mind. If what they do is merely for the purpose of reducing the cost of production, without the thought of suppressing competition by use of the bigness of the plant they are creating, then they can not be convicted at the time the union is made, nor can they be convicted later, unless it happen that later on they conclude to suppress competition and take the usual methods for doing so, and thus establish for themselves a monopoly. They can, in such a case, hardly complain if the motive which subsequently is disclosed is attributed by the court to the original combination.

Much is said of the repeal of this statute and of constructive legislation intended to accomplish the purpose and blaze a clear path for honest merchants and business men to follow. It may be that such a plan will be evolved, but I submit that the discussions which have been brought out in recent days by the fear of the continued execution of the anti-trust law have produced nothing but glittering generalities and have offered no line of distinction or rule of action as definite and as clear as that which the Supreme Court itself lays down in enforcing the statute.

. . .

. . . . This statute as construed by the Supreme Court must continue to be the line of distinction for legitimate business. It must be enforced, unless we are to banish individualism from all business and reduce it to one common system of regulation or control of prices like that which now prevails with respect to public utilities, and which when applied to all business would be a long step toward State socialism.

The anti-trust act is the expression of the effort of a freedom-loving people to preserve equality of opportunity. It is the result of the confident determination of such a people to maintain their future growth by preserving uncontrolled and unrestricted the enterprise of the individual, his industry, his ingenuity, his intelligence, and his independent courage.

For twenty years or more this statute has been upon the statute book. All knew its general purpose and approved. Many of its violators were cynical over its assumed impotence. It seemed impossible of enforcement. Slowly the mills of the courts ground, and only gradually did the majesty of the law assert itself. Many of its statesmen-authors died before it became a living force, and they and others saw the evil grow which they had hoped to destroy. Now its efficacy is seen; now its power is heavy; now its object is near achievement. Now we hear the call for its repeal on the plea that it interferes with business prosperity, and we are advised in most general terms, how by some other statute and in some other way the evil we are just stamping out can be cured, if we only abandon this work of twenty years and try another experiment for another term of years.

Black, Gilbert J., ed. *William Howard Taft, 1857–1930: Chronology—Documents— Biographical Aids.* Dobbs Ferry, N.Y.: Ocean Publishing, 1970, 51, 57, 58, 61, 62.

THEODORE ROOSEVELT—"THE TRUSTS, THE PEOPLE, AND THE SQUARE DEAL" (NOVEMBER 18, 1911)

The suit against the Steel Trust by the Government has brought vividly before our people the need of reducing to order our chaotic Government policy as regards business. As President, in Messages to Congress I repeatedly called the attention of that body and of the public to the inadequacy of the Anti-Trust Law by itself to meet business conditions and secure justice to the people, and to the further fact that it might, if left unsupplemented by additional legislation, work mischief, with no compensating advantage. . . .

It is a vitally necessary thing to have the persons in control of big trusts of the character of the Standard Oil Trust and Tobacco Trust taught that they are under the law. . . . But to attempt to meet the whole problem not by administrative governmental action but by a succession of lawsuits is hopeless from the standpoint of working out a permanently satisfactory solution. Moreover, the results sought to be achieved are achieved only in extremely insufficient and fragmentary measure by breaking up all big corporations, whether they have behaved well or ill, into a number of little corporations which it is perfectly certain will be largely, and perhaps altogether, under the same control. Such action is harsh and mischievous if the corporation is guilty of nothing except its size; and where, as in the case of the Standard Oil, and especially the Tobacco, trusts, the corporation has been guilty of immoral and anti-social practices, there is need for far more drastic and thoroughgoing action than any that has been taken, under the recent decree of the Supreme Court. In the case of the Tobacco Trust, for instance, the settlement in the Circuit Court, in which the representatives of the Government seem inclined to concur, practically leaves all of the companies still substantially under the control of the twenty-nine original defendants. Such a result is lamentable from the standpoint of justice. . . .

The Anti-Trust Law cannot meet the whole situation, nor can any modification of the principle of the Anti-Trust Law avail to meet the whole situation. The fact is that many of the men who have called themselves Progressives, and who certainly believe that they are Progressives, represent in reality in this matter not progress at all but a kind of sincere rural toryism. These men believe that it is possible by strengthening the Anti-Trust Law to restore business to the competitive conditions of the middle of the last century. Any such effort is foredoomed to end in failure, and, if successful, would be mischievous to the last degree. Business cannot be successfully conducted in accordance with the practices and theories of sixty years ago unless we abolish steam, electricity, big cities, and, in short, not only all modern business and modern industrial conditions, but all the modern conditions of our civilization. The effort to restore competition as it was sixty years ago, and to trust for justice solely to this proposed restoration of competition, is just as foolish as if we should go back to the flintlocks of Washington's Continentals as a substitute for modern weapons of precision. The effort to prohibit all combinations, good or bad, is bound to fail, and ought to fail; when made, it merely means that some of the worst combinations are not checked and that honest business is checked. Our purpose should be, not to strangle business as an incident of strangling combinations, but to regulate big corporations in thoroughgoing and effective fashion, so as to help legitimate business as an incident to thoroughly and completely safeguarding the interests of the people as a whole. . . .

Few will dispute the fact that the present situation is not satisfactory, and cannot be put on a permanently satisfactory basis unless we put an end to the period of groping and declare for a fixed policy, a policy which shall clearly define and punish wrong-doing, which shall put a stop to the iniquities done in the name of business, but which shall do strict equity to business. We demand that big business give the people a square deal; in return we must insist that when any one engaged in big business honestly endeavors to do right he shall himself be given a square deal; and the first, and most elementary, kind of square deal is to give him in advance full information as to just what he can, and what he cannot, legally and properly do. It is absurd, and much worse than absurd, to treat the deliberate lawbreaker as on an exact par with the man eager to obey the law, whose only desire is to find out from some competent Governmental authority what the law is, and then to live up to it. . . .

. . . We should not strive for a policy of unregulated competition and of the destruction of all big corporations, that is, of all the most efficient business industries in the land. Nor should we persevere in the hopeless experiment of trying to regulate these industries by means only of lawsuits, each lasting several years, and of uncertain result. We should enter upon a course of supervision, control, and regulation of these great corporations—a regulation which we should not fear.

The Outlook, November 18, 1911, 649, 652–655.

FUTURE OF THE REPUBLICAN PARTY AND THE 1912 ELECTION

After Taft, Roosevelt's hand-picked successor, won the 1908 presidential election and was inaugurated in 1909, Roosevelt sailed for Africa, confident that his agenda would endure. Most Americans believed that as well—a common joke at the time was that "Taft" stood for "Take Advice From Teddy." But Taft's vision differed in important ways from Roosevelt's, and their ultimate split reflects not just the mismatch between their philosophies, but discord within the Republican Party over a conservative versus a progressive agenda. When Taft and Roosevelt competed for the Republican presidential nomination in 1912, the party weathered a crisis over its identity.

The Taft-Roosevelt split was in part based on fairly petty, personal issues. For example, Roosevelt resented Taft's shuffling of some cabinet positions, and fumed over the U.S. Steel Corporation suit and its implications that Roosevelt had been duped into letting that company develop a monopoly. But, more basically, it was an outgrowth of their differing views on the core principles of American democracy. Roosevelt had grown increasingly convinced of the necessity for more powerful progressive reforms—such as increased popular input into government (through direct ballot measures and judicial recall provisions), restrictions on child labor, and workplace regulations—while Taft was more concerned with constitutional guidelines, legal precedent, and ordered governmental processes. The party itself was divided along these lines as well, with the progressive (insurgent) element favoring Roosevelt's views, and the conservative (old guard) faction aligned with Taft's philosophy.

In reality, these labels were not so clear cut, at least as they applied to Taft and Roosevelt. Many of the insurgents disliked Roosevelt and felt he was not a true progressive, given his autocratic tendencies. For example, while he claimed to favor democratic reforms, as president he had frequently bypassed the popularly elected Congress. And, given his somewhat inconsistent views on trusts, some felt that he had given in too much to the corporate interests that the progressives opposed. Alternatively, Taft (while growing to despise the Republican insurgents in Congress) still portrayed himself as a progressive and did favor several reforms. In 1909, he had supported a constitutional amendment to allow Congress to levy an income tax. He believed the tax was necessary both because it would finance essential federal programs, and because it would allow intensive governmental oversight of business and industry, two important facets of the progressive agenda.

But while the labels are somewhat imprecise, the two men had still come to be seen as the respective symbols of the progressive and conservative wings of the Republican Party—a characterization that was escalated and magnified by the volatile 1912 presidential campaign, launched in February when Roosevelt announced he was challenging Taft for the party nomination. A spirited, and sometimes *mean*-spirited, primary campaign ensued. Both men undertook speaking tours and seemed to inspire each other to more extreme positions. For Taft, who did not come as naturally to politics as his rival, the fervor and increasingly belligerent tone of the campaign was trying. He was driven to defend himself with such statements as "condemn me if you will but condemn me by other witnesses than Theodore Roosevelt. I was a man of straw, but I have been a man of straw long enough."[1] In addition to having to admit his own past weakness and dependence on his predecessor, he was simply hurt by the break with his old friend, who had taken to calling him names ("fathead" was one favorite) on the campaign trail.

In his primary speeches, such as the one given in Louisville, Kentucky, on April 3, 1912, Roosevelt argued that the Republican Party must turn against the reactionary tendencies of Taft and the conservatives and move to rectify the wrongs that had been perpeturated against the American people in favor of wealthy, special interests. He advocated reforms that would enable citizens to play a more active and meaningful role in their own governance. For his part, Taft was moved to proclaim several progressive reforms reckless and irresponsible. As noted in the statement to the *New York Times* after winning the nomination, he believed that a dangerous course that threatened not just the Republican Party but the very foundations of American government had been averted with Roosevelt's defeat.

Given Roosevelt's extremist attitudes, it was not surprising that party leaders shunned him and awarded Taft the nomination. But the almost frenzied level of popular support that Roosevelt continued to inspire had been made apparent during the primary campaign, and he capitalized on this through a third-party campaign. In August, the National Progressive Party (nicknamed the Bull-Moose Party) nominated the former president as their candidate. The three-way race between Taft, Roosevelt, and Democratic nominee Wilson led to a Wilson victory, but one in which the winner failed to achieve a majority of the popular vote. Taft received the fewest popular and electoral votes, with Roosevelt coming in a strong second, at least as measured by the popular vote. (Socialist candidate Eugene V. Debs also drew a respectable 6 percent of the popular vote.) Although Wilson also referred to himself as a progressive, the Bull-Moose platform represents the high point of progressivism by a viable party at the national level.

The conservative-insurgent split remained a factor within the Republican Party, but was never again as pronounced and divisive as it was in 1912. Many moderately progressive citizens put their faith in Wilson (according to Taft, this was because they were terrified of a Roosevelt victory), although many were ultimately disappointed in his fairly insubstantial reform vision. Nonetheless, by the time the Republican Party regained the presidency in 1920, progressives were a much smaller and less powerful element. On May 26, 1918, during a chance meeting in the dining room of Chicago's Blackstone Hotel, Roosevelt and Taft spoke for the first time since the election, and were apparently reconciled. As described by the *New York Times*, they shook hands and slapped each other on the back while "a fashionable company rose and cheered."[2]

NOTES

1. Henry F. Pringle, *The Life and Times of William Howard Taft*, vol. 2 (Hamden, Conn.: Archon Books, 1964), 782–783.

2. "Roosevelt Grips the Hand of Taft," *New York Times*, May 27, 1918, 1.

TAFT—STATEMENT UPON RECEIVING REPUBLICAN NOMINATION (JUNE 23, 1912)

Never before in the history of the country was such a pre-convention campaign fought. Precedents of propriety were broken in a President's taking the stump, much to the pain and discomfort of many patriotic, high-minded citizens, but the emergency was great and the course thus taken was necessary to avert a National calamity, and in view of the result it was justified.

A National convention of one of the great parties is ordinarily important only as a preliminary to a National campaign for the election of a President.

The Chicago Convention just ended is much more than this, and is in itself the end of a pre-convention campaign presenting a crisis more threatening and issues more important than those of the election campaign which is to follow between the two great National parties.

The question here at stake was whether the Republican Party was to change its attitude as the chief conservator in the Nation of constitutional representative government and was to weaken the constitutional guarantees of life, liberty, and property, and all other rights declared sacred in the Bill of Rights, by abandoning the principle of absolute independence of the judiciary essential to the maintenance of those rights.

The campaign carried on to seize the Republican Party and make it the instrument of reckless ambition and the unsettling of the fundamental principles of our Government was so sudden and unexpected that time was not given clearly to show the people and the party the dangers which confronted them.

It was sought to break the wise and valuable tradition against giving more than two terms to any one man in the Presidency, and the dangers from its breach could not be measured.

The importance of the great victory which has been achieved cannot be overestimated.

All over this country patriotic people to-night are breathing more freely, that a most serious menace to our republican institutions has been averted.

It is not necessary to-night to speak of the result in November or of the issues which will arise between the Republican and Democratic Parties in the Presidential campaign to follow.

It will be time enough to do that after the action of the Baltimore Convention.

It is enough now to say that, whatever may happen in November, a great victory for the Republican Party and the people of the United States has already been won.

The party remains as a great, powerful organization for carrying out its patriotic principles, as an agency of real progress in the development of the Nation along the constitutional lines upon which it was constructed and has ever been maintained, and its future opportunity for usefulness is as great as its achievements in the past.

New York Times. June 23, 1912

THEODORE ROOSEVELT—"WHAT A PROGRESSIVE IS"
(APRIL 3, 1912)

In his recent speech at Philadelphia, President Taft stated that he was a Progressive, and this raises the question as to what a Progressive is. More is involved than any man's say-so to himself. A well-meaning man may vaguely think of himself as a Progressive without having even the faintest conception of what a Progressive is. . . .

Every man who fights fearlessly and effectively against special privilege in any form is to that extent a Progressive. Every man who, directly or indirectly, upholds privilege and favors the special interests, whether he acts from evil motives or merely because he is puzzle-headed or dull of mental vision, or lacking in social sympathy, or whether he simply lacks interest in the subject, is a reactionary.

Every man is to that extent a Progressive if he stands for any form of social justice, whether it be securing proper protection for factory girls against dangerous machinery, for securing a proper limitation of hours of labor for women and children in industry, for securing proper living conditions of our great cities, for helping, so far as legislation can help, all the conditions of work and life for wage-workers in great centres of industry, or for helping by the action both of the National and State Governments, so far as conditions will permit, the men and women who dwell in the open county to increase their efficiency both in production on their farms and in business arrangements for the marketing of their produce, and also to increase the opportunities to give the best possible expression to their social life.

The man is a reactionary, whatever may be his profession and no matter how excellent his intentions, who opposes these movements, or who, if in high place, takes no interest in them and does not earnestly lead them forward. . . .

The Republican Party is now facing a great crisis. It is to decide whether it will be as in the days of Lincoln the party of the plain people, the party of progress, the party of social and industrial justice; or whether it will be the party of privilege and of special interest, the heir to those who were Lincoln's most bitter opponents, the party that represents the great interests within and without Wall Street which desire though their control over the servants of the public to be kept immune from punishment when they do wrong and to be given privileges to which they are not entitled. . . .

We are in a period of change; we are fronting a great period of further change. Never was the need more imperative for men of vision who are also men of action. Disaster is ahead of us if we trust to the leadership of the men whose hearts are seared and whose eyes are blinded, who believe that we can find safety in dull timidity and dull inaction. The unrest cannot be quieted by the ingenious trickery of those who profess to advance by merely marking time. It cannot be quieted by demanding only the prosperity which is to come to those who have much, in such quantity that some will drip through to those who have little.

Hagedorn, Hermann, ed. *The Works of Theodore Roosevelt.* Vol. 17. New York: Scribner's, 1926, 177, 180, 184, 186, 187.

PRESIDENTIAL POWER

One of the consistent assertions of Taft's administration, and one that influenced the president's position on many issues, was the limited nature of the powers of the office. During his four-year term, Taft acted in accordance with his views that the president was charged only with acting under the clear dictates of laws and the Constitution, and not in attempting to stretch legal limits in order to achieve a policy agenda. It was of course Roosevelt who had championed this latter, more activist model, and their differing conceptions of the presidency were one of the chief forces driving these two former allies apart by 1909.

In retrospect, Roosevelt's decision to anoint Taft as his chosen successor seems misguided, as they represent such drastically different personality types. However, in terms of actual policy positions, the two men did share some similar views, at least until Roosevelt grew more radical over the course of the 1912 election. Taft himself stated in a letter to Roosevelt in 1906, "I, with deference, have never met a man more strongly in favor of a strong government than you are and more insistently that courts shall not only have power to enforce the law, but should enforce the law."[1] And yet, even in this note of adulation, a key difference between them is revealed. For Taft maintained that the rule of law should reign supreme, especially for the president. All actions should be taken only as the law allows or mandates.

But Roosevelt had come to believe that actions not specifically prohibited by the law or Constitution were fair game for any president who enjoyed a mandate from the people. Given their divergent backgrounds, this disagreement makes sense. Taft, an attorney and future chief justice of the U.S. Supreme Court, was an avid devotee of the law. All of his public positions prior to the presidency were appointed—he had never run for office. Roosevelt, however, attended law school but never practiced law and was a politician through and through. In all of his elected positions, he saw himself as the delegate of the people. Thus, while they did largely agree on goals, they differed in their views of the proper means to attain them.

For Roosevelt, an activist model was justified by the president representing the will of the people, and the only danger was when presidents behaved in this manner without popular support. But for Taft, public support was not the key. Even when (perhaps especially when) the president was reflecting public preference, it was still important that the rule of law and the Constitution reign supreme.

One policy arena in particular provides a good illustration (as noted by Roosevelt in his autobiography) of their differing views on presidential power—the designation and preservation of public lands. By use of an executive order, Roosevelt set aside for protection sixteen million acres after Congress approved a bill barring such actions, but just before it actually became law. As Roosevelt noted, "while President I have *been* President emphatically."[2] Because the means were available to him, he utilized them, even though this action clearly violated the spirit of congressional intent.

Taft, in contrast, was disturbed by Roosevelt's decision and, after taking office, returned those questionable lands to public usage. It was not the earlier outcome that Taft opposed but the process by which it had been achieved. As there was no law or constitutional provision granting this authority to the president, Taft believed the power properly resided only with the U.S. Congress or state legislatures. This focus on procedure is underscored by the final result. Once Congress did authorize the president to remove such lands from development, Taft swiftly acted to do so. He favored the original outcome, but he wanted it achieved in the legally proper manner.

The battle over the propriety of an activist presidency brewed between Taft and Roosevelt over much of the Taft administration. It was one of the causes of the great rift that triggered Roosevelt's challenge to Taft in 1912. Their respective views on the controversy were clearly set down in writing after the acrimony of that election had passed. The disagreements on the proper scope of activity remained obvious, although the earlier hostilities seemed to have settled somewhat. So divergent were the views these two men held on this issue that today scholars refer not to the Buchanan versus Lincoln models that Taft and Roosevelt reference, but to the Taft versus Roosevelt models as representations of polar views on the exercise of presidential power.

NOTES

1. Paolo E. Coletta, *The Presidency of William Howard Taft* (Lawrence: University Press of Kansas, 1973), 14.

2. Ibid., 12.

TAFT—LECTURE ON PRESIDENTIAL POWER (1915)

The true view of the executive functions is, as I conceive it, that the President can exercise no power which cannot be fairly and reasonably traced to some specific grant of power or justly implied and included within such express grant as proper and necessary to its exercise. Such specific grant must be either in the federal Constitution or in an act of Congress passed in pursuance thereof. There is no undefined residuum of power which he can exercise because it seems to him to be in the public interest. . . . The grants of executive power are necessarily in general terms in order not to embarrass the executive within the field of action plainly marked for him, but his jurisdiction must be justified and vindicated by affirmative constitutional or statutory provision, or it does not exist.

There have not been wanting, however, eminent men in high public office holding a different view and who have insisted upon the necessity for an undefined residuum of executive power in the public interest. They have not been confined to the present generation. . . .

I may add that Mr. Roosevelt, by way of illustrating his meaning as to the differing usefulness of Presidents, divides the Presidents into two classes and designates them as "Lincoln Presidents" and "Buchanan Presidents." In order more fully to illustrate his division of Presidents on their merits, he places himself in the Lincoln class of Presidents and me in the Buchanan class. The identification of Mr. Roosevelt with Mr. Lincoln might otherwise have escaped notice, because there are many differences between the two, presumably superficial, which would give the impartial student of history a different impression.

It suggests a story which a friend of mine told of his little daughter Mary. As he came walking home after a business day, she ran out from the house to greet him, all aglow with the importance of what she wished to tell him. She said, "Papa, I am the best scholar in the class." The father's heart throbbed with pleasure as he inquired, "Why, Mary, you surprise me. When did the teacher tell you? This afternoon?" "Oh, no," Mary's reply was, "the teacher didn't tell me—I just noticed it myself."

My judgment is that the view of . . . Mr. Roosevelt, ascribing an undefined residuum of power to the President, is an unsafe doctrine and that it might lead under emergencies to results of an arbitrary character, doing irremediable injustice to private right. The mainspring of such a view is that the executive is charged with responsibility for the welfare of all the people in a general way, that he is to play the part of a universal Providence and set all things right, and that anything that in his judgment will help the people he ought to do, unless he is expressly forbidden not to do it. The wide field of action that this would give to the executive, one can hardly limit. . . .

There is little danger to the public weal from the tyranny or reckless character of a President who is not sustained by the people. The absence of popular support will certainly in the course of two years withdraw from him the sympathetic action of at least one House of Congress, and by the control that that House has over appropriations, the executive arm can be paralyzed, unless he resorts to a coup d'état, which means impeachment, conviction, and deposition. The only danger in the action of the executive under the present limitations and lack of limitation of his powers is when his popularity is such that he can be sure of the support of the electorate and therefore of Congress, and when the majority in the legislative halls respond with alacrity and sycophancy to his will.

This condition cannot probably be long continued. We have had Presidents who felt the public pulse with accuracy, who played their parts upon the political stage with histrionic genius and commanded the people almost as if they were an army and the President their commander in chief. Yet, in all these cases, the good sense of the people has ultimately prevailed and no danger has been done to our political structure and the reign of law has continued. In such times when the executive power seems to be all prevailing, there have always been men in this free and intelligent people of ours who, apparently courting political humiliation and disaster, have registered protest against this undue executive domination and this use of the executive power and popular support to perpetuate itself.

The cry of executive domination is often entirely unjustified, as when the President's commanding influence only grows out of a proper cohesion of a party and its recognition of the necessity for political leadership; but the fact that executive domination is regarded as a useful ground for attack upon a successful administration, even when there is no ground for it, is itself proof of the dependence we may properly place upon the sanity and clear perceptions of the people in avoiding its baneful effects when there is real danger. Even if a vicious precedent is set by the Executive and injustice done, it does not have the same bad effect that an improper precedent of a court may have; for one President does not consider himself bound by the policies or constitutional views of his predecessors.

The Annals of America. Vol. 14. Chicago: Encyclopaedia Britannica, 1968, 41–44.

THEODORE ROOSEVELT—PASSAGE FROM
AUTOBIOGRAPHY ON PRESIDENTIAL POWER (1913)

... The course I followed, of regarding the executive as subject only to the people, and, under the Constitution, bound to serve the people affirmatively in cases where the Constitution does not explicitly forbid him to render the service, was substantially the course followed by both Andrew Jackson and Abraham Lincoln. Other honorable and well-meaning Presidents, such as James Buchanan, took the opposite and, as it seems to me, narrowly legalistic view that the President is the servant of Congress rather than of the people, and can do nothing, no matter how necessary it be to act, unless the Constitution explicitly commands the action. Most able lawyers who are past middle age take this view, and so do large numbers of well-meaning, respectable citizens. My successor in office took this, the Buchanan, view of the President's powers and duties.

For example, under my Administration we found that one of the favorite methods adopted by the men desirous of stealing the public domain was to carry the decision of the Secretary of the Interior into court. By vigorously opposing such action, and only by so doing, we were able to carry out the policy of properly protecting the public domain. My successor not only took the opposite view, but recommended to Congress the passage of a bill which would have given the courts direct appellate power over the Secretary of the Interior in these land matters. ...

I acted on the theory that the President could at any time in his discretion withdraw from entry any of the public lands of the United States and reserve the same for forestry, for water-power sites, for irrigation, and other public purposes. Without such action it would have been impossible to stop the activity of the land thieves. No one ventured to test its legality by lawsuit. My successor, however, himself questioned it, and referred the matter to Congress. Again Congress showed its wisdom by passing a law which gave the President the power which he had long exercised, and of which my successor had shorn himself.

Perhaps the sharp difference between what may be called the Lincoln-Jackson and the Buchanan-Taft schools, in their views of the power and duties of the President, may be best illustrated by comparing the attitude of my successor toward his Secretary of the Interior, Mr. Ballinger, when the latter was accused of gross misconduct in office, with my attitude towards my chiefs of department and other subordinate officers. More than once while I was President my officials were attacked by Congress, generally because these officials did their duty well and fearlessly. In every such case I stood by the official and refused to recognize the right of Congress to interfere with me excepting by impeachment or in other Constitutional manner. On the other hand, wherever I found the officer unfit for his position, I promptly removed him, even although the most influential men in Congress fought for his retention. The Jackson-Lincoln view is that a President who is fit to do good work should be able to form his own judgment as to his own subordinates, and, above all, of the subordinates standing highest and in closest and most intimate touch with him. . . . My successor took the opposite, or Buchanan, view when he permitted and requested Congress to pass judgment on the charges made against Mr. Ballinger as an executive officer. These charges were made to the President; the President had the facts before him and could get at them at any time, and he alone had power to act if the charges were true. However, he permitted and requested Congress to investigate Mr. Ballinger. . . .

There are many worthy people who reprobate the Buchanan method as a matter of history, but who in actual life reprobate still more strongly the Jackson-Lincoln method when it is put into practice. These persons conscientiously believe that the President should solve every doubt in favor of inaction as against action, that he should construe strictly and narrowly the Constitutional grant of powers both to the National Government, and to the President within the National Government. In addition, however, to the men who conscientiously believe in this course from high, although as I hold misguided, motives, there are many men who affect to believe in it merely because it enables them to attack and to try to hamper, for partisan or personal reasons, an executive whom they dislike. There are other men in whom, especially when they are themselves in office, practical adherence to the Buchanan principle represents not well-thought-out devotion to an unwise course, but simple weakness of character and desire to avoid trouble and responsibility. Unfortunately, in practice it makes little difference which class of ideas actuates the President, who by his action sets a cramping precedent. Whether he is highminded and wrongheaded or merely infirm of purpose, whether he means well feebly or is bound by a mischievous misconception of the powers and duties of the National Government and of the President, the effect of his actions is the same. The President's duty is to act so that he himself and his subordinates shall be able to do efficient work for the people, and this efficient work he and they cannot do if Congress is permitted to undertake the task of making up his mind for him as to how he shall perform what is clearly his sole duty.

Roosevelt, Theodore. *An Autobiography*. New York: Scribner's, 1913, 362–365.

RECOMMENDED READINGS

Broderick, Francis L. *Progressivism at Risk: Electing a President in 1912*. New York: Greenwood Press, 1989.

Coletta, Paolo E. *The Presidency of William Howard Taft*. Lawrence: University Press of Kansas, 1973.

Manners, William. *TR & Will; A Friendship That Split the Republican Party*. New York: Harcourt, Brace and World, 1969.

Pinchot, Gifford. *Breaking New Ground*. Seattle: University of Washington Press, 1947.

Pringle, Henry F. *The Life and Times of William Howard Taft*. 2 vols. Hamden, Conn.: Archon Books, 1964.

Rosenberg, Emily S. *Financial Missionaries to the World: The Politics and Culture of Dollar Diplomacy, 1900–1930*. Cambridge: Harvard University Press, 1999.

Scholes, Walter V., and Marie V. Scholes. *The Foreign Policies of the Taft Administration*. Columbia: University of Missouri Press, 1970.

Shabecoff, Philip. *A Fierce Green Fire: The American Environmental Movement*. New York: Hill & Wang, 1992.

Taft, William Howard. *The President and His Powers*. New York: Columbia University Press, 1916.

3

WOODROW WILSON

(1913–1921)

INTRODUCTION

Woodrow Wilson's record in office may appear to be that of three distinct presidents. Over the course of his 1913–1921 administration, this Democratic chief executive achieved quite disparate records in the major policy realms. In the economic sphere, he was able to gain meaningful and necessary policy innovations, often by artfully converting opponents to his side. These achievements represent an important force for progressive change. In regard to social issues, Wilson symbolizes the division within progressivism itself in regard to government's treatment of particular groups. He sometimes appears to be a defender of the have-nots, and at other times lacks the convictions of the more committed reformers to provide meaningful improvements in the lives of all Americans. Finally, in the foreign policy realm, Wilson's record is complex and somewhat baffling. While providing firm and rational leadership to the nation in the war years, he displayed a puzzling tendency toward extreme inflexibility and self-defeatism both in regard to his policies toward Mexico, and his role in the peace process following the Great War.

By far, Wilson's most positive legacy came in the form of the economic policies that implemented the "New Freedom" platform of his 1912 campaign. Wilson believed that while the progressive antitrust agenda had been valuable to the extent that it limited the destructive powers of monopolies, it had in some ways gone too far and instilled a dangerously antibusiness mood in the nation. Thus, he sought to combine progressive regulation of harmful trusts with policies designed to free American business in general from an overly activist government, thereby restoring a healthy and less contentious climate. As president, Wilson's first effort was to drastically reduce the long-standing protective tariff system that William Howard Taft and other predecessors had been unable to scale back. Although faced with a blizzard of special interest opposition, the tariff overhaul bill was passed by the Democratic Congress, in large part as a result of Wilson's energetic advocacy.

Another aspect of the New Freedom, with a slight twist, was the creation of the Federal Reserve system. Differing from the other New Freedom programs in the sense that it represented an *increased* federal role in banking, it fit the general philosophy by offering a stable, regulated money supply that would return freedom to business by eliminating the destructive currency shortages and panics of recent years. Here, too, Wilson was able to forge a compromise between conservatives who wanted a system run by the bankers themselves, and progressives who advocated an even greater level of federal involvement.

Wilson also helped to gain passage of the Clayton Antitrust Act, a law clarifying and expanding the scope of existing limits on monopolies, and creation of the Federal Trade Commission (FTC), a business oversight agency. However, these two achievements do not bear Wilson's mark to the extent that tariff reduction and the Federal Reserve Act do. In fact, the FTC—an oversight body designed to help guide business to regulatory compliance—was advocated by Theodore Roosevelt during the campaign and, at that time, soundly rejected by Wilson, who instead favored the passage of more detailed legislation. Additionally, the original Clayton Act's strong declarations of restrictions on particular business activities, as supported by the president, were drastically weakened in the Senate. Still, despite their distance from Wilson's initial preferences, both policies represented a degree of reform.

It is difficult to reconcile this aggressive record with Wilson's generally more passive and conservative approach to social issues. Although social reforms occurred during his administration, he ignored or opposed several of them. As had become clear during the administrations of his two immediate predecessors, the progressive label was rather imprecise, and Wilson's version of progressivism was a fairly narrow one. This may be at least partly explained by his academic background. In comparison with Roosevelt's politically generated agenda, Wilson adhered to a much more scholarly version of progressivism that focused on making government more efficient and the commercial sector more fair, but not on the necessity of achieving *justice* through economic and social reforms.

While progressives had come to champion the causes of child labor, woman suffrage, and the plight of the farmer, for example, Wilson (at least in the early years of his administration) refused to support legislation for reforms. It is difficult to ascertain what his personal feelings on these issues were, but on record his opposition in all these areas rested on his philosophical rejection of attempts to enlarge the federal government, especially into areas of state discretion. In particular, he believed that matters of labor and suffrage should be left to state law. This resurgence of the states' rights viewpoint in the White House is perhaps traceable to Wilson's early years in the South, where that opinion remained dominant even after the Civil War. One important aspect of his presidency is that it represented a rejuvenated national voice advocating that view.

Additionally, Wilson's record on racial issues was fairly dismal. He refused to appoint a promised commission on race, and allowed for the segregation of several federal agencies and departments. Although this policy was ultimately dropped, Wilson did not respond well to criticisms from black leaders, insisting that this segregation was in their own best interest.

Thus, for Wilson, progressivism had a very limited meaning—it did not extend to reorganizing the social order. When Wilson wrote a public letter to Treasury Secretary William McAdoo stating that, as a result of passage of New Freedom economic polices, the tenets of progressivism had been fulfilled, he was lambasted by progressive Herbert Croly, who accused him of "utterly misunderstanding the meaning and task of American progressivism."[1] For Croly and other reformers, progressivism dictated remediation of fundamental social wrongs and injustices.

However, some genuine progressive social accomplishments did occur during the Wilson administration. Some simply happened in spite of his protests, such as the Nineteenth Amendment, which granted women the right to vote. It is illustrative that despite being the president who officially presided over this important reform (and did finally endorse it in 1917), Wilson was frequently burned in effigy by suffragists frustrated at his stubbornness on the issue.

In other cases, Wilson underwent a transformation in the summer of 1916, when his reelection was in some doubt. Advised that attracting the votes of Americans in favor of progressive reforms was essential, Wilson threw his support behind child labor regulations, rural credits (in which the federal government provided loans to farmers), eight-hour days for railroad employees, and workers' compensation bills. Although his statements upon passage of these laws suggested he had always favored them, Roosevelt's characterization that Wilson's words "may mean much or may mean little"[2] is apt. Ironically, though, Wilson's 1916 preelection transformation to active progressivism is quite similar in direction to Roosevelt's 1905 postelection shift.

But, there were a few Wilson positions that did seem to suggest a commitment to social justice. For example, he fought early in his administration for passage of a bill designed to protect the contractual rights and safety of merchant seamen. Additionally, he twice vetoed bills establishing literacy requirements for new immigrants. Paradoxically, the literacy tests were actually favored by many progressives, as immigration restrictions were fast becoming a major focus of the progressive agenda. In opposing this policy, Wilson allied himself with some of the more radical reformers who viewed the restrictions as unjust. With the exception of these final two examples, however, it is fair to say that in the realm of social policy, reforms passed in the Wilson administration may be somewhat deceiving in terms of the president's preferences and the advocacy role he played.

Finally, the third Woodrow Wilson is the architect of American foreign policy. In this realm, Wilson is perhaps most difficult to understand, as he carved out zealous, yet often untenable positions that bore the stamp of his own peculiar brand of progressivism. Progressives themselves were split on foreign policy doctrine. Some believed in an isolationist position, where all efforts could be focused on domestic reform; others advocated an American duty to serve as a global example of democracy and thus accepted some interaction with other nations. Wilson took this latter position even further, as he was seemingly driven to impose American ideals of democracy on the rest of the world through his Missionary Diplomacy approach.

The diplomatic episode of secondary importance in the Wilson administration involved the situation in Mexico. Here, Wilson exercised Missionary Diplomacy to the point of twice almost entangling the two nations in war. The president's disapproval of two successive Mexican leaders led him to initially support rebel leader Francisco "Pancho" Villa who, when Wilson decided to pursue a neutral position, retaliated by murdering several Americans in border raids. Opponents accused Wilson of both intervening and declaring neutrality at the most inopportune times. Once again, however, anticipation of the elections of 1916 seemed to have an effect, as cordial relations were reestablished in the summer of that year.

Of course, the dominant foreign issue by far for Wilson was the Great War, and he provided able leadership through most of this portion of U.S. history. However, he faced opposition at every juncture. While citizens generally welcomed his decision to remain neutral in the early stages of the war, preparedness advocates argued that this stance should not be pursued at the expense of military readiness, and urged additional military funding and a draft. When Wilson ultimately acceded to at least the demand for increased funds, he was criticized by those who feared he was steering the country too close to war. Finally, when he appealed to Congress for a declaration of war against Germany, he was again largely supported by the American people, but excoriated by a small group of progressive isolationists.

Wilson's spectacular failure came after the war, in the peace process.

The president's dogged pursuit of the acceptance of his Fourteen Points, specific provisions designed to secure peace, in the Versailles Treaty, and U.S. entry into the League of Nations led to his disappointment and embitterment. Because he had for so long (almost since the war had broken out) seen himself as the man who would lead the peace process, he seemed unable to compromise on his vision. The Allies rejected some of his treaty provisions including, ominously, his advocacy of only minimal German reparations. (The Allied desire for vengeance, and the destruction of the German economy, may have opened the door for the ascendance of Adolf Hitler.)

But his biggest battle was with the U.S. Senate, which ultimately rejected membership in the League of Nations. Domestically, the president's loosening grip on power had already been signaled by the election of a Republican-controlled Congress in 1918, and he was unable to utilize his old powers of persuasion here. Despite Wilson's cross-country journey to champion this provision, Americans had grown frightened of the implications of joining the league. Wilson did not help matters by refusing to give in on mitigating provisions, such as the insistence of independent sovereignty on matters of war, and ultimately lost the fight. At the height of this effort, in the autumn of 1919, Wilson suffered two strokes and thereafter was only a shell of his former self.

Thus, Wilson left three distinct legacies. First, he pursued an active economic agenda in the name of the New Freedom, and won important and innovative victories. Second, he presided over, but cannot be fully credited for, a series of social reforms, while at the same time failing to make any sort of advance (and in fact allowing a large step backward) on the racial issue. Finally, although ably leading the nation through the difficult war years, he pursued a sometimes puzzling and irrational foreign policy vision in which the leadership qualities of his early reforms seemed to elude him completely.

TARIFF REDUCTION

Wilson's first effort as president was to sharply curtail the long-standing and entrenched system of protective tariffs—that is, taxes levied on foreign goods entering the United States. While high tariffs were advocated by some politicians as a means to strengthen the American economy, critics felt the strategy was no longer necessary. Wilson adhered to this latter view and, despite opposition from organized interests, Republicans, and even members of his own party, won a victory early in his administration to drastically overhaul the system through the Underwood Tariff Act, a law that eliminated or reduced most existing tariffs.

The use of tariffs as a means to protect emerging American industries dates back to the early days of the nation. By artificially increasing the price of imported goods, tariffs gave domestic producers an edge that helped them gain entry into the market. Their utilization was intensified during the Civil War, when they were relied upon for revenue. But tariffs had grown increasingly controversial beginning in the late nineteenth century. For one thing, once the Civil War ended, the need for the additional source of revenue declined. Additionally, many argued that tariffs protected industries well beyond the point where they were needed, and that the system was in fact shielding perfectly healthy economic sectors from the global free market, thereby giving them an extra and unnecessary advantage.

Furthermore, the effect of tariffs on consumers was questioned. The pro-tariff forces argued that by protecting American producers from foreign competition, and thus virtually guaranteeing them the domestic market, prices would drop as a function of the ensuing high-sales volume. However, opponents asserted that, freed from the threat of cheaper imported products, industries could charge whatever they wanted for goods, and Americans would have no choice but to pay the higher prices.

In 1909, President Taft had advocated some tariff reductions, but was faced with powerful opposition. In the end, the tariff bill passed in his administration represented little change. By the Wilson administration, fairly clear coalitions had formed—Republicans opposed tariff reductions and most Democrats supported them.

Wilson was determined to force a dramatic change, believing that consumers and producers alike would benefit from sharp reductions. This issue fit with his New Freedom agenda, which stressed a reduced role for the federal government in economic matters. In April 1913, dressed in his most formal clothes, Wilson personally delivered his request for a tariff reduction bill to the U.S. Congress. In his message, Wilson stressed the theme that tariffs had moved beyond protection of infant industries to a privileged system of overprotection of quite vigorous industries, and recommended swift and meaningful change. He believed that as the new leader of the American people, it was his duty to personally shepherd this bill through Congress.

But Wilson was not prepared for the strength of organized opposition, as scores of lobbyists descended on Washington, D.C., to attempt to preserve tariffs protecting their own products. Additionally, Wilson's proposal faced opposition from members of his own party who represented agricultural regions. These congressmen supported tariff reductions on manufactured products (which would result in lower prices for goods their constituents purchased, such as farm implements) but wanted the protective tariffs to remain (or be increased) for domestically produced agricultural commodities. Especially vocal in their opposition were representatives of the sugar and wool sectors. In July, Senator Porter J.

McCumber, (R–ND) made a somewhat melodramatic speech in defense of the farmers and the effects this law would have on them. For Mc-Cumber, the small benefits to the consumer of ending agricultural tariffs could not outweigh the disastrous effects the change could have on farmers. He argued that farmers are never given the attention that other groups in America are granted.

Despite the opposition, the bill passed easily in the House, with Wilson's assistance. However, it bogged down in the Senate. In frustration at the entrenched interests that seemed to be impeding passage, Wilson issued a public statement in the spring of 1913 asserting that special interests were blocking necessary and beneficial legislation. He noted that "it is of serious interest to the country that the people at large should have no lobby and be voiceless in these matters, while great bodies of astute men seek to create an artificial opinion and to overcome the interests of the public for their private profit."[3] The letter created a public sensation. In a drive to embarrass the president by proving his assertions unfounded, Senate Republicans began hearings into the matter. The ploy backfired, however, as the hearings did uncover evidence of intense lobbying by organized interests. Furthermore, they showed that many senators who opposed reduction held stock in companies that would likely suffer financial losses if the tariff bill passed.

After the hearing debacle, the opposition was severely weakened, and the Senate approved the bill in September 1913. The new law did not give America completely free trade, but it did lower tariffs an average of 25 percent. It also totally eliminated tariffs on certain goods already marked by American dominance in the world market.

This was not the end of the tariff story, however, as many of the reductions were reversed in the Warren G. Harding administration. However, the episode is important for several reasons. It first of all worked to greatly enhance the image of the new president, and it gave him clout in future dealings with Congress. Additionally, although little remarked upon at the time, the Underwood Tariff Act assessed a very small income tax on the American people (as authorized by the Sixteenth Amendment) for the first time. The tax was seen as necessary to make up for the loss of tariff revenue. Finally, this represents a rare example where a president, in the face of entrenched special interests and opposition from the opposite party as well as his own, succeeded in getting a policy passed without major compromise.

NOTES

1. Herbert Croly, "Presidential Complecency," *The New Republic*, November 21, 1914, 7.

2. Mark Sullivan, *Our Times, 1900–1925*, vol. 5 (New York: Scribner's, 1939), 496.

3. Ray Stannard Baker and William E. Dodd, ed., *The Public Papers of Woodrow Wilson*, vol. 2, *The New Democracy* (New York: Harper and Brothers, 1926), 36.

WILSON—TARIFF MESSAGE TO CONGRESS
(APRIL 8, 1913)

I am very glad indeed to have this opportunity to address the two Houses directly and to verify for myself the impression that the President of the United States is a person, not a mere department of the Government hailing Congress from some isolated island of jealous power, sending messages, not speaking naturally and with his own voice—that he is a human being trying to co-operate with other human beings in a common service. After this pleasant experience I shall feel quite normal in all our dealings with one another.

I have called the Congress together in extraordinary session because a duty was laid upon the party now in power at the recent elections which it ought to perform promptly, in order that the burden carried by the people under existing law may be lightened as soon as possible, and in order, also, that the business interests of the country may not be kept too long in suspense as to what the fiscal changes are to be to which they will be required to adjust themselves. It is clear to the whole country that the tariff duties must be altered. They must be changed to meet the radical alteration in the conditions of our economic life which the country has witnessed within the last generation. While the whole face and method of our industrial and commercial life were being changed beyond recognition the tariff schedules have remained what they were before the change began, or have moved in the direction they were given when no large circumstance of our industrial development was what it is to-day. Our task is to square them with the actual facts. The sooner that is done the sooner we shall escape from suffering from the facts and the sooner our men of business will be free to thrive by the law of nature—the nature of free business—instead of by the law of legislation and artificial arrangement.

We have seen tariff legislation wander very far afield in our day—very far indeed from the field in which our prosperity might have had a normal growth and stimulation. No one who looks the facts squarely in the face or knows anything that lies beneath the surface of action can fail to perceive the principles upon which recent tariff legislation has been based. We long ago passed beyond the modest notion of "protecting" the industries of the country and moved boldly forward to the idea that they were entitled to the direct patronage of the Government. For a long time—a time so long that the men now active in public policy hardly remember the conditions that preceded it—we have sought in our tariff schedules to give each group of manufacturers or producers what they themselves thought that they needed in order to maintain a practically exclusive market as against the rest of the world. Consciously or unconsciously, we have built up a set of privileges and exemptions from competition behind which it was easy by any, even the crudest, forms of combination to organize monopoly; until at last nothing is normal, nothing is obliged to stand the tests of efficiency and economy, in our world of big business, but everything thrives by concerted arrangement. Only new principles of action will save us from a final hard crystallization of monopoly and a complete loss of the influences that quicken enterprise and keep independent energy alive.

It is plain what those principles must be. We must abolish everything that bears even the semblance of privilege or of any kind of artificial advantage, and put our business men and producers under the stimulation of a constant necessity to be efficient, economical, and enterprising, masters of competitive supremacy, better workers and merchants than any in the world. Aside from the duties laid upon articles which we do not, and probably can not, produce, therefore, and the duties laid upon luxuries and merely for the sake of the revenues they yield, the object of the tariff duties henceforth laid must be effective competition, the whetting of American wits by contest with the wits of the rest of the world.

It would be unwise to move toward this end headlong, with reckless haste, or with strokes that cut at the very roots of what has grown up amongst us by long process and at our own invitation. It does not alter a thing to upset it and break it and deprive it of a chance to change. It destroys it. We must make changes in our fiscal laws, in our fiscal system, whose object is development, a more free and wholesome development, not revolution or upset or confusion. We must build up trade, especially foreign trade. We need the outlet and the enlarged field of energy more than we ever did before. We must build up industry as well, and must adopt freedom in the place of artificial stimulation only so far as it will build, not pull down. In dealing with the tariff the method by which this may be done will be a matter of judgment exercised item by item. To some not accustomed to the excitements and responsibilities of greater freedom our methods may in some respects and at some points seem heroic but remedies may be heroic and yet be remedies. It is our business to make sure that they are genuine remedies. Our object is clear. If our motive is above just challenge and only an occasional error of judgment is chargeable against us, we shall be fortunate.

Congressional Record. 63rd Congress, 1st sess., 1913. Vol. 50, 130.

SENATOR PORTER J. McCUMBER—REMARKS ON THE
TARIFF (JULY 14, 1913)

For more than two months, behind carefully guarded doors and shaded windows, the Democratic members of the Finance Committee have been hatching a tariff measure. They have tenderly shielded it from the too chilling blasts of cold reason and from the too dazzling light of information. . . .

It seems to have been conceived in animosity against every American industry that really needed protection—the many small concerns of the country, the only competitors of the great concerns that need no legislative favors. While it bears the birthmark of ill will against nearly all, the special object of its choler and hate is the American farmer. It is especially endowed with tooth and talon for his injury and destruction. . . .

And so I shall address myself first to you, the Democratic Party, with reference to your assault upon the American farmer. In this year 1913 you are about to commit a greater crime against the American farmer than has ever been perpetrated by any political party against any class of people during any period of recorded history. You are about to rob him of sacred rights which he has paid for through long years of toil, self-denial, and patient waiting. . . .

Does the Democratic majority of the Senate concur in the sentiment that seems everywhere prevalent among city people, that the Almighty never intended that the tiller of the soil should have more than a mere existence, that his purpose in the world is simply to produce food for others to eat, for which economic arrangement he is to be accorded the right to live in a humble way—a honey bee to be hived and tolerated that drones may have honey to live on?

In all lines of business outside of farming the laborer must receive his wages. Neither frost, hail, blight, nor bug can affect him. The farmer, on the other hand, will lose at least a full crop once in 10 years, and will have many half crops during that period. Everyone acquainted with farm earnings knows that the labor of the farmer has always been the poorest paid labor in the United States; that the thing which the farmer sells always has represented and still represents twice as much expended energy in its production as the thing which he buys with it. . . . Why, then, do you want to further discriminate against the farmer . . . ?

A reduction of 10 cents a bushel on wheat will have no influence whatever upon the retail price of flour. The reduction bears such a small ratio to the value of a barrel of flour that it scarcely affects the wholesale price at all and is entirely lost sight of in the retail trade. . . . But suppose that by a 25 cents per bushel tariff of wheat the farmer does get 10 cents a bushel better price for his wheat, as has been demonstrated in the last 10 years. And suppose that this extra price of 10 cents a bushel is charged up to the ultimate consumer. The ultimate consumer uses about a barrel of flour per capita per year. That would increase the cost of a barrel of flour and make an added expense of 45 cents a year—3.8 cents a month. The ultimate consumer man would have to retrench in his expenses to meet this extra outlay to the extent of two-thirds of a 5-cent cigar a month. The ultimate consumer girl would have to retrench in her expenses 3 sticks of chewing gum per month. What an enormous burden this tax is upon the people who smoke and chew gum from 4 o'clock on, while the farmer is sweating in the field and worrying over reports of frost, hot winds, hail, noxious weeds, smut, chinch bugs, and grasshoppers.

But you say the people want cheaper bread. You know this reduction will not reduce the price of a loaf of bread a penny. What the people want is not cheaper bread but a better opportunity to earn good wages to buy that bread, and your proposed tariff measure will decrease that opportunity.

Congressional Record. 63rd Congress, 1st sess., 1913. Vol. 50, 2397, 2398, 2400.

FEDERAL RESERVE ACT

Organization of the nation's currency and banking system was another of Wilson's major domestic priorities upon taking office. Although representing an increased federal presence, it fit his New Freedom agenda by offering greater freedom and independence to American business. Passage of the law is generally viewed as one of the high points of his administration. However, while there was virtually unanimous agreement on the need for some restructuring, Wilson faced a difficult fight in the summer of 1913 over the particulars of this policy.

For several years there had been warnings, in the form of financial "panics," that America's banking system, made up of independent institutions solely responsible for their own money supplies, needed reform. Basically, panics were runs on banks in which many depositors sought to withdraw large amounts of currency, sometimes resulting in shortfalls. With banks having to worry about these potential shortages, credit was tightened (i.e., less money was lent out), and the entire economy suffered. For some, these periodic shortages were traceable to the so-called money trust—a small group of men who, through control of several of the nation's largest banks, were thought to be able to direct the supply of currency and credit to their own advantage. American business and investment were thus completely dependent on the decisions this trust made. Other observers felt that the problem was more one of logistics. Because of general seasonal- and market-based fluctuations, banks simply had more or less cash reserves at different times. Either way, the system was obviously flawed.

Whether viewed as the result of an unscrupulous money trust or as a matter of normal vacillations, it was clear that some sort of centralized system, through which banks could pool their resources and thus provide a more elastic source of currency and credit, was called for. But, there was a fundamental disagreement as to how this system would work. Although the details of competing plans were quite complex, the basic dispute involved the extent of federal involvement.

Bankers themselves wanted a privately controlled system, in which banks would remain individually owned but would join in a loose partnership that would provide an elastic money supply to all members. However, several members of Congress (i.e., progressives of both parties who strongly believed in the money trust explanation) advocated a federally controlled centralized system, and even one more rather extreme step—federal control of all banks. Bankers viewed this plan as dangerously socialistic.

As New Jersey governor and during the 1912 campaign Wilson had spoken out against the money trust, but upon becoming president he freely admitted that he did not understand the subtleties of the banking issue. He listened to arguments from both sides, and in the summer of 1913 helped to forge a compromise plan—a Federal Reserve system that would provide an elastic currency and credit supply to all member banks, but in which banks remained privately owned. Federal control was established by the fact that members of the main Federal Reserve Board as well as several regional boards were to be appointed by the president. The federal government would also issue a new form of currency—Federal Reserve notes—to help facilitate the flow of currency among member banks.

Wilson displayed an ability to compromise here that tended to elude him in later matters. It was important to him, however, to obtain passage of a law representing a positive stimulus to the economy as a companion measure to the tariff bill, which (although constructive in the long run) would have some immediately negative effects on certain businesses. In his address to Congress, he noted the freedom restored to American business by virtue of an assured supply of money and credit and stated that banks would now be the "instruments not the masters" of business. His secretary, Joe Tumulty, referred to this as a law that "set business free."[1]

The banking interests were not happy with the degree of federal control but were relieved that some action had been taken and that the government takeover had been averted. Alternatively, several midwestern and southern senators opposed the bill on the grounds that it had not gone far enough. Senator Robert La Follette's position, as outlined in a February 1912 speech, illustrates this view, arguing that "the people," through the federal government, must be allowed to control their own money. However, La Follette undermined his own position (and probably his own presidential aspirations for that year) in the delivery of this speech that, overall, was so unfocused, long, and rambling, that many in the audience believed he was suffering a nervous breakdown.

A different and more subtle response to the Federal Reserve Act was offered by Walter Lippmann, a progressive-socialist commentator, one year after passage. Lippmann helped to put this entire issue in perspective by rising above the controversy of whether banks and currency would be better served by public or private control. In this essay, he instead focused on how the American economy had changed so drastically in recent years that whether control was centered in the public or private sector was of little consequence. He warned that the Federal Reserve Act should not be seen as a return to more democracy in the sense of the average American being able to play a meaningful role in business or industry. For Lippman, the economy had been taken over by a small group of expert elites. Whether these came from the public or private sector was less important than the fact that small-scale capitalism, the individual initiative and enterprise referred to by Wilson, had largely vanished.

The Federal Reserve Act did fulfill its intended goals. Panics steadily decreased and then disappeared for a time after its passage. Within a decade after passage, 70 percent of U.S. banking resources were controlled by member banks. However, the system was not strong enough to prevent the bank runs and economic collapse of the Great Depression. Eventually, through the Banking Act of 1935, the Federal Reserve system was overhauled and strengthened.

NOTE

1. Joseph P. Tumulty, *Woodrow Wilson As I Know Him* (Garden City, N.Y.: Garden City Publishing, 1921), 170.

WILSON—ADDRESS TO CONGRESS ON THE FEDERAL RESERVE ACT (JUNE 23, 1913)

It is absolutely imperative that we should give the business men of this country a banking and currency system by means of which they can make use of the freedom of enterprise and of individual initiative which we are about to bestow upon them.

We are about to set them free; we must not leave them without the tools of action when they are free. We are about to set them free by removing the trammels of the protective tariff. Ever since the Civil War they have waited for this emancipation and for the free opportunities it will bring with it. It has been reserved for us to give it to them. Some fell in love, indeed, with the slothful security of their dependence upon the Government; some took advantage of the shelter of the nursery to set up a mimic mastery of their own within its walls. Now both the tonic and the discipline of liberty and maturity are to ensure. There will be some readjustments of purpose and point of view. There will follow a period of expansion and new enterprise, freshly conceived. It is for us to determine now whether it shall be rapid and facile and of easy accomplishment. This it can not be unless the resourceful business men who are to deal with the new circumstances are to have at hand and ready for use the instrumentalities and conveniences of free enterprise which independent men need when acting on their own initiative.

It is not enough to strike the shackles from business. The duty of statesmanship is not negative merely. It is constructive also. We must show that we understand what business needs and that we know how to supply it. No man, however casual and superficial his observation of the conditions now prevailing in the country, can fail to see that one of the chief things business needs now and will need increasingly as it gains in scope and vigor in the years immediately ahead of us is the proper means by which readily to vitalize its credit, corporate and individual, and its originative brains. What will it profit us to be free if we are not to have the best and most accessible instrumentalities of commerce and enterprise? What will it profit us to be quit of one kind of monopoly if we are to remain in the grip of another and more effective kind? How are we to gain and keep the confidence of the business community unless we show that we know how both to aid and to protect it? What shall we say if we make fresh enterprise necessary and also make it very difficult by leaving all else except the tariff just as we found it? The tyrannies of business, big and little, lie within the field of credit. We know that. Shall we not act upon the knowledge? Do we not know how to act upon it? If a man can not make his assets available at pleasure, his assets of capacity and character and resource, what satisfaction is it to him to see opportunity beckoning to him on every hand when others have the keys of credit in their pockets and treat them as all but their own private possession? It is perfectly clear that it is our duty to supply the new banking and currency system the country needs, and it will need it immediately more than it has ever needed it before.

The only question is, When shall we supply it—now or later, after the demands shall have become reproaches that we were so dull and so slow? Shall we hasten to change the tariff laws and then be laggards about making it possible and easy for the country to take advantage of the change? There can be only one answer to that question. We must act now, at whatever sacrifice to ourselves. It is a duty which the circumstances forbid us to postpone. I should be recreant to my deepest convictions of public obligation did I not press it upon you with solemn and urgent insistence.

The principles upon which we should act are also clear. The country has sought and seen its path in this matter within the last few years— sees it more clearly now than it ever saw it before—much more clearly than when the last legislative proposals on the subject were made. We must have a currency, not rigid as now, but readily, elastically responsive to sound credit, the expanding and contracting credits of everyday transactions, the normal ebb and flow of personal and corporate dealings. Our banking laws must mobilize reserves; must not permit the concentration anywhere in a few hands of the monetary resources of the country or their use for speculative purposes in such volume as to hinder or impede or stand in the way of other more legitimate, more fruitful uses. And the control of the system of banking and of issue which our new laws are to set up must be public, not private, must be vested in the Government itself, so that the banks may be the instruments, not the masters, of business and of individual enterprise and initiative.

Baker, Ray Stannard, and William E. Dodd, eds. *The Public Papers of Woodrow Wilson*. Vol. 1, *The New Democracy*. New York: Harper and Brothers, 1926, 37–40.

ROBERT M. LA FOLLETTE—REMARKS ON CURRENCY CONTROL (FEBRUARY 2, 1912)

The country is only just beginning to understand how completely great banking institutions in the principal money centres have become bound up with the control of industrial institutions, the railroads and franchise combinations.

. . .

The plain truth is that legitimate commercial banking is being eaten up by speculative banking. The greatest banks of the financial centre of the country have ceased to be agents of commerce and have become primarily agencies of promotion and speculation. By merging the largest banks, trust companies, and insurance companies masses of capital have been brought under one management, to be employed not as the servant of commerce, but as its master; not to supply legitimate business and to facilitate exchange, but to subordinate the commercial demands of the country upon the banks to call loans in Wall Street and to finance industrial organizations, always speculative, and often unlawful in character. Trained men, who a dozen years ago stood first among the bankers of the world as heads of the greatest banks of New York City, are, in the main, either displaced or do the bidding of men who are not bankers, but masters of organization.

The banks which were then managed by bankers as independent commercial institutions are now owned in groups by a few men, whose principal interests are in railroads, traction, telegraph, cable, shipping, iron and steel, copper, coal, oil, gas, insurance, etc.

. . .

With this enormous concentration of business it is possible to create, artificially, periods of prosperity and periods of panic. Prices can be lowered or advanced at the will of the "System." When the farmer must move his crops a scarcity of money may be created and prices lowered. When the crop passes into the control of the speculator the artificial stringency may be relieved and prices advanced, and the illegitimate profit raked off the agricultural industry may be pocketed in Wall Street.

If an effort is made to compel any one of these great "Interests" to obey the law, it is easy for them to enter into a conspiracy to destroy whoever may be responsible for the undertaking.

. . .

Our National Banking Law is a patchwork of legislation. It should be thoroughly revised. And all authorities agree that a comprehensive plan for an emergency currency is vitally important. When the basic principle of such a plan is once determined, when it is settled that government controlled banks are to be, *in fact*, controlled by the government *in the public interest*, the details can easily be worked out.

La Follette, Robert M. *A Personal Narrative of Political Experiences*. Madison, Wisc.: La Follette, 1911, 766, 780–781, 792.

WALTER LIPPMANN—"THE MAGIC OF PROPERTY" (1914)

There has been in recent years a great outcry against the concentrated control of credit. It was found that the decision as to how money should be invested had passed away from the people who owned the money.

The enormous power of Morgan consisted in his ability to direct the flow of capital. He was the head of a vast system which had taken out of the hands of investors the task of deciding how their money was to be used. It was no doubt a colossal autocracy.

There has been a great effort to break it up, to decentralize the power that concentrated about Morgan. But no one proposes to put back into the hands of the investor the decision as to the financing of industry. The investors are a scattered mob incapable of such decisions. The question of where money is to be applied is a matter for experts to answer. And so reform of the credit system does not consist in abolishing the financial expert. It consists in making him a public servant.

The Wilson Currency Bill seems to be an effort to make banking responsive to business needs all over the country. It gives businessmen a larger control over financial experts. How that control is to be extended to the citizens at large is one of the subtlest problems of democracy. I do not venture here to answer it. I wish rather to keep more closely to the fact that whatever system is devised, it will have to recognize that the investor no longer can decide in modern industry, that "foresight" has become an organized, technical profession, and is ceasing to be one of the duties of private property.

. . .

. . . The trusts have concentrated control and management, but ownership they have diffused and diluted till it means very little more than a claim to residual profits, after expenses are paid, after the bondholders are satisfied, and perhaps, after the insiders have decided which way they wish the stock market to fluctuate.

Let no stockholder come to the radical, then, and charge him with attacking the sanctity of private property. The evolution of business is doing that at a rate and with a dispatch which will make future historians gasp.

Lippmann Walter. *Drift and Mastery*. New York: Kennerly, 1914, 53–55, 58–59.

SEGREGATION IN THE FEDERAL GOVERNMENT

While progressives worked to improve the quality of life for many Americans, the lingering, widespread belief in the inequality of the races limited a true partnership between the progressive and civil rights movements in the early party of the twentieth century. For southern progressives in particular (who did not get as much attention as their brethren in other regions but existed nonetheless), racism was widely accepted as a core ideological principle—thus leading to a brand of progressivism that stressed only the betterment of whites. Wilson, attempting to reconcile his own southern background and at least somewhat progressive leanings, not surprisingly found himself embroiled in controversy over the issue of segregation in the federal government.

Although Wilson is not generally thought of as a southern president, he spent his first twenty-four years in the South, and had childhood memories of living in the Confederacy during the Civil War. Certainly, Wilson was quite apart from the virulently racist, extremely conservative southern Democrats who grew increasingly more powerful throughout this era. However, Wilson himself was committed only to a very limited concept of equal rights and was not willing to press even those moderate views, given the shifting balance of power in the Democratic Party. Thus, he presented a mixed message to blacks in America.

Just before his election in 1912, he had promised "fair dealing" with blacks. Still angered at both Roosevelt and Taft over the earlier Brownsville affair, writer and activist W.E.B. Du Bois had advised blacks to vote for Wilson, stating that "Mr. Wilson's personality gives us hope that reactionary Southern sentiment will not control him,"[1] and in fact the number of votes cast by African Americans for the Democratic candidate for president that year was the highest it had ever been at that point.

But once in office, Wilson proved to be a disappointment. First, he changed his mind in regard to appointing a commission to study the racial situation in America, citing the "delicacy and difficulty of the situation."[2] Most notably, however, he allowed several departments in the executive branch to practice racial segregation. Wilson did not order the segregation, and the idea originated not from the president himself but from members of his cabinet. But Wilson made no effort to stop it. Beginning in 1913, several departments and agencies, including the U.S. Post Office and the Treasury Department, began to separate white and black employees with segregated work areas, lunchrooms, and restrooms. In the Post Office Department, for example, many black employees were transferred to the dead-letter office, where they worked behind a row of lockers separating them from whites.

Although there had been some limited segregation of workers prior to this, it now was authorized by specific orders of Wilson's appointed cabinet members. However, there was no widespread reaction to the new policy in the mainstream press, thus suggesting that this was not an altogether shocking or disagreeable development for many Americans. A correspondent from *Harper's Weekly* magazine even wrote a very positive piece on the newly segregated Bureau of Engraving and Printing. Apparently trying hard to put an optimistic spin on the situation, he observed that the employees seemed happy with the arrangement and that the only noticeable difference in the segregated cafeterias was that "the negroes seem to have a better style of table than the white men."[3]

This article advocated a philosophy that was fairly widespread at the time—that equal rights and racial separation are not incompatible.

But a determined opposition to the policy did emerge. The editor of the *New York World*, a newspaper generally supportive of Wilson, called this a "small, mean, petty discrimination."[4] Du Bois referred to it as "plain, flat, disgraceful spitting in the face of people."[5] Publisher Oscar Garrison Villard, writing in the *North American Review*, offered one of the earliest responses to the new practice, criticizing both Wilson and Treasury Secretary McAdoo for the decision. He stressed in particular the dangerous precedent set by this policy—segregation by states and cities was one thing, but by the federal government quite another. For Villard, this action left African Americans feeling they had been abandoned completely by their own nation.

On November 12, 1914, a delegation of black leaders led by the minister William Monroe Trotter met with the president at the White House, but the meeting went badly. Wilson began by offering a statement in support of the practice, stressing the delicate nature of the situation, and the benefits of segregation to both races. But Trotter refused to be mollified and argued with the president. At the end of the session Wilson angrily informed Trotter that he was "the only American citizen that has ever come into this office who had talked to me with a tone with a background of passion that was evident," and that he had "spoiled the cause for which you came."[6]

Despite Wilson's indignation with Trotter and defensiveness toward the criticism in general, the opposition did seem to have an effect. Over the course of this administration, segregation was slowly phased out again, although there was never any official declaration of a policy rescission. General discrimination against black employees and military segregation remained characteristics of the executive branch, however, until the late 1940s when President Henry S Truman began to institute changes.

NOTES

1. Henry Lee Moon, ed., *The Emerging Thought of W.E.B. Du Bois* (New York: Simon and Schuster, 1972), 96.

2. Arthur S. Link, *The Papers of Woodrow Wilson*, vol. 28 (Princeton, N.J.: Princeton University Press, 1979), 202.

3. McGregor, "Segregation in the Departments," *Harper's Weekly*, December 26, 1914, 621.

4. Arthur S. Link, *Woodrow Wilson and the Progressive Era* (New York: Harper and Row, 1954), 66.

5. Moon, *Emerging Thought*, 331.

6. Link, *Papers of Woodrow Wilson*, vol. 31, 306.

WILSON—REMARKS AT MEETING WITH AFRICAN AMERICAN DELEGATION (NOVEMBER 12, 1914)

Now, I think that I am perfectly safe in stating that the American people, as a whole, sincerely desire and wish to support, in every way they can, the advancement of the Negro race in America. They rejoice in the evidences of the really extraordinary advances that the race has made—in its self-support, in its capacity for independent endeavor, in its adaptation for organization, and everything of that sort. All of that is admirable and has the sympathy of the whole country.

But we are all practical men. We know that there is a point at which there is apt to be friction, and that is in the intercourse between the two races. Because, gentlemen, we must strip this thing of sentiment and look at the facts, because the facts will get the better of us whether we wish them to or not.

Now, in my view the best way to help the Negro in America is to help him with his independence—to relieve him of his dependence upon the white element of our population, as he is relieving himself in splendid fashion. And the problem, as I have discussed it with my colleagues in the departments, is this, for I had taken it very seriously after my last interview with a committee of this organization. If you will leave with me all the instances you have just cited, I will look into them again. But the point that was put to me, in essence, was that they were seeking, not to put the Negro employees at a disadvantage, but they were seeking to make arrangements which would prevent any kind of friction between the white employees and the Negro employees.

Now, they may have been mistaken in judgment. But their objective was not to do what you gentlemen seem to assume—to put the Negro employees at an uncomfortable disadvantage—but to relieve the situation that does arise. We can't blink the fact, gentlemen, that it does arise when the two races are mixed.

Now, of course color outside is a perfectly artificial test. It is a race question. And color, so far as the proposition itself, is merely an evidence of the development from a particular continent; that is to say, from the African continent.

Now, it takes the world generations to outlive all its prejudices. Of course they are prejudices. They are prejudices which are embarrassing the Government of the United States just as much with other races, that is, some other races, as they are embarrassing us about the race that is derived from African descent. And so we must treat this thing with a recognition of its difficulties.

Now, I am perfectly willing to do anything that is just. I am not willing to do what may turn out to be unwise. Now, it is the unwise part that is debatable—whether we have acted in a wise way or not. If my colleagues have dealt with me candidly—and I think they have—they have not intended to do an injustice. They have intended to remedy what they regarded as creating the possibility of friction, which they did not want ever to exist. They did not want any white man made uncomfortable by anything that any colored man did, or a colored man made uncomfortable by anything that a white man did in the offices of the government. That, in itself, is essentially how they feel—that a man of either race should not make the other uncomfortable. It works both ways. A white man can make a colored man uncomfortable, as a colored man can make a white man uncomfortable if there is a prejudice existing between them. And it shouldn't be allowed on either end.

Now, what makes it look like discrimination is that the colored people are in a minority as compared with the white employees. Any minority looks as if it were discriminated against. But suppose that the Negroes were in the majority in the departments in the clerkships and this segregation occurred? Then it would look like discrimination against the whites, because it is always the minority that looks discriminated against, whereas the discrimination may not be intended against anybody, but for the benefit of both.

Link, Arthur S., ed. *The Papers of Woodrow Wilson*. Vol. 31. Princeton, N.J.: Princeton University Press, 1979, 301–302.

OSWALD GARRISON VILLARD—"THE PRESIDENT AND THE SEGREGATION AT WASHINGTON" (DECEMBER 1913)

On October 16, 1912, Woodrow Wilson, then the Democratic nominee for President, declared that: "Should I become President of the United States, they [the colored people] may count upon me for absolute fair dealing and for everything by which I could assist in advancing the interests of their race in the United States." This utterance gave complete satisfaction to those leaders of the colored people and the friends of the race who were urging them to break away from their thraldom to the Republican party and to vote for the Governor of New Jersey on the ground that the country would profit most by the election of the Democratic ticket. For decades previous the colored people, through their blind fealty to the Republican party, had been its pawns, to be used or shoved aside as the case might be. . . .

It was with dismay, therefore, that early in the Administration of Mr. Wilson, whose Cabinet is equally divided between Southerners and

Northerners, there became noticeable in certain quarters a distinct hostility to the colored people. . . .

Careful inquiry by a representative of the National Association for the Advancement of Colored People, and by newspaper men of the standing of Washington correspondents of the New York *Evening Post* and Boston *Advertiser*, has developed the fact that segregation of colored employees exists and is increasing, especially in the Bureau of Engraving and Printing, in the Post-Office Department, and in the office of the Auditor for the Post-Office, which is a part of the Treasury Department, and that it has begun in the Washington city post-office. As yet, segregation has not been introduced in the Treasury Building, where there are two hundred and seventy colored employees in the corridors and offices together with white clerks. It is defended by Mr. McAdoo as "an effort to remove causes of complaint and friction where white women have been forced unnecessarily to sit at desks with colored men." But there is no statement that there have been many such complaints or that they were heard of under previous Administrations. Nor is it explained why colored clerks are taken out of rooms in which their sole companions are white men, or why, if there should be segregation because of the women, the Government does not segregate all its women clerks. Nor does Mr. McAdoo record the fact that in many instances the white clerks, without respect to sex, have gone to their colored associates and expressed their complete dissent from the Government's caste undertaking. He indignantly denies that poorer quarters have been given to the segregated, but eye-witnesses have told of colored women shut off in an unpleasant alcove in one office; of others quietly forced out of the lunch-room they had been using for nine years past and compelled to go into lavatories at the lunch-hour, of men clerks segregated behind lockers in one corner of a room in the dead-letter division of the Post-Office Department. Poorer accommodations for the segregated are the invariable law of segregation. The assignment of separate toilet-rooms to the races under threats of prompt punishment for failure to obey the rules has been another of the deeply humiliating features of the Washington segregation. To the colored workers all this segregating has been more brutal than a slap in the face. It is as if the great Government of the United States had gone out of its way to stamp them publicly as lepers, as physically and morally contagious and unfit for association with white people. . . .

These colored people who are thus branded are not roustabouts, or corner loafers, or worthless laborers. They are educated men and women, college graduates many of them, from all over the country who have passed their civil-service examinations and entered the Government's employ with full faith in its justice, asking merely the right to serve on equal terms with their fellows. The readers of *The North American Review* will understand the bitter humiliation of the segregation orders if they can imagine themselves set apart as unworthy by brute authority, but they can hardly appreciate the added sense of injury which comes from the fact that this is an act of the Federal Government. . . .

Mr. Wilson has proved himself in many respects a noble and inspired leader with rare political intuition. No one, moreover, can deny that he finds himself in this matter in a terribly difficult position. He is between the devil and the deep sea; on one side the negro-haters so powerful in and out of Congress and official life; on the other side sympathy for the oppressed and disadvantaged, fair play, true democracy, justice, liberty, and an old freedom beckon to him. And his philosophy, if he remains silent and segregates further, will be wrong, his democracy gravely at fault; he has given us beautiful and worthy sentiments in his book called *The New Freedom*, and in his various speeches prior to and since his election to the Presidency. But nowhere thus far do we find any indication that his democracy is not limited both by the sex line and the color line. He fails utterly to see that to discriminate in his democracy against any one is to bring his whole carefully reared edifice crashing to the ground. The principles upon which our democracy rests must apply to everybody without discrimination, as exactly as a law of science, or they are open to doubt at once.

Villard, Oswald Garrison. "The President and the Segregation at Washington." *The North American Review* (December 1913): 800–806.

U.S.–MEXICAN RELATIONS

Although paling in comparison to the war in Europe, U.S. relations with Mexico were a major concern and controversy of the Wilson administration. Wilson's Missionary Diplomacy approach twice led the two nations to the brink of war. In both his initial advocacy of U.S. intervention and his later retreat from that position, Wilson faced opposition. The entire episode, in addition to providing a capstone to the history of U.S. intervention in Latin America, was also linked to the growing tensions in Europe and provides a clear illustration of Wilson's sometimes obdurate approach to foreign policy.

When Wilson took office in 1913, General Victoriano Huerta had already attained the presidency of Mexico in a violent coup in which his predecessor was murdered. There was a great deal of pressure on Wilson, largely from companies and individuals with financial investment in Mexico, to follow the lead of most European nations and officially recognize the Huerta regime. But Wilson was virtually obsessed with seeing this regime removed from power, viewing Huerta as "the bitter, implacable foe of everything progressive and humane in Mexico."[1] Additionally, Wilson could see that the growing Constitutionalist revolutionary movement, led by Venustiano Carranza, Francisco "Pancho" Villa and others, was gaining popular support.

Wilson proceeded to attempt to broker an agreement for elections that would exclude Huerta and include the Constitutionalists. All sides resented the intrusion, but it looked as though an arrangement might ensue. Before an election could take place, however, Huerta arrested several members of the Mexican legislature in the fall of 1913, and moved toward a clear dictatorship. Despite their reticence at his involvement (for they feared U.S. intervention in their nation more than they opposed Huerta), Wilson began to actively support the Constitutionalists. He allowed arms to be transferred to the revolutionary movement and stated to Congress in November his intent to intervene if necessary. This message came despite council from his own advisors that the position was extreme and unwarranted.

For Wilson, the necessity was provided by the purposefully intensified Tampico, Mexico, affair in April 1914. In that episode, after Mexican officials apologized for arresting the crew of a U.S. fishing vessel that had landed in Tampico without permission, Wilson supported Admiral Henry T. Mayo's further demand for a twenty-one gun salute to the American flag, which Huerta refused. This occurred at the same time that a German ship loaded with ammunition for Huerta's regime was about to land in Vera Cruz harbor. The two incidents together led to Wilson putting the intervention threat into action by occupying Vera Cruz, which drew a great deal of international and domestic opposition. A typical response is represented by an April 18, 1914, editorial in *The Economist* of London, proclaiming the entire Tampico affair an overreaction that could backfire on the United States.

Wilson was prepared at this point to go to war with Mexico. The situation was diffused for the short term when negotiations were undertaken by envoys from Argentina, Brazil, and Chile (the so-called ABC powers). Then, in July 1914 in the face of advancing revolutionary forces, Huerta resigned and Carranza assumed the presidency. That would seem to be the resolution of the story but it was only the beginning of part two.

A split soon emerged between Carranza and Villa, and a new Mexican revolution ensued. Still stung by Carranza's previous reluctance to accept U.S. assistance, Wilson supported Villa, although once again this was counter to advice he received from his staff. But as the civil war dragged on through 1914 and 1915, Wilson became less anxious to intervene, now stating that Mexicans should be left to settle their own problems.

It is difficult to know for sure what caused Wilson's change of heart but there are several key factors. For one thing, he did not feel nearly the disdain for Carranza that he had for Huerta, since Carranza had gained power in what Wilson believed to be a just and necessary revolution. And it did seem as though the situation would soon stabilize, as Carranza's forces appeared to be close to victory. The situation in Europe also influenced Wilson's decision. The sinking of the ship *Lusitania* by Germany (in which 128 Americans were killed) occurred on May 7, 1915, and Wilson, wary of a coming war with Germany, wanted to avoid fighting on two fronts. Given the fact that Germany appeared to be trying to goad the United States into war with Mexico, taking that bait seemed a particularly bad idea, although some Americans (including former president Theodore Roosevelt) believed that intervention on Villa's behalf was warranted.

As a result of Wilson's decision to avoid intervention and accept Carranza (who was officially recognized as the Mexican president by the United States on October 19, 1915), Villa turned against the United States. He began a murderous rampage on the U.S.–Mexican border in the spring of 1916, killing many civilians. Wilson was finally forced to dispatch General John J. Pershing and his expeditionary force of seven thousand troops to pursue Villa. But in the final twist to this story, Carranza saw this force as a threat to his own government and ordered it out of Mexico. When U.S. and Mexican forces battled in Carrizal on June 21, 1916, war once again seemed inevitable, and Wilson drafted a war message that that was averted at the last minute. Public opinion came out strongly against a war, especially after the press reported the Carrizal battle was provoked by the American forces, and Wilson bowed to this as well as to the other reasons in favor of neutrality.

The situation improved markedly through the summer of 1916 as the United States established cordial diplomatic relations with Carranza, and Mexico instituted liberal reforms. Carranza was overthrown in 1920 in a nonviolent revolution in which the United States played no role. This history represents the last time in this era in which a U.S. president overtly intervened in Latin American affairs on the grounds of a perceived American duty to instruct these nations in the proper exercise of democracy.

NOTE

1. Joseph P. Tumulty, *Woodrow Wilson As I Know Him* (Garden City, N.Y.: Garden City Publishing, 1921), 146.

WILSON—"OUR PURPOSES IN MEXICO" (NOVEMBER 24, 1913)

The purpose of the United States is solely and singly to secure peace and order in Central America by seeing to it that the processes of self-government there are not interrupted or set aside.

Usurpations like that of General Huerta menace the peace and development of America as nothing else could. They not only render the development of ordered self-government impossible; they also tend to set law entirely aside, to put the lives and fortunes of citizens and foreigners alike in constant jeopardy, to invalidate contracts and concessions in any way the usurper may devise for his own profit, and to impair both the national credit and all the foundations of business, domestic or foreign.

It is the purpose of the United States, therefore, to discredit and defeat such usurpations whenever they occur. The present policy of the Government of the United States is to isolate General Huerta entirely; to cut him off from foreign sympathy and aid from domestic credit, whether moral or material, and so to force him out.

It hopes and believes that isolation will accomplish this end, and shall await the results without irritation or impatience. If General Huerta does not retire by force of circumstances, it will become the duty of the United States to use less peaceful means to put him out. It will give other governments notice in advance of each affirmative or aggressive step it has in contemplation, should it unhappily become necessary to move actively against the usurper; but no such step seems immediately necessary.

Its fixed resolve is, that no such interruptions of civil order shall be tolerated so far as it is concerned. Each conspicuous instance in which usurpations of this kind are prevented will render their recurrence less likely, and in the end a state of affairs will be secured in Mexico and elsewhere upon this continent which will assure the peace of America and the untrammeled development of its economic and social relations with the rest of the world.

Beyond this fixed purpose the Government of the United States will not go. It will not permit itself to seek any special or exclusive advantages in Mexico or elsewhere for its own citizens, but will seek, here as elsewhere, to show itself the consistent champion of the open door.

In the meantime it is making every effort that the circumstances permit to safeguard foreign lives and property in Mexico and is making the lives and fortunes of the subjects of other governments as much its concern as the lives and fortunes of its own citizens.

Link, Arthur S., and William M. Leary Jr., eds. *The Diplomacy of World Power: The United States, 1889–1920.* New York: St. Martin's, 1970, 88–89.

THE ECONOMIST—THE UNITED STATES NAVY AND MEXICO (APRIL 18, 1914)

On Good Friday a launch from an American battleship flying the American flag put into Tampico for kerosene. The men on board, who were unarmed, were arrested and marched through the streets. They were shortly released, and President Huerta tendered his apology for what he explained as the mistake of a subordinate. This apology the United States refused to accept as adequate recognition of an offence which came as the culmination of a series of minor incidents, including the destruction of foreign property in Tampico. Admiral Mayo demanded that a salute should be fired to the American flag. A time limit was imposed; but though it was twice extended in the hope that Huerta would give way, his attitude remained unyielding. Accordingly on Tuesday the whole Atlantic fleet—12 battleships, with an appropriate number of cruisers—was ordered to Tampico. This demonstration in force undoubtedly appeared to constitute an ultimatum, and great excitement was roused in Washington. Whether better counsels prevailed—the foreign Ambassadors in Mexico City are, in some quarters, given the credit for peaceful persuasion—anyhow, General Huerta has now made a deft concession; he has expressed his willingness to salute the American flag if the Americans reply in kind—a courteous recognition that is usual. The ceremony will take place on Tuesday when the American fleet arrives at Tampico. With this the incident may be regarded as over. Upon it we would make this remark. The demand for a salute, in addition to the ample apology which was duly accorded was almost bound to be refused, if only because the United States have not recognised the Government of General Huerta. In any case, the offence committed was so trifling that the humiliating ceremony demanded by the American admiral was one which one sovereign was not likely to accord to another. On Thursday it seemed as if, because an unreasonable demand made by one of his admirals had not been complied with, President Wilson would embark on the conquest of Mexico. . . . If war is to be made on points of punctilio raised by admirals and generals, and if the Government of the United States is to set the example for this return to mediaeval conditions it will be a bad day for civilisation. President Wilson, indeed, declares that the citizens of the United States have received specially bad treatment from President Huerta. . . . But it must surely be clear to President Wilson that his unfriendly attitude towards Huerta and his patronage of the Carranzists provide at least some excuse for a de facto Government struggling against military and financial embarrassments. We can quite understand why in the first instance President Wilson refused to act with the other powers in recognising General Huerta after the shooting of Madero. But he went a good deal further. However, the course of events, we think, has amply shown that recognition was, and still is, the proper policy. It is not the business of foreigners to decide whether another country is constitutionally governed, or to refuse recognition to a military dictator because his power is founded upon a coup d'etat. . . . As it is, the action of the American admiral in demanding the salute and of the President in deciding to send an expedition in support of that demand, will probably cost the United States from 10 to 20 million dollars and (if the incident had not been settled) might for aught we know have involved ultimately an expenditure of 1,000 million dollars—that is to say, as much as the Boer War cost the taxpayers of this country. That the situation is an extremely difficult one for the Washington Government and that it would have been difficult even if Huerta had been recognised, we frankly admit. There is probably almost as much American capital invested in Mexico as British, and the guerilla warfare has already involved some loss of life as well as enormous loss of property and income to the citizens of the United States. But the pacification of Mexico by military invasion—far from restoring what has been lost—would almost necessarily involve further destruction of property on a gigantic scale. An invasion of Mexico would probably require at least 100,000 troops, and even that force might well prove inadequate to master all the railways and occupy all the principal towns. It is believed by those who know Mexico best that an American invasion would meet with national resistance, and that the guerilla forces now fighting against General Huerta would join him in opposing a common enemy. The effect upon the finances and upon the social and economic conditions of the United States might be disastrous.

The Economist. April 18, 1914, 906–907.

IMMIGRATION LITERACY TEST

Throughout the Wilson administration, attempts to limit immigration through federal legislation gained strength in Congress. In 1915 and again in 1917, President Wilson vetoed bills instituting literacy requirements for all immigrants to the United States. The debate pitted the president against a growing exclusionary nativist movement that opposed immigration in general, and highlighted some of the complex characteristics of both the progressive movement and Wilson's own political philosophy.

Up until this point, America had (with the exception of a minority of dissenters) prided itself on its open immigration policy. The only restrictions that had been imposed were on classes perceived as undesirable such as convicts, people with infectious diseases, and (reflecting the vicious prejudices of the time) some Asians. But the immigration bill approved by Congress in early 1915 included additional exclusions (adding Hindus, stowaways, and alcoholics to the list) as well as a literacy provision—the first mechanism designed to limit large numbers of immigrants based on a quality not in and of itself considered dangerous or intolerable.

There were a number of groups lobbying the government to enact limits in these years that followed a strong wave of immigration slowed only by the war in Europe. Some nativists reacted by asserting that the tide should now be stopped lest "they" begin to outnumber "us," even though the proportion of immigrants to native born was about where it was in the mid-nineteenth century. This group objected particularly to the newest wave that had begun arriving in large numbers since about 1890—southern and eastern Europeans who tended to be more dark skinned, spoke thoroughly unfamiliar languages, and were often Jewish or Catholic.

Labor unions feared that too many immigrants, who were generally willing to work for low wages, would decrease the earning potential for American citizens. Although business interests were always interested in cheap labor, they did not fight immigration restrictions because they had found a new source of this commodity in the form of southern blacks migrating to northern cities. A less hostile but still anti-immigration view came from sociologists and social workers who believed that too many newcomers would result in a decline in the quality of life for those already here.

While Wilson understood some of these concerns, he objected in both veto messages to the literacy test mechanism as a means to stem the tide. The policy was simply too far removed from the American tradition of welcoming all, and he disliked a doctrine that barred people who lacked exactly what they were coming to the United States to achieve—an education and a future.

Wilson's position revealed once again the difficulty of assessing the true legacy of the progressive movement, and his own rather uncomfortable fit with that label. Although progressives advocated many causes designed to improve the lives of immigrants, such as better working and living conditions, they were sometimes at odds with what the immigrants themselves desired. For example, reformers fought to "clean up" the urban political machines, but the machines and the bosses who ran them were seen by many new arrivals as their benefactors. Similarly, immigrants vigorously opposed the literacy test while many progressives insisted on its necessity. This highlights the question of whether this reform movement was designed to empower the underclasses or merely to work paternalistically in their perceived best interest.

University of Chicago sociologist Herman Hoyt's argument in favor of the literacy test is far from a nativist or prejudicial diatribe. In fact, he notes how the literacy test itself was a rather blunt and inefficient tool with which to address the perceived economic and social threat. However, he believed that immigration levels needed to be diminished quickly and the literacy test was probably the most politically expedient method by which to achieve this end, since there was not a great deal of organized opposition to it.

Congress overrode Wilson's second veto in early 1917, and the literacy test became law. More drastic immigration restrictions were to follow in the early 1920s; the literacy provision remained in place until 1952.

WILSON—IMMIGRATION LITERACY TEST VETO
(JANUARY 28, 1915)

It is with unaffected regret that I find myself constrained by clear conviction to return this bill . . . without my signature. Not only do I feel it to be a very serious matter to exercise the power of veto in any case, because it involves opposing the single judgment of the President to the judgment of a majority of both the Houses of the Congress, a step which no man who realizes his own liability to error can take without great hesitation, but also because this particular bill is in so many important respects admirable, well conceived, and desirable. Its enactment into law would undoubtedly enhance the efficiency and improve the methods of handling the important branch of the public service to which it relates. But candor and a sense of duty with regard to the responsibility so clearly imposed upon me by the Constitution in matters of legislation leave me no choice but to dissent.

In two particulars of vital consequence this bill embodies a radical departure from the traditional and long-established policy of this country, a policy in which our people have conceived the very character of their Government to be expressed, the very mission and spirit of the Nation in respect of its relations to the peoples of the world outside their borders. It seeks to all but close entirely the gates of asylum which have always been open to those who could find nowhere else the right and opportunity of constitutional agitation for what they conceived to be the natural and inalienable rights of men; and it excludes those to whom the opportunities of elementary education have been denied, without regard to their character, their purposes, or their natural capacity.

Restrictions like these, adopted earlier in our history as a Nation, would very materially have altered the course and cooled the humane ardors of our politics. The right of political asylum has brought to this country many a man of noble character and elevated purpose who was marked as an outlaw in his own less fortunate land, and who has yet become an ornament to our citizenship and to our public councils. The children and the compatriots of these illustrious Americans must stand amazed to see the representatives of their Nation now resolved, in the fullness of our national strength and at the maturity of our great institutions, to risk turning such men back from our shores without test of quality or purpose. It is difficult for me to believe that the full effect of this feature of the bill was realized when it was framed and adopted, and it is impossible for me to assent to it in the form in which it is here cast.

The literacy test and the tests and restrictions which accompany it constitute an even more radical change in the policy of the Nation. Hitherto we have generously kept our doors open to all who were not unfitted by reason of disease or incapacity for self-support or such personal records and antecedents as were likely to make them a menace to our peace and order or to the wholesome and essential relationships of life. In this bill it is proposed to turn away from tests of character and of quality and impose tests which exclude and restrict; for the new tests here embodied are not tests of quality or of character or of personal fitness, but tests of opportunity. Those who come seeking opportunity are not to be admitted unless they have already had one of the chief of the opportunities they seek, the opportunity of education. The object of such provisions is restriction, not selection.

If the people of this country have made up their minds to limit the number of immigrants by arbitrary tests and so reverse the policy of all the generations of Americans that have gone before them, it is their right to do so. I am their servant and have no license to stand in their way. But I do not believe that they have. I respectfully submit that no one can quote their mandate to that effect. Has any political party ever avowed a policy of restriction in this fundamental matter, gone to the country on it, and been commissioned to control its legislation? Does this bill rest upon the conscious and universal assent and desire of the American people? I doubt it. It is because I doubt it that I make bold to dissent from it. I am willing to abide by the verdict, but not until it has been rendered. Let the platforms of parties speak out upon this policy and the people pronounce their wish. The matter is too fundamental to be settled otherwise.

I have no pride of opinion in this question. I am not foolish enough to profess to know the wishes and ideals of America better than the body of her chosen representatives know them. I only want instruction direct from those whose fortunes, with ours and all men's, are involved.

Congressional Record. 63rd Congress, 3rd sess., 1915. Vol. 52, 2481–2482.

HOMER HOYT—"THE RELATION OF THE LITERACY TEST TO A CONSTRUCTIVE IMMIGRATION PROBLEM" (MAY 1916)

Since 1885 the immigrant stream from the older sources has been rapidly diminishing in volume, and in its place has come "the new immigration" from the south and east of Europe in even greater numbers than the "old immigration." The consensus of opinion seems to be that this new immigration is far less desirable than the old, because of its lower standards of living, industrial backwardness, lack of sympathy with our type of institutions, and its marked differences from our predominant stock in religion, race, literacy, and industrial training. It is pointed out that the literacy test would discriminate against these less desirable peoples, because if it had been applied during the ten years from 1899 to 1909, it would have excluded 35.6 per cent of the new immigration as contrasted with 2.7 per cent of the old immigration. The literacy test would therefore enable the United States to secure relatively more of the industrially advanced races and relatively less of the backward races.

Notwithstanding the earnestness with which the qualitative aspect of the literacy test has been emphasized, it is altogether unlikely that these selective arguments alone could have advanced the literacy test to the commanding position in the public favor that it occupies today. The relationship between illiteracy and crime and pauperism is not sufficiently convincing to enable the literacy test to win national approval without the assistance of another favorable circumstance. This supporting argument is to be found in the apparent need for the restriction of the volume of immigration.

· · ·

. . . If there is only a reasonable prospect of an increase of immigration after the war, some method of restriction should be adopted. The rate of increase of immigration for the past decade was far in excess of the rate of increase of the demand for labor in our industries, and it was far in excess of our capacity to assimilate and make good American citizens out of the aliens who are even advantageously employed industrially. If there is any doubt as to what will happen in the future, that doubt should be resolved against the person who asserts that the unusual and abnormal thing will happen, namely, that European immigration will not continue in the future in its accustomed volume. In view of the excessive rate of immigration in past years, it would be far better to err in the future by providing for some restriction when no restriction was needed, than to fail to provide for restriction of immigration when restriction was needed. It would be wise to insure against the possibility of a recurrence in the future of the same rate of immigration that obtained before the war by adopting some restrictive measure now.

The literacy test will probably be effective as a method of restricting post-war immigration. The war will undoubtedly have a tendency to set back the slow growth of compulsory education in Southeastern Europe for many years. The sacrificing of the needs of all other governmental functions to the supreme necessities of the war and the lessened educational opportunities that will come to orphan children will probably combine to make the number of European illiterates in the future at least as large, if not larger than the number in the past.

As long as illiteracy is a marked characteristic of any large element of European immigration, the literacy test will have a pronounced restrictive effect. It is true that the amount of restriction it secures will have no reference to the fluctuations in our economic demand for labor; and that it will have no necessary connection with the needs or lack of needs of our labor market. It will, however substantially reduce the volume of immigration and thereby relieve the pressure of too great numbers upon our economic standards and social institutions. This in itself will be a service of considerable value. The coming of so many immigrants within the last decade or so has made any restrictive measure welcome, even if it does not work with absolute precision in securing a correspondence between the supply of immigrant wage-earners and the demand of our employers for their labor. The literacy test will check the undoubted detrimental effect of the pronounced tendency of our alien population to grow faster than the opportunities for its employment at American standards of wages and its assimilation at American standards of culture. Even if it does not debar as many as our economic needs of restriction require, it will be better than no restriction at all. If it excludes so large a number that our employers are unable to get enough laborers at the prevailing rates of wages to satisfy their demands, the literacy test will operate to afford higher pay and better opportunity for the diminished number of immigrants that are allowed to enter, so that the ultimate effect will always be some improvement in the quality of our economic life at the expense of quantity. It is also possible that too much restriction in the future may compensate for too little restriction in the past.

The Journal of Political Economy 24 (May 1916): 447, 471–472.

REGULATION OF CHILD LABOR

Perhaps the most notable social reform of the Wilson administration, and arguably the Progressive Era, was passage of federal regulation of child labor in 1916. The policy was essential and significant, given the fact that the practice of hiring even young children to work in sometimes dangerous jobs in factories, mills, and mines had become widespread. While child labor was regulated by most states, many of those laws were vague and only weakly enforced. However, it is important to understand this federal policy in its true context. Although there were activists who had fought for a long time for this law, Wilson was not one of them. Passage of the act was the result of political expediency, and Wilson's part in it illustrates one of the differences between this president and progressive reformers.

Before attaining elective office, Wilson had been a strictly conservative Democrat. As president of Princeton University, he spoke out publicly against federal regulation in general, and was no advocate of progressivism. Once nominated for governor of New Jersey in 1910, however, he began to embrace progressive policies. As governor, he helped to promote passage of several reforms such as workmen's compensation and state control of railroads. But while he was instrumental in bringing these innovations to New Jersey, a key to Wilson's philosophy was that he remained a states' rights advocate. While he was willing to bring these reforms to his state, he did not support the federal government ordering them for all states. In regard to child labor in particular, he had written in 1908 that pending federal legislation on the issue "affords a striking example of a tendency to carry congressional power over interstate commerce beyond the utmost boundaries of reasonable and honest interference."[1]

Wilson's general philosophy became more defined in the New Freedom platform of his 1912 presidential campaign. This largely focused on freeing American business from government intervention, and stressed a similar theme in opposing most federal social regulation, asserting it made citizens little more than wards of the state. These policies clearly distinguished Wilson's campaign from Roosevelt's New Nationalism philosophy, which advocated federal intervention in both the economic and social realms, including child labor prohibitions.

But, despite the fact that the fight for federal-level child labor prohibitions was not one that Wilson came naturally to, a dramatic evolution in his public pronouncements on the topic occurred over the course of his administration. Shortly after his election, he met with leading social reformers who had successfully advocated the creation of a Children's Bureau in the Department of Labor in 1912. Wilson explained to the group that any attempts to move the bureau's mission beyond the mere collection of information on child labor would be seen as an infringement on states' rights.

But in 1916, Wilson's position quickly and sharply shifted. In this reelection year, he was informed by advisors that progressives were disappointed in his inaction on various social reforms, and saw child labor legislation as an important test. The Owen-Keating Federal Child Labor bill, which did not outlaw child labor but instituted bans on the products of child labor in interstate commerce (goods could not be produced by children under 14, or by children between the ages 14 and 16 working over eight hours a day or six days a week), had passed the House of Representatives early in the year, but was languishing in the Senate. Wilson was advised to push for passage, and he eventually complied.

The first evidence of the shift was the initial draft of the 1916 Democratic Party platform. Although Wilson was not the original author, he revised and authorized the document, which stated that child labor prohibition "should be urged" on the states. The final version of the statement, written several days later, had evolved to clearly advocating federal legislation.

Wilson's new commitment to the policy was evidenced in the letter written to a supporter of the bill in July. That same month he urged Senate Democratic leaders to bring the bill up for a vote. By the time the Senate passed the bill in September, his support was formalized through his remarks upon signing it into law. The press acknowledged that Wilson's enthusiasm was of recent origin, but lauded him nonetheless for pushing the bill to success.

Ironically, Wilson's earlier doubts as to the constitutionality of this policy were to be validated. Before the law went into effect, Roland Dagenhart of North Carolina challenged it on behalf of his two sons, who would have difficulty finding work under the new policy. An injunction was issued, thus keeping the law from being implemented, and in 1918 the Supreme Court declared it unconstitutional.

Although federal attorneys claimed the law was a valid exercise of Congress' power to control interstate commerce, a bare majority of the court disagreed. In the majority opinion in *Hammer v. Dagenhart*, Justice William R. Day stressed the difference between regulating commerce per se (which would be allowable) and, as was the case here, regulating based on the manner in which goods are produced. It was ruled a violation of the Tenth Amendment's grant of reserved powers to the states. Justice Oliver Wendell Holmes wrote one of his famous dissents in this decision, strenuously arguing that the law was fully within the purview of the interstate commerce clause.

In retrospect, child labor seems to be one of the most outrageous practices of this era, and the reluctance to prohibit it is puzzling. But it should be kept in mind that, for some families, it was a necessity for children to work. Furthermore, as Roosevelt stated in 1911, the issue "appeals to no great special interest."[2] While reformers pressed for federal regulation, there were no powerful forces fighting with them. Even President Wilson, although personally opposed to the practice of child labor, came on board only when political necessity seemed to warrant it. Passage of the Owen-Keating bill had sparked national interest in the issue, however, and interstate shipping of goods produced by minors was again prohibited in the 1938 Fair Labor Standards Act. When that law was challenged, the Supreme Court upheld it, noting that the earlier ruling "was a departure from the principles which have prevailed in the interpretation of the commerce clause both before and since the decision."[3]

NOTES

1. Woodrow Wilson, *Constitutional Government in the United States* (New York: Columbia University, Press, 1908), 179.

2. Hermann Hagedorn, ed., *The Works of Theodore Roosevelt*, vol. 16 (New York: Scribner's, 1920), 186.

3. *U.S. v. Darby Lumber Co.*, 312 U.S. 100 (1941), 115–116.

WILSON ON REGULATION OF CHILD LABOR

Remarks at Meeting with Social Workers (January 27, 1913)

With regard to the Children's Bureau another similar difficulty exists. My own party in some of its elements represents a very strong State's rights feeling. It is very plain that you would have to go much further than most interpretations of the Constitution would allow if you were to give to the Government general control over child labor throughout the country. It is important to make it generally understood that the purpose of your bureau is to collect and co-ordinate information on the subject.

Draft of Democratic Party Platform (June 10, 1916)

We hold that the life, health and strength of the individual men, women and children of the nation are its greatest asset, and that in the conservation of these the Federal Government, wherever it acts as the employer of labor, should both on its own account and as an example put into effect the following principles of just employment:

—The standards of the "Uniform Child Labor Law" wherever minors are employed. . . . We believe also that the adoption of similar principles should be urged and applied in the legislation of the states with regard to labor within their borders; that through every possible agency the life and health of the people of the nation should be conserved.

Final Democratic Party Platform (June 16, 1916)

We favor the speedy enactment of an effective Federal Child Labor Law.

Letter to Charles Samuel Jackson (July 24, 1916)

Thank you warmly for your telegram about the child labor legislation. I am going after it with all my heart and am hopeful of success.

Remarks upon Signing Child Labor Bill (September 1, 1916)

I want to say that with real emotion I sign this bill, because I know how long the struggle has been to secure legislation of this sort and what it is going to mean to the health and to the vigor of the country, and also to the happiness of those whom it affects. It is with genuine pride that I play my part in completing this legislation. I congratulate the country and felicitate myself.

Link, Arthur S. ed. *The Papers of Woodrow Wilson.* Princeton, N.J.: Princeton University Press, 1981. June 27, 1913: vol. 1, 78; June 10, 1916: vol. 37, 198–199; July 24, 1916: vol. 37, 469; Sept. 1, 1916: vol. 38, 123.
    Porter, Kirk H., and Donald B. Johnson, eds. *National Party Platforms, 1840–1964.* Urbana: University of Illinois Press, 1966, 207 (June 16, 1916).

JUSTICE WILLIAM R. DAY—MAJORITY OPINION IN *HAMMER V. DAGENHART* (JUNE 3, 1918)

A bill was filed in the United States District Court for the Western District of North Carolina by a father in his own behalf and as next friend of his two minor sons, one under the age of fourteen years and the other between the ages of fourteen and sixteen years, employees in a cotton mill at Charlotte, North Carolina, to enjoin the enforcement of the act of Congress intended to prevent interstate commerce in the products of child labor. . . .

The controlling question for decision is: Is it within the authority of Congress in regulating commerce among the states to prohibit the transportation in interstate commerce of manufactured goods, the product of a factory in which, within thirty days prior to their removal therefrom, children under the age of fourteen have been employed or permitted to work, or children between the ages of fourteen and sixteen years have been employed or permitted to work more than eight hours in any day, or more than six days in any week, or after the hour of 7 o'clock P.M., or before the hour of 6 o'clock A.M.?

The power essential to the passage of this act, the government contends, is found in the commerce clause of the Constitution which authorizes Congress to regulate commerce with foreign nations and among the states. . . .

It is further contended that the authority of Congress may be exerted to control interstate commerce in the shipment of childmade goods because of the effect of the circulation of such goods in other states where the evil of this class of labor has been recognized by local legislation, and the right to thus employ child labor has been more rigorously restrained than in the state of production. In other words, that the unfair competition, thus engendered, may be controlled by closing the channels of interstate commerce to manufacturers in those states where the local laws do not meet what Congress deems to be the more just standard of other states.

There is no power vested in Congress to require the states to exercise their police power so as to prevent possible unfair competition. Many causes may co-operate to give one state, by reason of local laws or conditions, an economic advantage over others. The commerce clause was not intended to give to Congress a general authority to equalize such conditions. . . .

That there should be limitations upon the right to employ children in mines and factories in the interest of their own and the public welfare, all will admit. That such employment is generally deemed to require regulation is shown by the fact that the brief of counsel states that every state in the Union has a law upon the subject, limiting the right to thus employ children. In North Carolina, the state wherein is located the factory in which the employment was had in the present case, no child under twelve years of age is permitted to work. . . .

A statute must be judged by its natural and reasonable effect. The control by Congress over interstate commerce cannot authorize the exercise of authority not entrusted to it by the Constitution. The maintenance of the authority of the states over matters purely local is as essential to the preservation of our institutions as is the conservation of the supremacy of the federal power in all matters entrusted to the nation by the federal Constitution.

In interpreting the Constitution it must never be forgotten that the nation is made up of states to which are entrusted the powers of local government. And to them and to the people the powers not expressly delegated to the national government are reserved. The power of the states to regulate their purely internal affairs by such laws as seem wise to the local authority is inherent and has never been surrendered to the general government. To sustain this statute would not be in our judgment a recognition of the lawful exertion of congressional authority over interstate commerce, but would sanction an invasion by the federal power of the control of a matter purely local in its character, and over which no authority has been delegated to Congress in conferring the power to regulate commerce among the states. . . .

In our view the necessary effect of this act is, by means of a prohibition against the movement in interstate commerce of ordinary commercial commodities to regulate the hour of labor of children in factories and mines within the states, a purely state authority. Thus, the act in a two-fold sense is repugnant to the Constitution. It not only transcends the authority delegated to Congress over commerce but also exerts a power as to a purely local matter to which the federal authority does not extend. The far reaching result of upholding the act cannot be more plainly indicated than by pointing out that if Congress can thus regulate matters entrusted to local authority by prohibition of the movement of commodities in interstate commerce, all freedom of commerce will be at an end, and the power of the states over local matters may be eliminated, and thus our system of government be practically destroyed. For these reasons we hold that this law exceeds the constitutional authority of Congress.

Hammer v. Dagenhart, 247 US 251 (1918).

U.S. NEUTRALITY IN THE GREAT WAR

When the assassination of Archduke Franz Ferdinand of Austria and his wife on June 23, 1914, by Gavrilo Princip quickly led to mobilization and war in Europe, Americans were surprised but unconcerned, assuming the conflict would not affect the United States. President Wilson reflected the nation's sentiment when he made an early and strong declaration of neutrality. But this was not the end of the story. The years preceding U.S. involvement in the Great War were marked by a gradually intensifying view that the nation must at least be prepared for war if it should come.

Because of the suddenness of the war, which had been anticipated by few, no national debate on the topic had occurred. In the summer of 1914, Wilson had also been personally distracted by the Mexico situation and the death of his first wife, Ellen, which left him devastated. But, despite the lack of planning and discussion, Wilson's statement of neutrality to the U.S. Senate on August 19 was widely supported. For the first few months of the war, at least, the expectation that America could remain neutral was quite reasonable. The outbreak of aggression had been triggered by the activation of European alliances (the Allies— France, Great Britain, and Russia—versus the Central Powers—Germany and Austria-Hungary) that the United States took no part in, and the nation's physical distance served as a further insulating factor. It was also assumed, at least until the stalemate precipitated by the Battle of the Marne in September, that the war would be over quickly.

Although the neutrality declaration was clear and received broad public approval, it was difficult to implement in practice. Questions over what neutrality in fact entailed led to some controversy. One major point of conflict was the rules of shipping. On the one hand, acceptance of Great Britain's severe interpretation of international law, which virtually halted U.S. trade with Germany, could be seen as favoritism to the Allies.

On the other hand, challenging this system could be seen as pro-Germany. Another issue was whether neutrality barred American loans to any of the warring nations.

Discussion over these specifics revealed that, while neutrality was supported in theory, there was growing dissent within the administration as to its practice. For example, the American ambassador to Great Britain was very "pro-Ally" and sometimes intervened on behalf of British interests. On the other side, Secretary of State William Jennings Bryan had become a rigid interpreter of neutrality, and believed that any bending of the rules constituted improper favoritism—usually in the Allies' favor.

This split was also reflected in the American people. In general, the overwhelming position was for staying out of the war. However, although in agreement with neutrality, many Americans did sympathize with the Allied cause, feeling a commonality and bond with the British people in particular. A smaller group, largely from the Midwest and South, felt some affinity for German interests. Many in this area were of German ancestry, and German-American newspapers (such as *The Fatherland*, which advocated "fair play for Germany and Austria-Hungary"[1]) were widely read. Several members of Congress from these regions took up this position as well.

But the biggest criticism of Wilson's neutrality policy was that it ignored the reality that American forces could conceivably be used at some point and so should at least be in a state of readiness. Preparedness advocates did not so much disagree with the neutrality position, but they did maintain it should be backed with reliable force. As Roosevelt (an increasingly outspoken critic of Wilson) noted, "When giants are engaged in a death wrestle as they reel to and fro they are certain to trample whoever gets in their way."[2]

Preparedness supporters were to be found within the administration as well. Major General Leonard Wood, erstwhile Rough Rider, and, in 1914, head of the eastern department of the U.S. Army, was the most vocal. In a series of speeches, Wood stressed the lack of readiness in the purely volunteer U.S. armed forces and advocated a draft, better military troop training, and expansion of material resources. He argued for preparedness as the best means to prevent war. As a result of these speeches, and his role as the guiding force behind the establishment of civilian training camps, Wood was sharply rebuked by Secretary of War Lindley M. Garrison, as ordered by Wilson. Garrison himself, though, was pro-preparedness and resigned in protest in 1916 over Wilson's opposition to a draft at that time.

Ultimately, Wilson did embrace preparedness. By late 1915, he urged Congress to provide funds for army and navy expansion, although stressing that the move was purely defensive. Thus, neutrality was still emphasized. Even in the wake of the German sinking of the British passenger ship *Lusitania* on May 7, 1915 (in which 128 Americans were killed), he resorted to diplomacy instead of force, with a series of messages to Germany demanding that submarine warfare against passenger vessels cease. Nonetheless, some critics saw the preparedness shift as dangerous and believed Wilson was drifting too far from neutrality and too close to war. Bryan resigned in protest over what he felt was the overly hostile tone of Wilson's *Lusitania* messages. Publisher Oswald Garrison Villard, editor of the *New York Evening Post*, wrote in 1916 that "we are to deprive the world of the one great beacon of light of a nation unarmed and unafraid, free from the admitted evils of militarism."[3]

But, a majority of Americans accepted that Wilson was doing a good job of maintaining the precarious balance between neutrality and defense of the national interest. Thus, the shift toward preparedness did not keep Wilson (running on the slogan "he kept us out of war") from winning reelection in 1916 against Charles Evans Hughes, although the race was close. The preparedness position did, however, work to alienate Wilson from progressives in both parties who believed that this policy violated the movement's focus on *domestic* agendas. Wilson had a quite different philosophy of neutrality (and progressivism), in which the United States could function as a peacemaker as well as a symbol of the superiority of democracy. Events would soon spin out of control and force Wilson to abandon this vision.

NOTES

1. Mark Sullivan, *Our Times, 1900–1925*, vol. 5 (New York: Scribner's, 1939), 137.
2. Ibid., 202.
3. Oscar Garrison Villard, "Preparedness Is Militarism," *Annals of the American Academy of Political and Social Science* (July 1916): 218.

WILSON—APPEAL TO THE SENATE FOR NEUTRALITY (AUGUST 19, 1914)

I suppose that every thoughtful man in America has asked himself, during these last troubled weeks, what influence the European war may exert upon the United States, and I take the liberty of addressing a few words to you in order to point out that it is entirely within our own choice what its effects upon us will be and to urge very earnestly upon you the sort of speech and conduct which will best safeguard the Nation against distress and disaster.

The effect of the war upon the United States will depend upon what American citizens say and do. Every man who really loves America will act and speak in the true spirit of neutrality, which is the spirit of impartiality and fairness and friendliness to all concerned. The spirit of the Nation in this critical matter will be determined largely by what individuals and society and those gathered in public meetings do and say, upon what newspapers and magazines contain, upon what ministers utter in their pulpits, and men proclaim as their opinions on the street.

The people of the United States are drawn from many nations, and chiefly from the nations now at war. It is natural and inevitable that there should be the utmost variety of sympathy and desire among them with regard to the issues and circumstances of the conflict. Some will wish one nation, others another, to succeed in the momentous struggle. It will be easy to excite passion and difficult to allay it. Those responsible for exciting it will assume a heavy responsibility, responsibility for no less a thing than that the people of the United States, whose love of their country and whose loyalty to its Government should unite them as Americans all, bound in honor and affection to think first of her and her interests, may be divided in camps of hostile opinion, hot against each other, involved in the war itself in impulse and opinion if not in action.

Such divisions amongst us would be fatal to our peace of mind and might seriously stand in the way of the proper performance of our duty as the one great nation at peace, the one people holding itself ready to play a part of impartial mediation and speak the counsels of peace and accommodation, not as a partisan, but as a friend.

I venture, therefore, my fellow countrymen, to speak a solemn word of warning to you against that deepest, most subtle, most essential breach of neutrality which may spring out of partisanship, out of passionately taking sides. The United States must be neutral in fact as well as in name during these days that are to try men's souls. We must be impartial in thought as well as in action, must put a curb upon our sentiments as well as upon every transaction that might be construed as a preference of one party to the struggle before another.

My thought is of America. I am speaking, I feel sure, the earnest wish and purpose of every thoughtful American that this great country of ours, which is, of course, the first in our thoughts and in our hearts, should show herself in this time of peculiar trial a Nation fit beyond others to exhibit the fine poise of undisturbed judgment, the dignity of self-control, the efficiency of dispassionate action; a Nation that neither sits in judgment upon others nor is disturbed in her own counsels and which keeps herself fit and free to do what is honest and disinterested and truly serviceable for the peace of the world.

Shall we not resolve to put upon ourselves the restraints which will bring to our people the happiness and the great and lasting influence for peace we covet for them?

Baker, Ray Stannard, and William E. Dodd, eds. *The Public Papers of Woodrow Wilson*. Vol. 1, *The New Democracy*. New York: Harper and Brothers, 1926, 157–159.

LEONARD WOOD—"THE MILITARY OBLIGATION OF CITIZENSHIP" (1915)

I always have impressed upon me at meetings of this kind the evident failure on the part of members of the conference to appreciate the position of officers of the Army and Navy with reference to the military situation. The officers of the Army and Navy are the professional servants of the Government in matters pertaining to the military establishment, and its agents in the conduct of military operations when such become necessary. They do not initiate wars. You are mostly business men engaged in trade and commerce. Nine-tenths of all wars have their origin directly or indirectly in issues arising out of trade. You the people make war; the Government declares it; and we, the officers of the Army and Navy, are charged with the responsibility of terminating it with such means and implements as you may give us.

Being more or less familiar with the requirements of the military situation, we naturally try to impress upon you the necessity of a reasonable degree of preparedness, both in the way of personnel, proper organization and material resources. We realize far more fully than you how necessary organized preparation is, especially in these days when our possible opponents are so thoroughly equipped and entirely ready for military activity.

There is a tendency at all these conferences to invoke the advice of Washington, Jefferson, Adams and other of our presidents and statesmen, given in the past to our countrymen on many matters, but I have heard no reference this year or last as to their advice on the question of military preparedness. You all, of course, know how earnestly Washington, Jefferson, Adams and many others urged upon our people the vital importance of preparedness as the best means of preventing war. Washington frequently urges this upon the attention of our people, as does Jefferson in messages and in his letters to Monroe. Adams states it tersely to the effect that it is the only means by which we can preserve peace. The soundness and correctness of this advice is apparent to all soldiers and it has been again and again brought to the attention of our people. . . .

. . . I want to impress upon you who know so little of war, that those of us whose business it is to know something of it and the requirements in the way of preparation, are most deeply concerned, not only from the standpoint of military efficiency, but also on the broad general grounds of common humanity, in establishing a system under which our young men may receive that degree of training which will better fit them to discharge with a reasonable degree of efficiency their duties as soldiers in the defence of the country in case they are needed and thereby tend to reduce to the lowest possible terms the cost in blood and treasure and to make such expenditure as is inevitable, efficient and of value, instead of wasting precious lives without avail. . . .

There are several things which have rendered preparedness necessary to a greater extent than ever before; the first is the great improvement in transportation. In the days when Washington, Jefferson and Adams were urging upon us the necessity of preparedness, our possible enemies were without anything like the military establishment of the great powers of today. Transportation over the sea was by sailing ship, and was slow and very difficult, and consequently considerable time was given for preparation. Indeed, there is no department connected with military preparedness in which there has been a greater advance than in means of transportation. There has also been a great advance made in the power and efficiency of weapons. They have become more complex, many of them are very intricate machines which require a great degree of skill in their handling, with resulting long period of instruction on the part of the personnel. The advance in weapons is quite as notable as that in transportation, and the weapon of today is as far ahead of the weapon in the times of Washington as is the vestibule train ahead of the cart of those days. In other words on one side we have a greatly increased condition of preparedness and greatly shortened period of approach through betterment in the means of transportation, and on the other hand we have consequently a shortened period to get ready combined with the necessity of familiarizing ourselves not with the simple weapons of our fathers but with the complex and intricate weapons of today requiring a high degree of skill in their use; the unprepared, unready defense labors under greater embarrassments than ever and the prepared aggressor has more in his favor than ever before.

. . .

. . . We are working not for war, but for preparation in the first place against it and in the second place for preparation which if it comes will render it as short and bloodless as possible. While cherishing our ideals and hopes for the future and continuing our efforts to bring about desired results in the way of world peace, we must not be misled or unmindful of the actual conditions which surround us today and will surround us for an indefinite period of time; in other words, we can not without jeopardizing the best interests of our country fail to make proper preparations against possible war; such preparations will exert the largest measure of influence for peace, and in case war is forced upon us, will enable us to conduct it with the least possible expenditure of blood and treasure.

Wood, Leonard. *The Military Obligation of Citizenship.* Princeton, N.J.: Princeton University Press, 1915, 40–46, 48–49.

U.S. ENTRY INTO THE GREAT WAR

On April 2, 1917, spurred by German aggression, President Wilson gave up hopes for neutrality and asked Congress for an official declaration of war. Where the neutrality issue had been quite complex, the declaration of war was plain and uncomplicated. There was no matter of interpretation here, and Americans could either be for or against Wilson's position. Mostly, they were for it, but a core group of midwestern, progressive members of Congress in particular opposed the president on the arming of merchant ships, the declaration itself, and the attendant military conscription plan.

Actually, a period of optimism preceded the war declaration. After the sinking of the *Lusitania*, submarine attacks on passenger ships had declined sharply. When, in December 1916, Germany proposed the commencement of armistice talks, Wilson saw himself in the peacemaker role. In early 1917, Wilson addressed the U.S. Senate with his plan for "peace without victory" among the belligerent nations. If the warring factions would agree to his ideas, he would broker the negotiations. Although neither side seemed particularly interested in Wilson's vision for peace, and Americans became concerned that Wilson was becoming far too involved in the conflict, he was still sanguine about the prospects.

On January 31, 1917, however (eight days after the Senate address), Wilson's hopes were dashed when Germany informed the United States that "all sea traffic will be stopped with every available weapon and without further notice."[1] There would however be one exception to this mandate: Germany would allow a single American ship, painted in red and white stripes, to travel to the English port of Falmouth once a week on a specific course and schedule. This single allowance was humiliating and added insult to the injury of the ban itself. Relations were, if possible, strained even further by the revelation of the Zimmerman note, a German diplomatic message stating that if Mexico would engage in a war against the United States, Germany would ally with them and ensure the return of lands currently in the state of Texas.

Wilson was crushed and left at a loss by this turn of events. After quickly announcing the termination of all diplomatic relations with Germany, he had to be urged by his cabinet to request congressional permission to arm American merchant ships. This measure passed in the House, but was bogged down by a Senate filibuster led by eleven mid-westerners. This opposition seemed to revitalize Wilson, who exploded, referring to them as "a little group of willful men" who "have rendered the great government of the United States helpless and contemptible."[2] Wilson undertook the action without congressional approval.

But this was just the first step to be taken. Since the January communiqué, three American vessels had been sunk by German U-boats and, for Wilson, there was now no question but that war must be declared. He addressed a special session of Congress on April 2, 1917, to request an official declaration of war against Germany.

It is undeniable that Wilson had a gift for writing and speech making. Some thought it was a destructive talent, which lent itself to misleading the American people; others thought it an essential and trustworthy aspect of his leadership qualities. Either way, the declaration of war likely represented the pinnacle of his persuasive abilities. The president spoke to Americans of the war not as a matter of competing national interests but as a matter of essential human rights that were being violated by Germany. But neither did he demonize the German people, a position he knew would be somewhat unpopular, focusing instead on the evils perpetrated by the German government. He also covered his vision of the end of the war in this speech by focusing on the peace without victory aspect and the need for a partnership of democratic nations. Although confident about the war's necessity and potential impact, Wilson had no illusions about the cost. After delivering the war message and returning to the White House on streets thronged with cheering crowds, Wilson stated to his secretary Joseph Tumulty, "My message today was a message of death for our young men. How strange it seems to applaud that."[3]

Ultimately, six senators and fifty representatives voted against the declaration of war. (The final vote has 82–6 in the Senate, and 373–50 in the House.) Robert La Follette, the progressive Republican senator from Wisconsin, challenged Wilson on his idealistic human rights assertion, reminding the nation of the inhuman impact of the war on the German people, and of the wartime behavior of the Allies, which he believed to be no less despicable than that of the Germans. The same members of Congress who opposed the arming of merchant ships and the war declaration not surprisingly resisted the draft as well. It was portrayed as heavy-handed and undemocratic.

In general, though, Wilson's speech did seem to convince Americans of the need to go to war. One indication of this is acceptance of conscription, which was potentially the most unattractive provision of the war message. This was only the second time in American history that a national draft would be instituted, and the first instance had led to rioting. But the American people generally accepted the draft. The first national day of registration, June 5, 1917, when all men between the ages of twenty-one and thirty-one were to report to local draft centers, triggered patriotism and war enthusiasm, but little protest. A second day, in August, in which the age range was expanded from eighteen to forty-five resulted in even more registrations than was thought possible. The early preparedness advocates were vindicated, however, by the fact that the armed forces had difficulty responding to this sudden influx. Draftees were instructed to bring their own blankets and "an olive-drab shirt of the kind issued to soldiers,"[4] and many had to train with broomsticks instead of rifles.

In less than three years, the war in Europe had evolved from a conflict for which Americans had little concern to a national sacrifice. The initial troops of the American Expeditionary Force reached France by late autumn, and the first American casualties were reported in November 1917.

NOTES

1. Mark Sullivan, *Our Times, 1900–1925*, vol. 5 (New York: Scribner's, 1939), 256.
2. Ibid., 269.
3. Joseph P. Tumulty, *Woodrow Wilson As I Know Him* (Garden City, N.Y.: Garden City Publishing, 1921), 256.
4. U.S Department of War, "Important Notice to All Men Selected for Military Service," P.M.G.O. Form 1028A.

WILSON—WAR MESSAGE (APRIL 2, 1917)

I have called the Congress into extraordinary session because there are serious, very serious, choices of policy to be made, and made immediately, which it was neither right nor constitutionally permissible that I should assume the responsibility of making.

. . .

The present German submarine warfare against commerce is a warfare against mankind. It is a war against all nations. American ships have been sunk, American lives taken in ways which it has stirred us very deeply to learn of; but the ships and people of other neutral and friendly nations have been sunk and overwhelmed in the waters in the same way. There has been no discrimination. The challenge is to all mankind.

Each nation must decide for itself how it will meet it. The choice we make for ourselves must be made with a moderation of counsel and a temperateness of judgment befitting our character and our motives as a nation. We must put excited feeling away. Our motive will not be revenge or the victorious assertion of the physical might of the nation, but only the vindication of right, of human right, of which we are only a single champion.

. . .

Armed neutrality is ineffectual enough at best; in such circumstances and in the face of such pretensions it is worse than ineffectual: it is likely only to produce what it was meant to prevent; it is practically certain to draw us into the war without either the rights or the effectiveness of belligerents. There is one choice we cannot make, we are incapable of making: we will not choose the path of submission and suffer the most sacred rights of our nation and our people to be ignored or violated. The wrongs against which we now array ourselves are no common wrongs; they cut to the very roots of human life.

With a profound sense of the solemn and even tragical character of the step I am taking and of the grave responsibilities which it involves, but in unhesitating obedience to what I deem my constitutional duty, I advise that the Congress declare the recent course of the Imperial German government to be in fact nothing less than war against the government and people of the United States; that it formally accept the status of belligerent which has thus been thrust upon it; and that it take immediate steps, not only to put the country in a more thorough state of defense but also to exert all its power and employ all its resources to bring the government of the German Empire to terms and end the war.

. . .

Our object now, . . . is to vindicate the principles of peace and justice in the life of the world as against selfish and autocratic power and to set up among the really free and self-governed peoples of the world such a concert of purpose and of action as will henceforth ensure the observance of those principles. Neutrality is no longer feasible or desirable where the peace of the world is involved and the freedom of its peoples, and the menace to that peace and freedom lies in the existence of autocratic governments backed by organized force which is controlled wholly by their will, not by the will of their people. We have seen the last of neutrality in such circumstances. We are at the beginning of an age in which it will be insisted that the same standards of conduct and of responsibility for wrong done shall be observed among nations and their governments that are observed among the individual citizens of civilized states.

We have no quarrel with the German people. We have no feeling toward them but one of sympathy and friendship. It was not upon their impulse that their government acted in entering this war. It was not with their previous knowledge or approval. It was a war determined upon as wars used to be determined upon in the old, unhappy days when peoples were nowhere consulted by their rulers and wars were provoked and waged in the interest of dynasties or of little groups of ambitious men who were accustomed to use their fellowmen as pawns and tools.

. . .

It is a distressing and oppressive duty, gentlemen of the Congress, which I have performed in thus addressing you. There are, it may be, many months of fiery trial and sacrifice ahead of us. It is a fearful thing to lead this great peaceful people into war, into the most terrible and disastrous of all wars, civilization itself seeming to be in the balance. But the right is more precious than peace, and we shall fight for the things which we have always carried nearest our hearts—for democracy, for the right of those who submit to authority to have a voice in their own governments, for the rights and liberties of small nations, for a universal dominion of right by such a concert of free peoples as shall bring peace and safety to all nations and make the world itself at last free.

To such a task we can dedicate our lives and our fortunes, everything that we are and everything that we have, with the pride of those who know that the day has come when America is privileged to spend her blood and her might for the principles that gave her birth and happiness and the peace which she has treasured. God helping her, she can do no other.

Congressional Record. 65th Congress, 1st sess., 1917. Vol. 55, 102–104.

ROBERT M. LA FOLLETTE—OPPOSITION TO WAR MESSAGE (APRIL 4, 1917)

I had supposed until recently that it was the duty of senators and representatives in Congress to vote and act according to their convictions on all public matters that came before them for consideration and decision. Quite another doctrine has recently been promulgated by certain newspapers, which unfortunately seems to have found considerable support elsewhere, and that is the doctrine of "standing back of the President" without inquiring whether the President is right or wrong.

For myself, I have never subscribed to that doctrine and never shall. I shall support the President in the measures he proposes when I believe them to be right. I shall oppose measures proposed by the President when I believe them to be wrong. The fact that the matter which the President submits for consideration is of the greatest importance is only an additional reason why we should be sure that we are right and not to be swerved from that conviction or intimidated in its expression by any influence of power whatsoever.

. . .

Mr. President, many of my colleagues on both sides of this floor have from day to day offered for publication in the *Record* messages and letters received from their constituents. I have received some 15,000 letters and telegrams. They have come from forty-four states in the Union. They have been assorted according to whether they speak in criticism or commendation of my course in opposing war. Assorting the 15,000 letters and telegrams by states in that way, 9 out of 10 are an unqualified endorsement of my course in opposing war with Germany on the issue presented.

. . .

Mr. President, let me make a . . . suggestion. It is this: that a minority in one Congress—mayhap a small minority in one Congress—protesting, exercising the rights which the Constitution confers upon a minority, may really be representing the majority opinion of the country, and if, exercising the right that the Constitution gives them, they succeed in defeating for the time being the will of the majority, they are but carrying out what was in the mind of the framers of the Constitution; that you may have from time to time in a legislative body a majority in numbers that really does not represent the principle of democracy; and that if the question could be deferred and carried to the people it would be found that a minority was the real representative of the public opinion. . . .

The poor, sir, who are the ones called upon to rot in the trenches, have no organized power, have no press to voice their will upon this question of peace or war; but, oh, Mr. President, at some time they will be heard. I hope and I believe they will be heard in an orderly and a peaceful way. I think they may be heard from before long. . . .

What is the thing the President asks us to do to these German people of whom he speaks so highly and whose sincere friend he declares us to be? Here is what he declares we shall do in this war. We shall undertake, he says—

The utmost practicable cooperation in council and action with the governments now at war with Germany, and as an incident to that, the extension to those governments of the most liberal financial credits in order that our resources may, so far as possible, be added to theirs.

"Practicable cooperation!" Practicable cooperation with England and her allies in starving to death the old men and women, the children, the sick and the maimed of Germany. The thing we are asked to do is the thing I have stated. It is idle to talk of a war upon a government only. We are leagued in this war, or it is the President's proposition that we shall be so leagued, with the hereditary enemies of Germany. Any war with Germany, or any other country for that matter, would be bad enough, but there are not words strong enough to voice my protest against the proposed combination with the Entente Allies.

. . .

Countless millions are suffering from want and privation; countless other millions are dead and rotting on foreign battlefields; countless other millions are crippled and maimed, blinded, and dismembered; upon all and upon their children's children for generations to come has been laid a burden of debt which must be worked out in poverty and suffering, but the "whole force" of no one of the warring nations has yet been expended; but our "whole force" shall be expended, so says the President. We are pledged by the President, so far as he can pledge us, to make this fair, free, and happy land of ours the same shambles and bottomless pit of horror that we see in Europe today.

Congressional Record. 65th Congress, 1st sess., 1917. Vol. 55, 223–227.

VERSAILLES TREATY AND THE LEAGUE OF NATIONS

When the armistice was declared on November 11, 1918, Wilson looked forward to the role he had anticipated all along—guiding the warring nations toward a fair and just peace as well as the creation of an organization of democratic states. But in the end the peace negotiations and the attendant struggles with the U.S. Senate over the League of Nations provision broke Wilson's health and spirit.

When Wilson arrived in Paris on December 14 as the leader of the U.S. delegation to the Versailles Peace Conference, cheering throngs greeted him. But things did not go well for the president in the coming months. In fact, he had made one of a series of miscalculations even before the armistice was declared. In October, he had appealed to Americans to return Democratic majorities to Congress in the November elections because, "a Republican majority would be interpreted on the other side of the water as repudiation of my leadership."[1] But Americans did not appreciate the rather scolding tone of this message. The Republicans won narrow majorities in both chambers, and Wilson's statement became a self-fulfilling prophecy, with Roosevelt stating, "Mr. Wilson has no authority whatever to speak for the American people at this time. His leadership has just been emphatically repudiated by them."[2]

Perhaps due to this factor, or more likely because they simply had their own goals, the other conferees did not fully adhere to Wilson's Fourteen Points, the specific provisions he believed necessary to ensure peace. In particular, the provision for complete freedom of the seas was challenged, and severe reparation payments were imposed on Germany. It should have been clear to Wilson that the peace treaty would involve compromise, and that not all would agree to his focus on fairness—especially after President Georges Clemenceau of France stated that "Mr. Wilson bores me with his Fourteen Points," and in light of the fact that Prime Minister David Lloyd George of Britain had campaigned on the slogan, "Make Germany Pay."[3] However, with a few exceptions, Wilson rigidly refused compromise, and as a result many of his provisions were omitted.

A similar attitude doomed U.S. entry into the League of Nations, which for Wilson was the vital provision of the treaty. The stated purpose of the league was to "promote international co-operation and to achieve international peace and security."[4] But, while most Americans initially supported membership, U.S. senators (who would have to ratify any agreement by a two-thirds majority) were concerned about two aspects in particular: the provisions that members would "undertake to respect and preserve as against external aggression the territorial integrity and existing political independence of all State members of the League," and that "any threat of war is a matter of concern to all members."[5] The fear was that membership would amount to the entangling alliance with European nations that America had historically avoided.

Aware of growing dissent, Wilson announced that the league provision would be embedded in the peace treaty itself, so that rejection of the league would delay the official declaration of the end of the war. But this was not a credible threat, as the war, for all intents and purposes, was over. Failure to sign a peace agreement right away would not have any real implications.

Wilson returned home in the summer of 1919 and commenced a cross-country speaking tour in support of the league. He was welcomed in these appearances, but public opinion was swayed by the opposition—in particular by a group of "irreconcilables" (those opposed to the league in any form) who trailed the president, sometimes appearing in the same hall the night after Wilson spoke. Wilson, ever more bitter and despondent in his speeches, seemed unable to understand the growing reluctance to join an organization that some perceived could lead to another war. His speech at Pueblo, Colorado, on September 25, 1919, portrayed league membership as a moral necessity that would not threaten American independence. It was reported that the president broke down in tears during its delivery. After giving this speech, Wilson suffered an attack and returned immediately to Washington, D.C., where a more serious and incapacitating stroke occurred ten days later. For several weeks, only Wilson's doctor and wife were allowed to see him. They insisted that he was capable of performing his duties, though members of Congress discussed his possible removal from office.

Senators continued their debate, and it was clear that many were willing to vote for membership if certain changes were made. These involved provisions respecting national sovereignty, allowances for members to opt out of multilateral military actions, and promises that the Monroe Doctrine would be respected. Senator Henry Cabot Lodge (R–Mass.), who as chairman of the Foreign Policy Committee was a key player in the debates, claimed to be willing to accept membership with these provisions. But Lodge seemed to hold a personal vendetta against Wilson, and his comments in the Senate in August dispute the very concept of the league.

In the summer of 1919, Wilson had hinted to an interviewer that he might be willing to compromise. But upon his gradual (but limited) recovery, he refused any proposed changes, maintaining that only the original form of the treaty would be acceptable. It is not clear whether his refusal to yield to these changes would have mattered. The Senate voted on both the original and a revised version of the treaty in November 1919. Another vote in March 1920 also resulted in rejection. However, if Wilson had worked with the Senate and been a more positive and flexible advocate, the outcome might have been different.

Wilson refused to give up on the matter. In another tactical error, he beseeched Americans to make the 1920 presidential election a referendum on the league. Although this was not the only issue of the campaign, it was a major topic, and in seeming repudiation of Wilson, the antileague, Republican Warren G. Harding was elected. Harding pronounced the league issue dead, and on July 2, 1921, a simple declaration ending the war was finally approved.

The League of Nations was formed and remained in existence until the end of World War II. The United States even participated informally in some of its activities, such as a plan to restrict the opium market. Ultimately, the league was replaced with the United Nations that the United States did join and that included the sovereignty provisions whereby nations would preserve their independence in matters of war.

NOTES

1. Mark Sullivan, *Our Times, 1900–1925*, vol. 5 (New York: Scribner's, 1939), 531.

2. Samuel E. Morrison and Henry S. Commager, eds., *Growth of the American Republic, 1865–1937* (New York: Oxford University Press, 1937), 489.

3. Ibid., 490.

4. Ibid., 492.

5. Sullivan, *Our Times*, 551.

WILSON—SPEECH IN DEFENSE OF THE LEAGUE OF NATIONS (SEPTEMBER 25, 1919)

The chief pleasure of my trip has been that it has nothing to do with my personal fortunes, that it has nothing to do with my personal reputation, that it has nothing to do with anything except great principles uttered by Americans of all sorts and of all parties which we are now trying to realize at this crisis of the affairs of the world. But there have been unpleasant impressions as well as pleasant impressions, my fellow citizens, as I have crossed the continent. I have perceived more and more that men have been busy creating an absolutely false impression of what the treaty of peace and the Covenant of the League of Nations contain and mean. . . .

. . . There is only one power to put behind the liberation of mankind, and that is the power of mankind. It is the power of the united moral forces of the world, and in the Covenant of the League of Nations the moral forces of the world are mobilized. For what purpose? Reflect, my fellow citizens, that the membership of this great League is going to include all the great fighting nations of the world, as well as the weak ones. It is not for the present going to include Germany, but for the time being Germany is not a great fighting country. All the nations that have power that can be mobilized are going to be members of this League, including the United States. And what do they unite for? They enter into a solemn promise to one another that they will never use their power against one another for aggression; that they never will impair the territorial integrity of a neighbor; that they never will interfere with the political independence of a neighbor; that they will abide by the principle that great populations are entitled to determine their own destiny and that they will not interfere with that destiny; and that no matter what differences arise amongst them they will never resort to war without first having done one or other of two things—either submitted the matter of controversy to arbitration, in which case they agree to abide by the result without question, or submitted it to the consideration of the council of the League of Nations, laying before that council all the documents, all the facts, agreeing that the council can publish the documents and the facts to the whole world, agreeing that there shall be six months allowed for the mature consideration of those facts by the council, and agreeing that at the expiration of the six months, even if they are not then ready to accept the advice of the council with regard to the settlement of the dispute, they will still not go to war for another three months. In other words, they consent, no matter what happens, to submit every matter of difference between them to the judgment of mankind, and just so certainly as they do that, my fellow citizens, war will be in the far background, war will be pushed out of that foreground of terror in which it has kept the world for generation after generation, and men will know that there will be a calm time of deliberate counsel. . . .

When you come to the heart of the Covenant, my fellow citizens, you will find it in Article X, and I am very much interested to know that the other things have been blown away like bubbles. There is nothing in the other contentions with regard to the League of Nations, but there is something in Article X that you ought to realize and ought to accept or reject. Article X is the heart of the whole matter. What is Article X? I never am certain that I can from memory give a literal repetition of its language, but I am sure that I can give an exact interpretation of its meaning. Article X provides that every member of the League covenants to respect and preserve the territorial integrity and existing political independence of every other member of the League as against external aggression. Not against internal disturbance. There was not a man at that table who did not admit the sacredness of the right of self-determination, the sacredness of the right of any body of people to say that they would not continue to live under the Government they were then living under, and under Article XI of the Covenant they are given a place to say whether they will live under it or not. For following Article X is Article XI, which makes it the right of any member of the League at any time to call attention to anything, anywhere, that is likely to disturb the peace of the world or the good understanding between nations upon which the peace of the world depends. . . .

You will say, "Is the League an absolute guarantee against war?" No; I do not know any absolute guarantee against the errors of human judgment or the violence of human passion, but I tell you this! With a cooling space of nine months for human passion, not much of it will keep hot. . . . It is true of the passions of men however you combine them. Give them space to cool off. I ask you this: If it is not an absolute insurance against war, do you want no insurance at all? Do you want nothing? Do you want not only no probability that war will not recur, but the probability that it will recur? The arrangements of justice do not stand of themselves, my fellow citizens. The arrangements of this treaty are just, but they need the support of the combined power of the great nations of the world. And they will have that support. Now that the mists of this great question have cleared away, I believe that men will see the truth, eye to eye and face to face. There is one thing that the American people always rise to and extend their hand to, and that is the truth of justice and of liberty and of peace. We have accepted that truth and we are going to be led by it, and it is going to lead us, and through us the world, out into pastures of quietness and peace such as the world never dreamed of before.

Link, Arthur S., and William M. Leary Jr., eds. *The Diplomacy of World Power: The United States, 1889–1920.* New York: St. Martin's, 1970, 166, 167, 169, 172, 178.

SENATOR HENRY CABOT LODGE—OPPOSITION TO THE LEAGUE OF NATIONS (AUGUST 12, 1919)

Never forget that this league is primarily—I might say over-whelmingly—a political organization, and I object strongly to having the politics of the United States turn upon disputes where deep feeling is aroused but in which we have no direct interest. . . .

It has been reiterated here on this floor, and reiterated to the point of weariness, that in every treaty there is some sacrifice of sovereignty. That is not a universal truth by any means, but it is true of some treaties and it is a platitude which does not require reiteration. The question and the only question before us here is how much of our sovereignty we are justified in sacrificing. In what I have already said about other nations putting us into war I have covered one point of sovereignty which ought never to be yielded—the power to send American soldiers and sailors everywhere, which ought never to be taken from the American people or impaired in the slightest degree. Let us beware how we palter with our independence. We have not reached the great position from which we were able to come down into the field of battle and help to save the world from tyranny by being guided by others. Our vast power has all been built up and gathered together by ourselves alone. We forced our way upward from the days of the Revolution, through a world often hostile and always indifferent. We owe no debt to anyone except to France in that Revolution, and those policies and those rights on which our power has been founded should never be lessened or weakened. It will be no service to the world to do so and it will be of intolerable injury to the United States. We will do our share. We are ready and anxious to help in all ways to preserve the world's peace. But we can do it best by not crippling ourselves.

I am as anxious as any human being can be to have the United States render every possible service to the civilization and the peace of mankind, but I am certain we can do it best by not putting ourselves in leading strings or subjecting our policies and our sovereignty to other nations. The independence of the United States is not only more precious to ourselves but to the world than any single possession. Look at the United States to-day. We have made mistakes in the past. We have had shortcomings. We shall make mistakes in the future and fall short of our own best hopes. But none the less is there any country to-day on the face of the earth which can compare with this in ordered liberty, in peace, and in the largest freedom? I feel that I can say this without being accused of undue boastfulness, for it is the simple fact, and in making this treaty and taking on these obligations all that we do is in a spirit of unselfishness and in a desire for the good of mankind. But it is well to remember that we are dealing with nations every one of which has a direct individual interest to serve, and there is grave danger in an unshared idealism. Contrast the United States with any country on the face of the earth to-day and ask yourself whether the situation of the United States is not the best to be found. I will go as far as anyone in world service, but the first step to world service is the maintenance of the United States. . . .

We hear much of visions and I trust we shall continue to have visions and dream dreams of a fairer future for the race. But visions are one thing and visionaries are another, and the mechanical appliances of the rhetorician designed to give a picture of a present which does not exist and of a future which no man can predict are as unreal and short lived as the steam or canvas clouds, the angels suspended on wires and the artificial lights of the stage. They pass with the moment of effect and are shabby and tawdry in the daylight. Let us at least be real. Washington's entire honesty of mind and his fearless look into the face of all facts are qualities which can never go out of fashion and which we should all do well to imitate.

. . .

No doubt many excellent and patriotic people see a coming fulfilment of noble ideals in the words "League for Peace." We all respect and share these aspirations and desires, but some of us see no hope, but rather defeat, for them in this murky covenant. For we, too, have our ideals, even if we differ from those who have tried to establish a monopoly of idealism. Our first ideal is our country, and we see her in the future, as in the past, giving service to all her people and to the world. Our ideal of the future is that she should continue to render that service of her own free will. She has great problems of her own to solve, very grim and perilous problems, and a right solution, if we can attain to it, would largely benefit mankind. We would have our country strong to resist a peril from the West, as she has flung back the German menace from the East. We would not have our politics distracted and embittered by the dissensions of other lands. We would not have our country's vigor exhausted, or her moral force abated, by everlasting meddling and muddling in every quarrel, great and small, which afflicts the world. Our ideal is to make her ever stronger and better and finer, because in that way alone, as we believe, can she be of the greatest service to the world's peace and to the welfare of mankind.

Link, Arthur S., and William M. Leary Jr., eds. *The Diplomacy of World Power: The United States, 1889–1920*. New York: St. Martin's, 1970, 163–166.

RECOMMENDED READINGS

Auchincloss, Louis. *Woodrow Wilson*. New York: Penguin Group, 2000.

Blumenthal, Henry. "Woodrow Wilson and the Race Question." *Journal of Negro History* 48 (1963): 1–21.

Clements, Kendrick A. *The Presidency of Woodrow Wilson*. Lawrence: University Press of Kansas, 1992.

———. *Woodrow Wilson, World Statesman*. New York: Ivan R. Dee, 1999.

Dimock, Marshall E. "Woodrow Wilson as Legislative Leader." *Journal of Politics* 19 (1957): 3–19.

Ferrell, Robert H. *Woodrow Wilson and World War I*. New York: Harper and Row, 1985.

Gilderhus, Mark T. *Diplomacy and Revolution: U.S.–Mexican Relations under Wilson and Carranza*. Tucson: University of Arizona Press, 1977.

Knock, Thomas J. *To End All Wars: Woodrow Wilson and the Quest for a New World Order*. New York: Oxford University Press, 1992.

Link, Arthur S. *Wilson*. 5 vols. Princeton, N.J.: Princeton University Press, 1947–1963.

———. *Woodrow Wilson: A Brief Biography*. Chicago: Quadrangle Books, 1963.

———. *Woodrow Wilson and the Progressive Era, 1910–1917*. New York: Harper and Row, 1954.

Roosevelt, Theodore. "Our Responsibility in Mexico." *New York Times Magazine*, 6 December 1914.

Smith, Gene. *When the Cheering Stopped: The Last Years of Woodrow Wilson*. New York: Morrow, 1964.

Tuchman, Barbara. *The Zimmerman Telegram*. New York: Viking Press, 1958.

Walworth, Arthur. *Woodrow Wilson and His Peacemakers: American Diplomacy at the Paris Peace Conference, 1919*. New York: W.W. Norton, 1986.

Wood, Stephen B. *Constitutional Politics in the Progressive Era, Child Labor and the Law*. Chicago: University of Chicago Press, 1968.

4

WARREN G. HARDING

(1921–1923)

INTRODUCTION

Warren G. Harding, who served as president only from 1921 until his death from a cerebral hemorrhage while on a speaking tour in 1923, inherited the task of restoring the nation to postwar "normalcy," as he put it. While generally taking a fairly passive approach and lacking a vision of governance, Harding provided direction to the nation, not through an innovative new agenda, but in attempts to grapple with existing problems. Specifically, he tried to soothe lingering fears and animosities in the foreign policy realm, rein in the unstable economy, and, in the social realm, even provide some leadership in regard to ongoing racial tensions. Despite his short term in office, and the distracting influence of high-profile political scandals, there are several notable and affirmative accomplishments of the Harding administration, although the ultimate effect of some of these are questionable.

Harding was a former newspaper editor whose political career (which included being elected to the U.S. Senate from Ohio) was largely driven by Republican Party leaders who saw him as an ideal candidate. Handsome, dignified, and relaxed, his career (presaging future electoral trends) was largely built on the image he projected, as opposed to his governing ideas. Thus, no one was particularly surprised when this new president came into office with an agenda tied not to change but to a restoration of prewar conditions. But this return to the past implied conservatism—old, progressive notions of previous administrations were not part of the plan. The goal in general was to shrink the federal government, although the specific policies Harding advocated were sometimes inconsistent in this regard. This was clearly a welcome message to the American people who, in addition to returning Republican majorities to Congress, elected Harding with 60.2 percent of the popular vote over Democrat James M. Cox—the most any presidential candidate had received to that point in the nation's history.

Naturally, the biggest issue facing Harding was how to ameliorate the lingering effects of the Great War. Although the fighting in Europe had ended over two years before he took office, many war-based issues remained unsettled, partly due to Woodrow Wilson's postwar lack of leadership. As a result of the impasse between Wilson and the Senate over inclusion of the League of Nations provision in the peace pact, even an official American declaration of the end of the war was still lacking. Upon taking office, Harding declared the league issue dead and in the summer of 1921, Congress passed, and the president signed, a simple statement that the war was over.

But a continuing fear of future acts of global aggression remained. In one of his most energetic acts of leadership, Harding convened the Washington Conference on Arms Limitation to settle issues of international relations, and convinced the Senate to approve all nine treaties that emerged from the meetings. These included an agreement among the United States, Great Britain, Japan, France, and Italy to limit battleship construction, and a controversial document signed by nine nations agreeing to respect each other's territories in the Pacific, and to confer if any one was threatened by an outside power. There were some fears that this latter agreement in particular involved the United States in dreaded entangling alliances, but in the long run these treaties were not particularly meaningful. Their immediate value, however, was to restore optimism and calm to the postwar world.

Another foreign policy of note, one that illustrated the degree to which international politics had changed from the days of Theodore Roosevelt's paternalistic treatment of Latin America, was approval of a compensatory treaty with Colombia on April 20, 1921. Essentially a document of apology (although the word "apology" was struck as too controversial) and repayment for America's role in the events surrounding the Panamanian revolution, this treaty guaranteed payment of $25 million. Harding was successful in getting this agreement approved by the U.S. Senate, where Wilson had failed, largely because lingering Latin American hostilities over the incident showed no signs of weakening, and had become a troubling bar to trade in that region. Additionally, its biggest opponent, Roosevelt, had died on January 6, 1919.

In the economic realm, Harding also faced continued aftereffects of the war. As the economy rose and fell in a typical postwar adjustment, Americans were confronted with stagnant wages and increasing prices. The agricultural sector in particular was in poor shape and farmers were suffering. Harding attempted to lower war-level taxes as a means of relief, but the real success there would not occur until the Calvin Coolidge administration. Harding's most notable economic accomplishment came instead with the restoration of tariffs, which Wilson had eliminated or reduced in 1913. Actually, this return to government-mandated protections of specific goods from foreign competition (one of the exceptions to Harding's promise to trim back government activity) was mandated by the Republican return to power. Thus, it was more of a party effort than one that can be attributed to Harding himself. However, he did help push the bill through Congress and also insisted on a degree of flexibility, through the inclusion of a tariff advisory board empowered to make adjustments without legislative approval. In retrospect, the tariff restorations were probably not what the postwar economy called for and, while the decision was generally popular with the American people, Harding faced criticism for caving in to special interests.

Linked to both the war and the push for the restoration of economic stability were the issues of the repayment of war debts by American allies, and the soldiers' bonus. In regard to the former, Harding worked to gain congressional approval of a more workable repayment agreement with Great Britain, but the topic was mostly uncontroversial. However, the question of a "bonus" paid to veterans by the federal government was quite contentious. Harding vetoed the bill, citing its huge drain on the national treasury. While this appears to have been the fiscally responsible decision, Harding was attacked by many members of Congress anxious to please the returning soldiers. They accused the president of hypocrisy for being willing to help a particular class of Americans (those who profited from protected industries) through tariff restoration, but refusing to grant this dispensation to deserving veterans.

Finally, while his personal style and philosophy of governance worked to inhibit Harding in providing a visionary or reform agenda, he did put some effort into social issues. First, he was a forceful and unwavering advocate of Prohibition. Although the battle over the Eighteenth Amendment preceded his election (and though he still drank, at least through a portion of his term), he committed himself to a strong defense of the policy. Yet in this attempt, he appeared somewhat out of step with the times. Many Americans were turning against national temperance, as they began to doubt the wisdom and practicability of the effort to stamp out drinking as a national pastime; both his predecessor and successor were much more tepid supporters of the policy. While providing the most zealous moral support of any president to Prohibition, Harding was not, however, able to ameliorate the severe problems of enforcement.

On a more activist note, Harding tried, but failed, to achieve a federal-level Department of Public Welfare. He envisioned this as a unit where all programs having to do with health and welfare issues could be centralized. Although the scope was fairly limited and did not really expand government's role, the idea was daring for these conservative times. Even during the earlier, reform-minded administrations, when public demand for such a federal department was much stronger, the policy had not been so decisively advocated at the presidential level.

Similarly, Harding fought for improvements in the nation's race relations. By virtue of a speech given in Birmingham, Alabama, on October 26, 1921, where he noted the importance of granting political and economic equality to blacks, the national dialogue on the issue was advanced. Although criticized both by conservative southerners who thought the concept was simply unacceptable, as well as those who saw his acknowledgment of the unacceptability of social equality as inherently racist, the speech was a breakthrough in the sense that no president had yet articulated this sort of guidance. Ironically, for this conservative president this policy also had reformist roots. The notion that blacks must achieve political and economic parity is traceable to radical populists of the late nineteenth century who believed it was necessary in order that the people of America could unify and thereby more effectively fight corporate domination.

Harding thus represented a mostly soothing palliative to the shaken America of the postwar period. The scandals of his administration, which tend to draw the majority of attention today, did not play a dominant role during his term. In particular, the Teapot Dome debacle, involving bribery in the granting of federal oil leases and allegations that Harding had fathered a child out of wedlock, did not emerge until after his death. Two earlier suicides by administration figures accused of wrongdoing also failed to greatly harm the president's reputation, since he had cut ties with both of these men upon learning of their unethical behavior.

Although some of Harding's ideas may have been ultimately ineffectual, or even detrimental, in terms of negating the effects of the war he provided at least the sense that someone was in charge—not a president who would try to change things a great deal, but one who would allow the nation to settle down again. Along the way, Harding even introduced a few fairly reformist notions that were to be resurrected in later years.

COMPENSATORY TREATY WITH COLOMBIA

One of the first items Harding fought for as president was Senate ratification of a compensatory treaty with Colombia in regard to the Panama Canal. This promise of a $25 million payment to mitigate lingering resentments over America's role in the Panamanian revolution and the subsequent construction of the canal outside of Colombian borders had been on hold, awaiting Senate approval, since early in the Wilson administration. Harding was able to gain ratification in just a few months, and the treaty was widely hailed as a positive step toward improving diplomatic and economic relations in Central and South America. But support was not universal, and the fight for this treaty placed Harding, who took office more than two years after the death of Roosevelt, in the position of having to contend with the legacy of this former president.

Controversy over the U.S. role in the 1903 Panamanian revolution, which had resulted in Colombia's loss of expected revenues from the canal, had been revitalized by Roosevelt's March 23, 1911, speech in which he boasted of having "taken" the canal zone. Many Americans were coming to the conclusion that the nation's (or at least Roosevelt's) role in that episode may have violated standards of justice and fairness. In response, a treaty was drafted in 1913 offering monetary compensation as well as a statement of sincere regret. It was immediately signed by Colombia but never voted on by the U.S. Senate. Although President Wilson supported it, there was a great deal of opposition to the apologetic tone in particular. Roosevelt actively fought ratification and, since he still commanded a great deal of loyalty, helped to block a vote. In addition, many Republican senators used rejection of the treaty as a political ploy to embarrass Wilson.

Harding was determined to get the treaty passed however, and began to advocate ratification even before his inauguration in early 1921. For the new president, as noted in his brief message on March 9, passage of the agreement was key to the reestablishment of friendly relations not just with Colombia but with all Latin American nations. The wisdom of this philosophy was even more widely accepted in 1921 than it had been in 1914. As noted by the outgoing Secretary of State Bainbridge Colby, refusal to sign "has caused us to be represented in Latin American minds as indifferent to justice."[1]

Additionally, after the experience of the Great War, Americans were in the mood for expanded economic opportunity, not smoldering international hostilities, and the treaty fit these purposes. As noted by Secretary of the Interior Albert Fall, the opening of Colombian petroleum fields to U.S. companies would be threatened by rejection of the treaty, thus leaving these vast reserves to other nations. For Fall this was of particular import. He argued that the war had illustrated that nations controlling large oil reserves maintain the advantage in sea commerce.

Some senators, however, objected to the treaty on these very grounds, seeing the compensatory payment as an indirect and expensive subsidy to American oil companies. In retrospect, the argument made by Fall, later convicted for taking bribes in return for granting lucrative oil drilling leases in the Teapot Dome scandal, does seem a bit suspect. Additionally, Republican senators who had opposed the treaty when advocated by the Democrat Wilson but supported it after Harding's election were accused of playing politics with the nation's diplomacy.

But the more vocal arguments were centered on the impact of the treaty on the nation's reputation. Although the 1921 version omitted the clear statement of apology, some senators, such as Frank B. Kellogg (R–Minn.), believed that the payment itself implied the United States was apologizing for wrongdoing, and thus made the nation appear weak and open to future similar demands from other nations for compensation in regard to diplomatic or military actions. For Kellogg, if earlier discussions had not led to the conclusion that Colombia had been wronged by the United States, it was hypocritical to change the official position on that now. The *Philadelphia North American* referred to the payment as nothing more than "belated blackmail."[2]

Furthermore, given the impact Roosevelt had on the Panamanian revolution and the construction of the canal, his posthumous presence in this debate was inevitable. The ratification issue in 1921, while triggering some rehashing of the question of Roosevelt's actions, also included a more subtle examination of the propriety of potentially damaging the former president's legacy. For example, the *Chicago Tribune* accused Harding of supporting a treaty that was "a miserable and humiliating thing concocted by Mr. Wilson for the express purpose of casting discredit upon President Roosevelt."[3] And there is an elegiac tone to Kellogg's concern for the impact on the reputation of one of "America's greatest Presidents," as well as in the unanimous consent agreement to include in the *Congressional Record* a chapter Roosevelt had written in opposition to the treaty.

Ultimately, the opponents lost this fight and the treaty was ratified by the Senate on April 20 by a vote of sixty-nine to nineteen (thus exceeding the ⅔ vote necessary for treaty ratification). As predicted by Harding and other advocates, diplomatic and trade relations between the United States and Colombia immediately and markedly improved. The episode illustrates well the changing nature of U.S. foreign policy through the early twentieth century. Not only had a domineering American presence in Latin America been rejected, but also recompense (and at least an implied apology) for such earlier actions, staunchly opposed in previous years, passed with ease in 1921.

NOTES

1. "The Colombia Rumpus Up Again," *Literary Digest*, March 26, 1921, 12.
2. Ibid.
3. "A Graceful Transition," *New York Times*, March 12, 1921, 10.

HARDING—MESSAGE TO THE SENATE ON THE
COLOMBIAN TREATY (MARCH 9, 1921)

I very respectfully invite the attention of the Senate to the pending treaty which has been negotiated between the United States and the Republic of Colombia which is in the hands of your honorable body, with full information relating to its negotiation and its later modification and revision.

The early and favorable consideration of this treaty would be very helpful at the present time in promoting our friendly relationships. There have been many and long delays in dealing with this treaty until we have been made to seem unmindful, when in truth we have had no thought but to deal with this sister Republic in a most cordial consideration. I believe the revised treaty to be a fair expression of our just and friendly relationship with the Republic of Colombia, and I would rejoice to have our example in dealing with the Republic of Colombia to be made an assurance of that promptness and firmness and justice which shall invite added confidence in our Government and a new regard for our own Republic.

Congressional Record. 67th Congress, 1st sess., 1921. Vol. 61, 157.

SENATOR FRANK B. KELLOGG—REMARKS ON THE
COLOMBIAN TREATY (APRIL 13, 1921)

I sincerely regret that circumstances compel me to state to the Senate the reasons why I can not vote for the ratification of this treaty. I had hoped that a new treaty would be negotiated on a basis consistent with the honor of the Nation; but there is an evident desire to press for the ratification of this treaty. . . .

I am opposed to this treaty because it writes the word "shame" across the pages of American history. I am opposed to this treaty because it is an acknowledgment of guilt, and I believe we are not guilty. I am opposed to this treaty because I do not believe the good will and friendship of nations is to be bartered in international markets. It is, rather, to be won by honorable dealing. If we have wronged Colombia, we should apologize. If we have not wronged Colombia, we should not.

I inquire at the outset, why are we paying $25,000,000 to Colombia? Disguise it as you may, the verdict of history will be that we are paying this sum as compensation to Colombia for the loss of Panama, under the claim that we encouraged the revolution, violated her rights under the treaty of 1846 and under international law, and wrested from her by force one of her Provinces. This was substantially the claim made by the distinguished Senator from Colorado, Mr. Thomas, I believe, in January or February of this year, in a long speech in this Chamber. He claimed, as a reason for the ratification of this treaty, that we had violated our treaty with Colombia and encouraged the revolution, and he laid at the door of Col. Roosevelt these unlawful acts. It was the only argument he made for ratification of the treaty.

But, it is well understood by the public, and the press announced, that this treaty is to be adopted to compensate Colombia for the loss of Panama. The people of this country and of the world will so understand it. . . .

Now, what is the position of Colombia? She has always been consistent. She claimed in 1903, and ever since has claimed, that the United States violated her treaty of 1846 with New Granada, to which Colombia succeeded; that we failed to maintain her sovereignty over Panama, that we violated the principles of neutrality by intervening with armed forces, and prevented Colombia from putting down the rebellion and that we are responsible, and should make reparation to Colombia. . . .

I have no wish to bring this into politics, but I might add that this position of Colombia has been taken by the principal Democratic leaders in the Senate of the United States since 1904, and I assume that the Democratic Party is now to be congratulated on finally getting some of the leaders of the Republican Party to agree with them. . . .

If this Government was guilty of the acts charged by the minority party in 1903 and 1904, we should have made reparations then. If the treaty which is now submitted to the Senate is a good treaty at this date, it was a good treaty eight years ago, when negotiated by the Democratic administration. I realize as much as anyone that our foreign relations should not be made the subject of partisan strife, but they were so made in 1903 and 1904, and were so made by the negotiation of this treaty immediately after the inauguration of President Wilson in 1913. . . .

I am not so much concerned about the pecuniary loss to the United States—deeply as we are involved in debt and burdened by taxation— as I am concerned about the fair name of the United States. I am concerned lest we go on record by the pusillanimous act of this ratification, and thereby cast a shadow on the brightest page of the history of American accomplishments. I am concerned because by this act we will place a stain upon the name and fame of one of America's greatest Presidents.

Congressional Record. 67th Congress, 1st sess., 1921. Vol. 61, 191–192.

RACIAL EQUALITY

After the era of Reconstruction following the Civil War, the question of African American rights received little political notice. Despite the postwar passage of legislation and constitutional amendments designed to secure basic freedoms, blacks in the American South were simply treated as second-class, inferior citizens. As a result of the compromise made in response to the disputed election of 1876, in which the presidency was granted to Republican Rutherford B. Hayes in return for a scaling back of the federal presence in the South, the southern states had been largely left alone in regard to their treatment of blacks. The Jim Crow system of state-sanctioned segregation and discrimination in all areas of life continued unfettered. While the rights question had received brief attention during the Roosevelt and Wilson administrations, it was President Harding who most energetically focused national attention on the topic.

By the 1920s, it was becoming difficult for Americans to continue to ignore this issue. Although the majority of blacks still lived in the South, a northern migration had begun, spurred by the decline of southern agriculture as well as the growth of northern industrialization and its need for new workers during the war. As a result, states outside of the South were now facing questions involving the rights of this expanding portion of their citizenry. Additionally, the notion of the basic inferiority of blacks was beginning to be publicly challenged by both races. This dialogue was encouraged by newly formed African American interest groups such as the National Association for the Advancement of Colored People (NAACP) and respected black leaders such as Booker T. Washington.

Parties and politicians were also starting to pay attention to this matter. Given the increasing black presence in the North, northern Democrats began to question the virulently racist position of their southern brethren. Although black voters had been traditionally faithful to the Republican Party since being granted the right to vote, northern Democrats saw a rational logic in fighting for this group's support. On the other side, the Republicans' comfortable reliance on the black vote was being threatened by the reemergence of this party in the South. Although some factions of southern Republicans welcomed black voters, others favored a "lily-white" strategy, in which blacks were denied participation. Thus, in both parties, a split was emerging between politicians who wanted to court the black vote by focusing on issues of interest to that group, and those who wanted to reinforce a racist ideology.

Harding was politically sophisticated enough to realize that the time had come for a presidential candidate to incorporate this rights issue into his campaign. Although in modern terms his approach appears to be quite conservative, his position was in fact fairly liberal for his time. During his campaign, he promised to fight for a federal antilynching bill, criticized U.S. intervention in the black republic of Haiti, and made some general statements in support of civil rights. He was attacked for these positions by many Democrats (the Ohio Democratic Party distributed an anti-Harding pamphlet entitled, "The Threat of Negro Domination") and some Republicans. Once in office, Harding pressed for the antilynching bill in his first message to Congress, but never again advocated passage of that or any other federal civil rights policy.

On October 26, 1921, however, Harding focused national attention on the issue through a speech given in Birmingham Alabama, on the occasion of the city's semicentennial celebration. Choosing this setting for his statement of at least moderate support for civil rights was a bold and courageous decision. Birmingham fully embraced the Jim Crow system, which segregated the races in almost every conceivable activity (including spectators for this speech). In 1930, the city would even pass an ordinance making it "unlawful for a Negro and a white person to play together or in company with each other"[1] at dominoes or checkers. Later, as the civil rights movement gained momentum in the 1960s, Birmingham became the site for some of the most hard-fought and violent battles in the struggle for equality.

This speech was delivered in Birmingham's Woodrow Wilson Park to several thousand spectators. It was the seventh speech the president made that day. After opening with a tribute to the Confederate South and its war heroes, Harding went on to the race issue. His opening theme was quite conservative and traditional, rejecting the notion of social equality between the races, and even stating that it would be helpful to eliminate the word "equality" from consideration in this regard. However, the speech then moved to a plea for economic and political equality for blacks, advocating specific reforms such as voting rights, educational opportunity, and greater economic freedom. Although acknowledging that this was no longer just a southern problem, he beseeched the South to begin the reform process. Harding also appealed to the self-respect of the "colored race," stressing that blacks must strive for their own identity and not seek merely to become imitations of white men.

There was a great deal of support for the speech, as many Americans viewed it as a reasonable statement whose time had come. There was pointed opposition from two quarters, however. Not unexpectedly, some southerners believed the speech to be far too radical and accused the president of trying to force untenable change on the South. This position is represented here by the comments of Senator Byron P. ("Pat") Harrison, a Democrat from Mississippi.

On the other hand, Harding's basic acceptance of the social inequality of blacks attracted negative comment, largely from the black press. W.E.B. Du Bois, a prominent black academic whose Niagara movement had led to formation of the NAACP, focused on the weakness of the speech in this regard in his December 1921 editorial in *The Crisis* magazine. Although commending the president for his support of economic and political equity, Du Bois believed the social inequality message to be dangerous and backwards.

The effects of this debate are difficult to gauge. There was no official action taken in the Harding administration, or for a long time to come, in support of civil rights. In fact, even the federal antilynching legislation did not pass until after World War II. However, the impact of the words of the president in support of at least some basic equality likely had an effect on the hearts and minds of this generation.

NOTE

1. C. Vann Woodward, *The Strange Career of Jim Crow* (New York: Oxford University Press, 1974), 118.

HARDING—SPEECH ON RACIAL EQUALITY (OCTOBER 26, 1921)

Men of both races may well stand uncompromisingly against every suggestion of social equality. This is not a question of social equality, but a question of recognizing a fundamental, eternal, inescapable difference.

Racial amalgamation there cannot be. Partnership of the races in developing the highest aims of all humanity there must be if humanity is to achieve the ends which we have set for it. The black man should seek to be, and he should be encouraged to be, the best possible black man and not the best possible imitation of a white man.

The World War brought us to full recognition that the race problem is national rather than merely sectional. There are no authentic statistics but it is common knowledge that the World War was marked by a great migration of colored people to the North and West. They were attracted by the demand for labor and the higher wages offered. It has brought the question of race closer to North and West, and, I believe, it has served to modify somewhat the views of those sections on this question. It has made the South realize its industrial dependence on the labor of the black man and made the North realize the difficulties of the community in which two greatly differing races are brought to live side by side. . . .

Politically and economically there need be no occasion for great and permanent differentiation, for limitations of the individual's opportunity, provided that on both sides there shall be recognition of the absolute divergence in things social and racial. When I suggest the possibility of economic equality between the races, I mean it in precisely the same way and to the same extent that I would mean it if I spoke of equality of economic opportunity as between members of the same race. In each case I would mean equality proportioned to the honest capacities and deserts of the individual.

Men of both races may well stand uncompromisingly against every suggestion of social equality. Indeed, it would be helpful to have that word "equality" eliminated from this consideration; to have it accepted on both sides that this is not a question of social equality, but a question of recognizing a fundamental, eternal and inescapable difference. We shall have made real progress when we develop an attitude in the public and community thought of both races which recognizes this difference.

Take the political aspect. I would say let the black man vote when he is fit to vote; prohibit the white man voting when he is unfit to vote. Especially would I appeal to the self-respect of the colored race. I would inculcate in it the wish to improve itself as a distinct race, with a heredity, a set of traditions, an array of aspirations all its own. . . . Out of such racial ambitions and pride will come natural segregations, without narrowing and rights, such as are proceeding in both rural and urban communities now in Southern States, satisfying natural inclinations and adding notably to happiness and contentment.

On the other hand I would insist upon equal educational opportunity for both. This does not mean that both would become equally educated within a generation or two generations or ten generations. Even men of the same race do not accomplish such an equality as that. There must be such education among the colored people as will enable them to develop their own leaders, capable of understanding and sympathizing with such a differentiation between the races as I have suggested—leaders who will inspire the race with proper ideals of honorable destiny; and important participation in the universal effort for advancement of humanity as a whole. Racial amalgamation there cannot be. Partnership of the races in developing the highest aims of all humanity there must be if humanity, not only here but everywhere, is to achieve the ends which we have set for it.

I can say to you people of the South, both white and black, that the time has passed when you are entitled to assume that this problem of races is peculiarly and particularly your problem. More and more it is becoming a problem of the North. . . .

It is a matter of the keenest national concern that the South shall not be encouraged to make its colored population a vast reservoir of ignorance, to be drained away by the processes of migration into all other sections. That is what has been going on in recent years at a rate so accentuated that it has caused this question of races to be, as I have already said, no longer one of a particular section. Just as I do not wish the South to be politically entirely one party; just as I believe that is bad for the South, and for the rest of the country as well so I do not want the colored people to be entirely of one party. I wish that both the tradition of a solidly Democratic South and the tradition of a solidly Republican black race might be broken up. Neither political sectionalism nor any system of rigid groupings of the people will in the long run prosper our country.

With such convictions one must urge the people of the South to take advantage of their superior understanding of this problem and to assume an attitude toward it that will deserve the confidence of the colored people. Likewise, I plead with my own political party to lay aside every program that looks to lining up the black man as a mere political adjunct. Let there be an end of prejudice and of demagogy in this line. Let the South understand the menace which lies in forcing upon the black race an attitude of political solidarity.

Every consideration, it seems to me, brings us back at last to the question of education. When I speak of education as a part of this race, I do not want the States or the nation to attempt to educate people, whether white or black, into something they are not fitted to be. I have no sympathy with the half-baked altruism that would overstock us with doctors and lawyers, of whatever color, and leave us in need of people fit and willing to do the manual work of a workaday world. But I would like to see an education that would fit every man not only to do his particular work as well as possible but to rise to a higher plane if he would deserve it. For that sort of education I have no fears, whether it be given to a black man or a white man. From that sort of education, I believe, black men, white men, the whole nation, would draw immeasurable benefit.

New York Times. October 27, 1921.

SENATOR PAT HARRISON—COMMENTS ON HARDING'S RACIAL EQUALITY SPEECH (OCTOBER 27, 1921)

The President's speech was unfortunate. To have made it in the heart of the South, where, in many States, the negro population predominates, was unfortunate in the extreme. Of course, every rational being desires to see the negro protected in his life, liberty, and property. I believe in giving to him every right under the law to which he is entitled, but to encourage the negro, who, in some States, as in my own, exceeds the white population, to strive through every political avenue to be placed upon equality with the whites, is a blow to the white civilization of this country that will take years to combat.

If the President's theory is carried to its ultimate conclusion, namely, that the black person, either man or woman, should have full economic and political rights with the white man and white woman, then that means that the black man can strive to become President of the United States, hold a Cabinet position and occupy the highest places of public trust in the nation. It means white women should work under black men in public places, as well as in all trades and professions.

I am against any such theory because I know it is impracticable, unjust and destructive of the best ideals of America. Place the negro upon political and economic equality with the white man or woman and the friction between the races will be aggravated.

New York Times. October 28, 1921.

W.E.B. DU BOIS—"PRESIDENT HARDING AND SOCIAL EQUALITY" (DECEMBER 1921)

And now comes President Harding's Birmingham speech when unwittingly or deliberately the President brings the crisis. We may no longer dodge nor hesitate. We must all, black or white, Northerner or Southerner, stand in the light and speak plain words.

The President must not for a moment be blamed because, when invited to the semicentennial of a great Southern city of industry, he talked of the Negro instead of the results of profitable mining. There is but one subject in the South. The Southerners themselves can speak no other, think no other, act no other. The eternal and inevitable Southern topic is and has been and will be the Black Man.

Moreover, the President laid down three theses with which no American can disagree without a degree of self-stultification almost inconceivable, namely:

1. The Negro must vote on the same terms that white folk vote.

2. The Negro must be educated.

3. The Negro must have economic justice.

The sensitive may note that the President qualified these demands somewhat, even dangerously, and yet they stand out so clearly in his speech that he must be credited with meaning to give them their real significance. And in this the President made a braver, clearer utterance than Theodore Roosevelt ever dared to make or than William Taft or William McKinley ever dreamed of. For this let us give him every ounce of credit he deserves.

But President Harding did not stop here. Indeed, he did not begin here. Either because he had no adequate view of the end of the fatal path he was treading or because, in his desire to placate the white South, he was careless of consequences, he put *first* on his program of racial set-tlement a statement which could have been understood and was under-stood and we fear was intended to be understood to pledge the nation, the Negro race and the world to a doctrine so utterly inadmissible in the twentieth century, in a Republic of free citizens and in an age of Hu-manity that one stands aghast at the motives and the reasons for the pronouncement.

It may to some seem that this statement is overdrawn. Some puzzled persons may say: But Negroes themselves have told me that they repu-diate "social equality" and amalgamation of race; in fact, right there at Birmingham, Negro applause of the President was audible.

All this does not minimize—rather, it emphasizes—the grave crisis precipitated by the President's speech. It emphasizes the fact of our men-tal skulking or transparent and deliberate dishonesty in dealing with the Negro.

Social equality may mean two things. The obvious and clear meaning is the right of a human being to accept companionship with his fellow on terms of equal and reciprocal courtesy. In this sense the term is un-derstood and defended by modern men. It has not been denied by any civilized man since the French Revolution. It is the foundation of de-mocracy, and to bring it into being the world went through revolution, war, murder and hell.

But there is another narrow, stilted and unreal meaning that is some-times dragged from these words, namely: social equality is the right to demand private social companionship with another.

Or, to put it more simply: the real meaning of "social equality" is eligibility to association with men, and the forced and illogical meaning is the right to demand private association with any particular person. Such a demand as the latter is idiotic and was never made by any sane person; while, on the contrary, for any person to admit that his character is such that he is physically and morally unfit to talk or travel or eat with his fellow men, or that he has no desire to associate with decent people, would be an admission which none but a leper, a criminal or a liar could possibly make. . . .

Let us sweep away all quibbling: Let us assume that the President was sane and serious and could not and did not mean by "social equality" anything so inconceivable as the right of a man to invite himself to an-other man's dinner table. No. Mr. Harding meant that the American Negro must acknowledge that it was a wrong and a disgrace for Booker T. Washington to dine with President Roosevelt!

The answer to this inconceivably dangerous and undemocratic de-mand must come with the unanimous ring of twelve million voices, en-forced by the voice of every American who believes in Humanity.

Let us henceforward frankly admit that which we hitherto have always known; that *no system of social uplift which begins by denying the manhood of a man can end by giving him a free ballot, a real education and a just wage.*

Moon, Henry Lee, ed. *The Emerging Thought of W.E.B. Du Bois*. New York: Simon and Schuster, 1972, 300–302.

RESTORATION OF TARIFFS

One of the postwar difficulties faced by President Harding was the dramatic twists and turns of the nation's economy. Although the relatively free trade policies instituted by Wilson in 1913 were not the immediate cause of these later problems, many Americans looked to a reinstatement of tariff protections as a solution. As a traditional Republican (i.e., not one of the more liberal members of the party), Harding also favored a dramatic increase in these taxes charged on foreign goods sold in the American market. The plan was opposed, however, by some who believed the change to be unnecessary and potentially disastrous.

The postwar economy in America was extremely complex and rather difficult even for experts to explain or forecast. In the two years immediately following the war, the prices of manufactured goods skyrocketed. For example, the average price of a pair of shoes jumped from $3 to over $10. Yet wages had remained stagnant, leading many Americans to participate in an informal buyers strike, resisting purchase of all but the most necessary products, and sometimes refusing to pay their rent. Farmers, in particular, suffered during these years. While the high monetary return on crops they had grown used to during the war years dropped sharply, they, like all other consumers, were forced to pay higher prices for manufactured goods. This period of inflation, which peaked in 1920, was replaced by prices that declined so dramatically that businesses failed and unemployment rose dangerously. In response to these hardships, many Americans began to demand the policy that had been somewhat simplistically (and perhaps erroneously) advocated as an economic cure-all: the return to high tariffs to shield domestic goods from foreign competition.

In 1921, an emergency tariff act was passed, but Harding pushed for more permanent legislation. In his first State of the Union speech, in December 1921, he argued that a more complete and perpetual system was necessary to return the nation to prosperity. His proposal was ultimately introduced in Congress as the Fordney-McCumber bill. This called for the reinstatement of tariffs at or exceeding the levels prior to 1913, the year in which Wilson pushed through dramatic reductions. This bill also added a new element to tariff policy—discretionary power to the chief executive. In consultation with an appointed Tariff Commission, the president could revise the newly established tariffs upward or downward by up to 50 percent without first having to secure legislative approval.

Congressional consideration of this bill followed the general pattern established in 1909 and 1913, with lobbyists and legislators fighting to protect particular economic sectors. As usual, agricultural interests argued for protections on their own goods but free trade for the manufactured products that farmers had to purchase. In the final bill, signed into law on September 21, 1922, agricultural commodities did receive the greatest protections, but tariffs were sharply increased on virtually all goods. Thus, while there was some congressional opposition to the bill per se, the major battles (particularly in the Senate) were fought over the details.

The most important and portentous criticisms of the bill, generally voiced by commentators outside of Congress, were based on a perceived illogic. To understand this theme of opposition, it is necessary to grasp one additional economic consequence of the Great War. During the war, the United States had been transformed from a borrowing to a lending nation. After the armistice, America was free of prewar debts to European nations (many of the debts had been liquidated to raise quick cash or had been paid off in agricultural commodities), and many now owed money to the United States and had to at least begin making payments on the interest.

But as critics pointed out, by establishing protective tariffs the United States was implementing a policy that made imported products prohibitively expensive in the domestic market. That is, the United States had precluded the best chance these nations had for raising money to pay their debts: selling their goods to Americans. European countries would thus be forced to default or to pay in currency, thus depleting their supplies and plunging them into economic depressions.

This scenario proved to be accurate. In addition, because of the worsening economic state of many European nations, combined with their own imposition of retaliatory protective tariffs, there was no longer an overseas market for American agricultural goods, further harming the farm economy. Although Harding acknowledged some of these concerns in his speech, he offered only vague statements in regard to the desire to be fair in trade dealings with all nations.

Without going so far as to warn of dire consequences, Harvard economist F.W. Taussig presented a reasoned opposition to Harding's plan. In particular, Taussig criticized the simplistic arguments underlying the new tariff law. He examined the very heart of the matter—whether tariff protections can ever stimulate the domestic economy, or if they do more harm than good. In his view, the tariff reductions of 1913 were never given a fair chance, as the war distorted the economy for several years, and he felt there was no basis for declaring them a failure at such an early stage. Taussig was particularly disturbed by the degree to which tariffs had become a solely political issue to the extent that whether or not America had a protective trade system in place depended on which party was dominant. Although clearly favoring less protection, and thus the old limited tariff system, he argued that business and consumers can adjust to just about any consistent policy. It is the constant, politically motivated revisions that put the economy at risk.

HARDING—COMMENTS TO CONGRESS ON TARIFF RESTORATION (DECEMBER 6, 1921)

There is before you the completion of the enactment of what has been termed a "permanent" tariff law, the word "permanent" being used to distinguish it from the emergency act which the Congress expedited early in the extraordinary session, and which is the law today. I can not too strongly urge an early completion of this necessary legislation. It is needed to stabilize our industry at home; it is essential to make more definite our trade relations abroad. More, it is vital to the preservation of many of our own industries which contribute so notably to the very lifeblood of our Nation.

There is now, and there always will be, a storm of conflicting opinion about any tariff revision. We can not go far wrong when we base our tariffs on the policy of preserving the productive activities which enhance employment and add to our national prosperity.

Again comes the reminder that we must not be unmindful of world conditions, that peoples are struggling for industrial rehabilitation and that we can not dwell in industrial and commercial exclusion and at the same time do the just thing in aiding world reconstruction and readjustment. We do not seek a selfish aloofness, and we could not profit by it, were it possible. We recognize the necessity of buying wherever we sell, and the permanency of trade lies in its acceptable exchanges. In our pursuit of markets we must give as well as receive. We can not sell to others who do not produce, nor can we buy unless we produce at home. Sensible of every obligation of humanity, commerce and finance, linked as they are in the present world condition, it is not to be argued that we need destroy ourselves to be helpful to others. With all my heart I wish restoration to the peoples blighted by the awful World War, but the process of restoration does not lie in our acceptance of like conditions. It were better to remain on firm ground, strive for ample employment and high standards of wage at home, and point the way to balanced budgets, rigid economies, and resolute, efficient work as the necessary remedies to cure disaster.

Everything relating to trade, among ourselves and among nations, has been expanded, excessive, inflated, abnormal, and there is a madness in finance which no American policy alone will cure. We are a creditor Nation, not by normal processes, but made so by war. It is not an unworthy selfishness to seek to save ourselves, when the processes of that salvation are not only not denied to others, but commended to them. We seek to undermine for others no industry by which they subsist; we are obligated to permit the undermining of none of our own which make for employment and maintained activities.

Every contemplation, it little matters in which direction one turns, magnifies the difficulty of tariff legislation, but the necessity of the revision is magnified with it. Doubtless we are justified in seeking a more flexible policy than we have provided heretofore. I hope a way will be found to make for flexibility and elasticity, so that rates may be adjusted to meet unusual and changing conditions which can not be accurately anticipated. There are problems incident to unfair practices, and to exchanges which madness in money have made almost unsolvable. I know of no manner in which to effect this flexibility other than the extension of the powers of the Tariff Commission, so that it can adapt itself to a scientific and wholly just administration of the law.

I am not unmindful of the constitutional difficulties. These can be met by giving authority to the Chief Executive, who could proclaim additional duties to meet conditions which the Congress may designate.

At this point I must disavow any desire to enlarge the Executive's powers or add to the responsibilities of the office. They are already too large. If there were any other plan I would prefer it.

The grant of authority to proclaim would necessarily bring the Tariff Commission into new and enlarged activities, because no Executive could discharge such a duty except upon the information acquired and recommendations made by this commission. But the plan is feasible, and the proper functioning of the board would give us a better administration of a defined policy than ever can be made possible by tariff duties prescribed without flexibility.

. . .

In this proposed flexibility, authorizing increases to meet conditions so likely to change, there should also be provision for decreases. A rate may be just to-day, and entirely out of proportion six months from to-day. If our tariffs are to be made equitable, and not necessarily burden our imports and hinder our trade abroad, frequent adjustment will be necessary for years to come. Knowing the impossibility of modification by act of Congress for any one or a score of lines without involving a long array of schedules, I think we shall go a long ways toward stabilization, if there is recognition of the Tariff Commission's fitness to recommend urgent changes by proclamation.

I am sure about public opinion favoring the early determination of our tariff policy. There have been reassuring signs of a business revival from the deep slump which all the world has been experiencing. Our unemployment, which gave us deep concern only a few weeks ago, has grown encouragingly less, and new assurances and renewed confidence will attend the congressional declaration that American industry will be held secure.

Israel, Fred L., ed. *The State of the Union Messages of the Presidents*. Vol. 3. New York: Chelsea House, 1967, 2619–2621.

F.W. TAUSSIG—"THE TARIFF ACT OF 1922" (NOVEMBER 1922)

The tariff act of 1913 was in force nine years. A glance at the dates of the acts of similar scope passed during the last forty years—1883, 1890, 1894, 1897, 1909, 1913—shows that one only, that of 1897 had a longer life. The application of moderate duties for nearly a decade, from 1913 to 1922, might have been expected to yield useful experience on some at least of the disputed points of the controversy.

True, it is only on a limited range of questions that helpful conclusions could reasonably be looked for. No trained observer would expect that experience could contribute much toward settling the fundamental question—the effect of such legislation on the general welfare through the greater or less output of material goods. We have here the familiar case of the intermingling of conflicting factors, of confused currents and cross currents. There is no way of disentangling the effects of a change in tariff legislation from those of the many other influences.

It might be otherwise, however, with one important phase of the controversy. What is the effect of a moderation of duties on the protected industries themselves? Would wool-growing, for example, quite disappear from the United States under free wool? Would foreign competition practically sweep away the domestic woolen manufacture under a simple duty of 35 percent on woolen goods? Would sugar continue to be made at all in Louisiana and the states producing beet sugar if imports were free of duty? In all these cases, and in many more, the protectionists predicted that disaster would ensue from such reductions as were made in the act of 1913. The revisionists, on the other hand, maintained that the rates of 1913, on manufactured goods at all events, were high enough to be "competitive"; that they were such as to enable these protected industries to hold their own, even tho importations might be somewhat larger and competition from abroad somewhat sharper. For myself I have long been of the opinion that the extent to which most of the manufacturing industries depend on high protection is habitually exaggerated, and that the industrial readjustment consequent on legislation like that of 1913 would not be far reaching. Certainly the scientific observer would watch the outcome with no little curiosity; and a decade of experience under normal conditions would go far toward supplying an answer.

But, alas! as everyone knows, the years during which the tariff act of 1913 was in force were as far from normal as could possibly be imagined. The war turned everything topsy-turvy. To American manufacturing industries it served as protection more effective than any tariff legislation could possibly be. Not only was foreign importation of competing products completely eliminated, but American goods such as previously had been made at home only under the shelter of high duties were exported to neutral markets. And the years immediately following the war were no less abnormal. We are not a whit wiser than before concerning the extent to which the manufacturing industries, great and small, depend for their existence on the unflinching maintenance of high protection. Consequently when the election of 1920 brought the Republicans into power again and made it certain that the tariff policy of 1913 would be reversed, the debates, so far as concerns this point, were carried on as much in the air as ever. The protectionists predicted ruin unless high duties were restored, but their predictions rested on no more secure basis than in 1913. Those who believed that a considerable reduction of duties could be made without causing an industrial overturn could only argue on the same lines of general reasoning as before. The experiment of 1913 was quite inconclusive.

. . .

Rash as it is to make predictions, I take it on me to state my expectation that a reaction will come. A complete overturn of the protectionist policy is not indeed to be looked for at any time in the visible future. But a return to a more moderate procedure than that of 1922 is fairly to be expected. Sooner or later the wheel of fortune will bring another party into power, or another combination of parties and factions. Then revision of a tariff act like that of 1922 will be peremptorily demanded. The tariff question is not settled; it is likely to remain on the political battlefield for years to come. And this is to be lamented. The industry of the country can accommodate itself to any system, if once the system be settled. The country can adjust itself to extreme protection or high protection or moderate protection or even to free trade, and can go on prosperously under any one of them. But constant vacillations are a great evil. They are not an intolerable evil, for the simple reason that the influence of the protective system on our industrial system, whether for good or ill, is not so far-reaching as most people think. But an influence it has, and that influence is particularly bad in so far as it is inconstant and uncalculable. Much the wiser course, if a protective system must be accepted as part of the settled order of things, would be to shape it in such form that it would endure for a considerable stretch of time; to eliminate the extreme and vulnerable features, and make a serious and honest endeavor to establish a régime with which the community might remain content. Only in this way is it possible—for a period at least—really to take the tariff out of politics. The tariff act of 1922 can serve no such purpose.

Quarterly Journal of Economics 37 (November 1922): 1–3, 27–28.

WASHINGTON CONFERENCE ON THE LIMITATION OF ARMAMENT

Although opposed to U.S. membership in the League of Nations, President Harding did not ignore the issue of how to limit future international disputes. On November 12, 1921, he convened the Washington Conference on the Limitation of Armament, which resulted in a set of treaties designed to avert acts of aggression. International and domestic support for the effort was generally strong, but Harding did face the seemingly inevitable opposition from some senators who argued that even these moderate treaties left the United States in a weakened position and would lead to entangling alliance agreements. Ultimately, the treaties were all approved by the Senate, but the effects were in some ways merely a symbolic end to world tensions.

While the years following the Great War were characterized by a global push for peaceful resolutions to international disputes, there were some disturbing trends that, left unchecked, might have threatened this stability. The most troubling was the incipient naval arms race involving the United States, Great Britain, and Japan. Although the three nations had been allied in the war, America's projected postwar naval expansion (potentially resulting in a fleet of fifty battleships) greatly concerned the other two, who anticipated their own disadvantage, particularly in the Pacific. Many Americans opposed this race for dominance as well, preferring to spend money on domestic needs, and fearing that too much preparation would inevitably lead to war. Furthermore, an arms race with long-time ally Great Britain seemed particularly unpalatable, and one with Japan was frightening, given the more tenuous American relationship with that nation, as well as Japan's apparent aspirations to empire building.

Responding to these national and international concerns, Harding called for a conference to assemble in November 1921. In addition to Great Britain and Japan, delegations from France, Italy, China, Belgium, the Netherlands, and Portugal were invited. The conference began dramatically, with a ceremony at the Tomb of the Unknown Soldier at Arlington National Cemetery on Armistice Day. Harding made an emotional plea that day that "his sacrifice, and that of the millions of dead, shall not be in vain."[1]

The following day, Secretary of State (and head of the U.S. delegation) Charles Evans Hughes made a stunning speech to the delegation. Although the conferees were prepared to discuss arms reductions, Hughes startled the group with very specific recommendations for naval limitations based on a 5:5:3 ratio of battleship tonnage to the United States Great Britain, and Japan, respectively. This in itself was not especially surprising, as it roughly reflected the existing balance of battleship strength. But Hughes proposed to formalize this benchmark by scrapping ships under construction, and scuttling some ships that were already built. Despite the shocked reaction (especially from the head of the British navy), the delegates cheered for ten minutes at the completion of the speech. These proposals formed the basis of one of the major accomplishments of the conference—the Five Power Treaty, signed by the United States, Great Britain, Japan, Italy, and France (each granted a 1.75 tonnage ratio).

After working for three months, the delegates completed six additional treaties. With the exception of one agreement outlawing the use of poison gases in war, these focused on stabilizing the Pacific region. In addition to the Five Power Treaty, two others were notable. The Nine Power Treaty was an agreement by all delegations to respect the so-called Open Door policy of nonaggression and mutual trade opportunities in China. But, of greatest consternation to some senators was the Four Power Treaty, signed by the United States, Great Britain, Japan, and France, which provided for the signatories to "communicate with each other fully and frankly in order to arrive at an understanding as to the most efficient measures to be taken, jointly or separately,"[2] in the event that the insular possessions of any one were threatened by a nation outside of the pact. Although the wording did not mandate defensive partnerships, this clause was seen as a trigger to potentially entangling alliances. Additionally, confusion over whether the agreement would extend to the islands of the Japanese nation itself (in the final version, it did not) led to accusations that the wording was designed to mislead the American people. Before the treaties even got to a full Senate vote, a reservation clause stating the United States would be under no obligation to join in any military action was added by the Senate Foreign Relations Committee.

As noted in his message to the Senate advocating approval of all the treaties, Harding saw no dangers in the agreements, and emphasized the contribution to future global stability that these pacts represented. He was somewhat annoyed by the added reservation clause, feeling it to be unnecessary, but did not fight it. Opposition to the treaties, particularly the Four Power Treaty, was largely comprised of the previous irreconcilable critics of the League of Nations. Senator James A. Reed (D–Miss.) led the fight with a two-day speech focusing on the potential dangers of U.S. approval.

But, this issue did not generate nearly the same level of hostilities as the League of Nations had. Most senators recognized the nonbinding nature of the agreements, and Harding had avoided Wilson's earlier mistake of excluding the Senate from negotiations by making sure to include three senators (two Republicans and a Democrat) in the U.S. delegation. Additionally, public opinion was generally supportive of the agreements and the nation's newspapers widely recommended approval.

By April 1922, all of the treaties had been approved by the Senate. Although Japan was somewhat dissatisfied with the outcome (there would be much later discussion over whether the treaties ultimately strengthened or weakened Japan's military capabilities), one triumph of the Washington Conference was an at least short-term optimism among all participant nations. In terms of longer lasting effects, the Five Power Treaty did have a noticeable, limiting influence on the role of the battleship in naval engagements. But whether this brought about a decline in the level of future hostilities is debatable. With construction of these ships largely halted, attention turned instead to innovation and development of other instruments of naval warfare such as cruisers, aircraft carriers, and airplanes. The Four Power Treaty was never invoked, and was abrogated in the 1930s.

NOTES

1. Robert K. Murray, *The Harding Era* (Minneapolis: University of Minnesota Press, 1969), 149.

2. "Reed Fights Treaty as Japan's Victory," *New York Times*, December 17, 1921, 1.

HARDING—ADDRESS TO THE SENATE ON THE WASHINGTON CONFERENCE (FEBRUARY 10, 1922)

I have come to make report to you of the conclusions of what has been termed the Washington Conference on the Limitation of Armament, and to lay before you the series of treaties which the United States and the other powers participating in the conference have negotiated and signed, and have announced to the world. Apart from the very great satisfaction in reporting to the Senate, it is a privilege as well as a duty to ask that advice and consent which the Constitution requires to make these covenants effective. . . .

I am not unmindful, nor was the conference, of the sentiment in this Chamber against Old World entanglements. Those who made the treaties have left no doubt about their true import. Every expression in the conference has emphasized the purpose to be served and the obligations to be assumed. Therefore, I can bring you every assurance that nothing in any of these treaties commits the United States, or any other power, to any kind of an alliance, entanglement, or involvement. It does not require us or any power to surrender a worth-while tradition. It has been said, if this be true, these are mere meaningless treaties, and therefore valueless. Let us accept no such doctrine of despair as that. If nations may not establish by mutual understanding the rules and principles which are to govern their relationship; if a sovereign and solemn plight of faith by leading nations of the earth is valueless; if nations may not trust one another, then, indeed, there is little on which to hand our faith in advancing civilization or the furtherance of peace. Either we must live and aspire and achieve under a free and common understanding among peoples, with mutual trust, respect, and forbearance, and exercising full sovereignty, or else brutal, armed force will dominate, and the sorrows and burdens of war in this decade will be turned to the chaos and hopelessness of the next. We can no more do without international negotiations and agreements in these modern days than we could maintain orderly neighborliness at home without the prescribed rules of conduct which are more the guaranties of freedom than the restraint thereof. . . .

The four-power treaty contains no war commitment. It covenants the respect of each nation's rights in relation to its insular possessions. In case of controversy between the covenanting powers it is agreed to confer and seek adjustment, and if said rights are threatened by the aggressive action of any outside power, these friendly powers, respecting one another, are to communicate, perhaps confer, in order to understand what action may be taken, jointly or separately, to meet a menacing situation. There is no commitment to armed force, no alliance, no written or moral obligation to join in defence, no expressed or implied commitment to arrive at any agreement except in accordance with our constitutional methods. It is easy to believe, however, that such a conference of the four powers is a moral warning that an aggressive nation, given affront to the four great powers ready to focus world opinion on a given controversy, would be embarking on a hazardous enterprise.

Frankly, Senators, if nations may not safely agree to respect each other's rights, and may not agree to confer if one to the compact threatens trespass, or may not agree to advise if one party to the pact is threatened by an outside power, then all concerted efforts to tranquilize the world and stabilize peace must be flung to the winds. Either these treaties must have your cordial sanction, or every proclaimed desire to promote peace and prevent war becomes a hollow mockery. . . .

We have convinced the on-looking and interested powers that we covet the possessions of no other power in the Far East, and we know for ourselves that we crave no further or greater governmental or territorial responsibilities there. Contemplating what is admittedly ours, and mindful of a long-time and reciprocal friendship with China, we do wish the opportunity to continue the development of our trade peacefully, and on equality with other nations, to strengthen our ties of friendship, and to make sure the righteous and just relationships of peace.

Holding the possessions we do, entertaining these views, and confessing these ambitions, why should we not make reciprocal engagements to respect the territory of others and contract their respect of ours, and thus quiet apprehension and put an end to suspicion?

There has been concern. There has been apprehension of territorial greed, a most fruitful cause of war. The conference has dissipated both, and your ratification of the covenants made will stabilize a peace for the breaking of which there is not a shadow of reason or real excuse. We shall not have less than before. No one of us shall have less than before. There is no narrowed liberty, no hampered independence, no shattered sovereignty, no added obligation. We have new assurances, new freedom from anxiety, and new manifestations of the sincerity of our own intentions; a new demonstration of that honesty which proclaims a righteous and powerful republic.

I am ready to assume the sincerity and the dependability of the assurances of our neighbors of the Old World that they will respect our rights, just as I know we mean to respect theirs. I believe there is an inviolable national honor, and I bring to you this particular covenant in the confident belief that it is the outstanding compact of peace for the Pacific, which will justify the limitation of armament and prove a new guarantee to peace and liberty, and maintained sovereignty and free institutions.

Congressional Record. 67th Congress, 2nd sess., 1922. Senate Docs., vol. 10, no. 126, 7, 10–13.

SENATOR JAMES A. REED—REMARKS
ON THE WASHINGTON CONFERENCE TREATIES
(DECEMBER 15–16, 1921)

We all long for the day when the substance of the people of the world will not be consumed in preparations for war, and when the race in the creation of armaments shall have ceased. To the realization of such a hope we are all devoted.

But, the reduction of the number of ships of the United States Navy and a corresponding reduction in the number of ships of the navies of the other nations of the world has no proper relation to an American-Anglo Franco-Japanese alliance. The plain truth is that an attempt is being forced to make the proposition of reduction of armaments the pack horse upon whose sagging back shall be loaded a quadruple alliance made for the protection of the interests of Japan and Great Britain in the Orient, to compel the United States of America to underwrite, in the blood of its sons, the ambition and avarice of Great Britain and Japan in the Pacific Ocean. . . .

The language employed in treaties is not the language which is employed between individuals. Phrases have a peculiar meaning. No nation preparing to form an offensive alliance has ever written in to the treaty that it is forming such alliance for the purpose of destroying or making war on some other nation. The universal language of such a treaty is that the nations are joined together for the purpose of preserving the peace, for the purpose of mutual protection, for the purpose of saving themselves or the world from destruction. Whenever the agreement is made that they will stand by each other, there is but one construction placed upon that kind of proposition, when it comes to a practical test, and that is that they shall make war side by side. It has been true in every period of history. . . .

Now, let us suppose that some of these islands are attacked by some power and that thereupon we consult together and we come to the rescue of the country whose islands are being attacked. Suppose we do that. Does the Senator from North Carolina [Senator Lee S. Overman] think—I am sure he does not—that the fight would be confined to that island? Certainly, the fight would not be started until it would be spread to every vessel of the two nations upon the sea, to their entire commerce, and to attack upon their mainland, if necessary.

Let us be practical. War is war, and once war has been started it can not be confined to a particular spot of earth. Do we need any other illustration than the events of the last few years? An Austrian archduke went across the line into Serbia. A single individual shot him.

That was the spark that lighted the conflagration that blazed around the world. . . .

To talk of confining a war to the Pacific or to the islands of the Pacific would be childish, because a war once started is a war that involves both nations at least and all their members and all parties to the controversy wherever their trade and territory may lie. . . .

I wish we could bring the President back to the sound, solid ground, the ground that Washington took [as stated by Harding]:

"We sense the call of the human heart for fellowship, fraternity, and cooperation. We crave friendship and harbor no hate."

Beautiful words, and very true, although I could always get enough fellowship somewhere within the confines of the United States. I never found myself getting homesick for some foreign stepmother. We have been indulging in a good deal of verbal mush lately, talking about our hearts longing for fellowship with countries we never saw and with people whose language we can not understand. It would be more consistent with good sense if we said: We respect the peoples of other lands; we ask them to respect us and our rights. . . .

But it is proposed here that we shall enter into an agreement which I say no honest man can deny binds us to submit great and vital questions to the arbitrament of three other powers associated with us. Not the American conscience in that case, but mayhap the Japanese conscience will command us. . . .

I wonder how much confidence springs to the hearts of the American people when they think: "If any of our possessions in the Pacific should be attacked, we have Japan to rely on." With what serene confidence we could go to bed at night and say, "Japan is looking after the Phillippines"! Why not junk our Navy altogether, and just trust this whole thing to Japan and Great Britain?

What do we receive from this treaty? . . . We have no oriental possessions except the Philippine Islands. We ought to give the Phillippines their liberty, and I am in favor of doing it . . .

What, then, do we get? Substantially nothing.

What do the other parties to this compact get? All the islands of the Pacific Ocean, outside of the Philippines and the Hawaiian Islands, are owned by these other nations, or controlled by them, or claimed by them. They get our contract to defend these islands that are "scattered like lilies" over the ocean. They get our contract to defend the whole domain of Japan; for, as I have shown, Japan is all insular. They get our contract to preserve their peace, even though China might rise some day to demand back the loot. They get our contract to defend these islands, even though Russia should some day seek to drive the Japs from her soil, and in so doing contract that we, with our men and our money, with our blood and our treasure, with our Army and our Navy, will respond to the "understanding as to the most efficient measures to be taken, jointly or separately, to meet the exigencies of the particular occasion"—which is a war, as shown by the context.

Congressional Record. 67th Congress, 2nd sess., 1921. Vol. 62, 436, 440, 442, 446–447.

THE SOLDIERS' BONUS

In his attempt to restore the postwar economy to "normalcy," Harding clashed with Congress over a bipartisan effort to provide payments to veterans. The president's opposition to the so-called soldiers' bonus on the grounds that it would represent a serious financial setback to the national budget received little sympathy from legislators anxious to please the returning veterans and the groups representing their interests. Although several newspapers lauded the president's decision as courageous and responsible, many members of Congress portrayed his position as one that ignored the needs of a deserving class of Americans.

America's Great War veterans did not generally enjoy a triumphant homecoming. Many of these men, whose only previous notions of warfare were idealized versions of the glories of the Civil War, returned shocked and disillusioned with their own experiences with trench warfare, poison gas, tanks, and machine guns. Furthermore, they returned to a volatile economy, and many had trouble getting jobs and restarting their civilian lives. Some states provided small monetary sums to help these men make the transition, but the demand for a larger, federal source of assistance to help them catch up began to grow. While this was not a key issue in the 1920 presidential campaign, an initial "adjusted compensation" bill was taken up in the Senate in the summer of 1921.

Harding was extremely concerned with this proposal because it contained no provision for financing—money would be spent, but it was not clear where it would come from. This was just the sort of law that the new president did not want passed at that time. His immediate focus was to cut the income tax rate that had been increased sharply (especially on higher incomes) to help finance the war effort, and policies requiring additional expenditures were antithetical to this goal. At that time, Harding personally delivered a speech in the Senate asking that the bonus bill be at least temporarily delayed, as it represented a potential disaster to the nation's finances. The Senate acquiesced, but the issue would soon return.

By the spring of 1922, many members of Congress, especially Republicans (who already feared that they might suffer from the public's aversion to some of the president's policies) became convinced that passing the bonus bill was an important factor in their potential reelection. It is difficult to judge whether this was a correct assessment. The nation's major newspapers almost unanimously opposed the very costly bill as fiscally irresponsible, and there is no clear indication of any sort of great public demand for the law. However, the American Legion and other groups supporting veterans' issues threatened legislators with the loss of veterans' votes if the bill failed. Thus, the House passed the bill in March and the Senate in August.

The Soldiers' Adjusted Compensation Act provided payments of $1 per day of service within the United States, and $1.25 per day for overseas service. Certificates issued to each veteran could be immediately cashed, or saved and allowed to accrue interest. A public bond was to be issued to help provide financing.

Harding vetoed the bill on September 19, 1922, just days before Congress adjourned for the election recess. In his veto message, he stressed the importance of fiscal accountability, and stated that the bill would have been much more palatable if an immediate and certain source of funds had been mandated, such as a sales tax. Harding also opposed the bill in more general terms, arguing against the use of any "class" legislation designed solely to benefit a single group of Americans, and questioning whether it was proper to reward the patriotic sacrifice of military service with cash. The veto message also noted the substantial federal aid that had been given to injured veterans and would be paid out in future soldiers' pensions.

Members of Congress reacted angrily to the veto. Senator James A. Reed in particular gave an impassioned speech on the Senate floor that was greeted with applause from the public galleries. Reed had a field day attacking Harding's seemingly thoughtless assertion that many veterans "came forth physically, mentally, and spiritually richer for the great experience." Additionally, he tied the bonus issue to Harding's advocacy of the tariff, ridiculing the president for referring negatively to the bonus bill as class legislation when the restoration of tariffs would protect the very wealthy class of American manufacturers.

A veto override (requiring a ⅔ majority) was narrowly defeated, and the soldiers' bonus would not come up again in the Harding administration. Republicans did suffer losses in the November elections (although they retained a majority in both houses), but it is impossible to gauge how much of this can be attributed to failure of the bonus bill. This issue returned in the Coolidge administration, when a bill providing bonuses in the form of paid up life insurance policies that could be cashed out in twenty years was passed over the president's veto. In 1932, veterans demanded that the policies be eligible for immediate cash out. President Herbert Hoover's refusal to comply led to the arrival, encampment, and ultimate National Guard dispersal of an impoverished veterans "Bonus Army" in Washington, D.C., one of the most dismal chapters of the Great Depression.

HARDING—VETO OF SOLDIERS' BONUS
(SEPTEMBER 19, 1922)

Herewith is returned, without approval, a bill "to provide adjusted compensation for the veterans of the World War, and for other purposes."

With the avowed purpose of the bill to give expression of a nation's gratitude to those who served in its defense in the World War I am in accord, but to its provisions I do not subscribe. The United States never will cease to be grateful; it can not and never will cease giving expression to that gratitude.

In legislating for what is called adjusted compensation Congress fails, first of all, to provide the revenue from which the bestowal is to be paid. Moreover, it establishes the very dangerous precedent of creating a Treasury covenant to pay which puts a burden variously estimated between four and five billions upon the American people, not to discharge an obligation which the Government always must pay, but to bestow a bonus which the soldiers themselves while serving in the World War did not expect.

It is not to be denied that the Nation has certain very binding obligations to those of its defenders who made real sacrifices in the World War, and who left the armies injured, disabled, or diseased so that they could not resume their places in the normal activities of life. These obligations are being gladly and generously met. . . .

Though undying gratitude is the meed of everyone who served, it is not to be said that a material bestowal is an obligation to those who emerged from the great conflict not only unharmed but physically, mentally, and spiritually richer for the great experience. If an obligation were to be admitted, it would be to charge the adjusted compensation bill with inadequacy and stinginess wholly unbecoming our Republic. Such a bestowal, to be worth while, must be generous and without apology. Clearly the bill returned herewith takes cognizance of the inability of the Government wisely to bestow, and says, in substance, "We do not have the cash; we do not believe in a tax levy to meet the situation, but here is our note; you may have our credit for half its worth." This is not compensation, but rather a pledge by the Congress, while the executive branch of the Government is left to provide for payments falling due in ever-increasing amounts.

When the bill was under consideration in the House I expressed the conviction that any grant of bonus ought to provide the means of paying it, and I was unable to suggest any plan other than that of a general sales tax. Such a plan was unacceptable to the Congress, and the bill has been enacted without even a suggested means of meeting the cost. . . .

It is worth remembering that the public credit is founded on the popular belief in the defensibility of public expenditures as well as the Government's ability to pay. Loans come from every rank in life, and our heavy tax burdens reach, directly or indirectly, every element of our citizenship. To add one-sixth of the total sum of our public debt for a distribution among less than 5,000,000 out of 110,000,000, whether inspired by grateful sentiment or political expediency, would undermine the confidence on which our credit is builded and establish the precedent of distributing public funds whenever the proposal and the numbers affected make it seem politically appealing to do so. . . .

It is sometimes thoughtlessly urged that it is a simple thing for the rich Republic to add four billions to its indebtedness. This impression comes from the readiness of the public response to the Government's appeal for funds amid the stress of war. It is to be remembered that in the war everybody was ready to give his all. Let us not recall the comparatively few exceptions. Citizens of every degree of competence loaned and sacrificed, precisely in the same spirit that our armed forces went out for service. The war spirit impelled. To a war necessity there was but one answer, but a peace bestowal on the ex-service men, as though the supreme offering could be paid for with cash, is a perversion of public funds, a reversal of the policy which exalted patriotic service in the past, and suggests that future defense is to be inspired by compensation rather than consciousness of duty to flag and country. . . .

I confess a regret that I must sound a note of disappointment to the many ex-service men who have the impression that it is as simple a matter for the Government to bestow billions in peace as it was to expend billions in war. I regret to stand between them and the pitiably small compensation proposed. I dislike to be out of accord with the majority of Congress which has voted the bestowal. The simple truth is that this bill proposes a Government obligation of more than four billions without a provision of funds for the extraordinary expenditure, which the executive branch of the Government must finance in the face of difficult financial problems, and the complete defeat of our commitment to effect economies. I would rather appeal, therefore, to the candid reflections of Congress and the country, and to the ex-service men in particular, as to the course better suited to further the welfare of our country. These ex-soldiers who served so gallantly in war, and who are to be so conspicuous in the progress of the Republic in the half century before us, must know that nations can only survive where taxation is restrained from the limits of oppressions, where the Public Treasury is locked against class legislation, but ever open to public necessity and prepared to meet all essential obligations. Such a policy makes a better country for which to fight, or to have fought, and affords a surer abiding place in which to live and attain.

Congressional Record. 67th Congress, 2nd sess., 1922. Vol. 62, 12981–12982.

SENATOR JAMES A. REED—REMARKS ON VETO OF SOLDIERS' BONUS (SEPTEMBER 20, 1922)

I dislike very much to criticize any document prepared by the President of the United States or under his direction, but I can not refrain from calling attention to the President's very remarkable veto of the bonus bill. I affirm first that a fair reading of the veto message will convince any man that it is the fixed purpose of the administration to kill every bonus bill which may be devised. As we read through the document and encounter the various arguments, verbal subterfuges, and special pleadings the conviction that there is no provision made in the bill for funds with which to pay the bonus, is after all, only a plausible excuse back of which there is no merit, and that it is thrust forward for the purpose of covering the real intent of the administration, which is to deny the bonus in toto and as a finality. . . .

All through the document runs the idea that there is no obligation, that there is no duty upon Congress, but that what we are giving to the soldiers and sailors of the war is in the nature of a gift, and a gift unjustifiable and unwarranted. If that is true, what is the use of longer spending our time discussing the questions? If that is the position taken by the administration, then the administration is taking it not only for to-day, not because the bill does not carry a revenue provision in it out of which to compensate the soldiers; but it is a finality. If the arguments be true, the bonus never should be paid, and that is the position taken by the administration.

If the administration is right when it states that every man who entered the war and came out without being maimed or crippled received a physical development and was "mentally and spiritually richer for the great experience," then war, instead of being a curse is, after all, a blessing and we ought to take the figure of Justice from above the Capitol of the Nation and put up a brass figure of the god Mars. What say the boys who went into the struggle? Do they think it was a spiritual and physical and mental uplift which conferred benefits upon all the millions and offset any sacrifice they may have made, and therefore they shall be paid nothing on account of financial loss?

A little later in the instrument the President declares that when the war was being waged all classes of people rallied to support the Government. That is true. I apprehend, then if they all rallied to support the Government that they all got the same spiritual and mental uplift that the soldier did who went to the front. Yet when we are presented with this proposition, what is the position of the administration? The proposition is that the soldier who went to the front and suffered financial loss peculiar to his having gone to the front and springing directly from his having been taken away from his home and his business, shall not receive any money because he enjoyed a spiritual and mental uplift. . . .

I utterly repudiate the idea that the bill provides a gift or that it is a bonus. . . . It is calculated only to equalize as far as practicable the financial loss the soldiers sustained through going into the war with what he would have received if he had not gone into the war. . . .

Moreover, the President's excuse is that no revenue is provided. When did it happen that in time of war the Government never incurred an obligation until the revenue was provided? I class this as a war measure, for it springs out of the war; it is the last, the final payment, perhaps, of the war. We settled our other obligations after the war was over, and we settled them out of the proceeds of the sale of bonds. . . .

The President, however, says that this obligation which springs out of the war can not be incurred because the money is not in sight. . . . So far as I am concerned, so long as we can issue bonds to pay for the goods we obtained in the war—and that was proper—I contend that we ought not to refuse to issue bonds, if necessary, to pay a compensation to the soldiers of the war which is morally due to them. . . .

Finally, we get to the humor of this message—and the President is always a humorist; perhaps an unconscious one, but a humorist just the same—when he says: ". . . the public treasury is locked against class legislation."

And yet, as his veto message has been delivered to this Chamber while I have been speaking, there is being carried to the other end of the Capitol the final amendment to a tariff bill which is nothing but class legislation from the first line to the last word; legislation in favor of the great manufacturing class; legislation in favor of the great moneyed class. . . .

Class legislation! This morning we have levied a tax upon every man and woman who drinks a cup of coffee with a little sugar in it, and we have levied that for a class of citizens dealing in sugar.

Class legislation! We have levied a tax upon wool, so that every man, woman, and child in this country who wears a woolen garment shall pay a tax to the classes that are interested in the production of wool and its manufacture. . . .

Class legislation! Let us have a little legislation in favor of that class who stood on the red line of battle, who looked into the mouth of hell, whose brothers went to their death with cheers upon their lips; that class of boys whose hearts beat strong and whose eyes were clear when they floated in the air 10,000 feet above the earth—class legislation for the men that saved the United States of America. Let us not hear the words, "class legislation" from those whose hands are polluted by the robbery of the American people which you have just perpetrated.

Congressional Record. 67th Congress, 2nd sess., 1922. Vol. 62, 12976–12978.

PROHIBITION

One of the more difficult issues that Harding inherited as president was Prohibition. When he took office, the Eighteenth Amendment, which prohibited the manufacture, sale, and transport of alcoholic beverages, had been in effect for a little over a year. Although it seemed as though acceptance of the amendment would have finally laid the long controversy between "wets" (Prohibition opponents) and "drys" (Prohibition supporters) to rest, the debate continued. Harding was forced to strongly defend this new policy as it was becoming clear to many Americans that it was just not working.

When Prohibition became constitutional law in 1920, it represented the culmination of a protracted and changing battle over a century in duration. As early as 1820, groups had formed in support of temperance, at that time a social movement merely encouraging moderation in drinking. By the late nineteenth century, the movement had evolved into the advocacy of laws banning liquor entirely. Although Prohibition is sometimes seen as a progressive reform, the success of the Eighteenth Amendment was attributable more to conservative, rural interests than to the traditional liberal, urban progressive coalition. Many advocates of Prohibition also tended to support immigration restrictions, anti-Catholic and anti-Jewish sentiment, and white supremacy, as they associated the evils of liquor with foreigners and blacks.

While Harding did not preside over the adoption of Prohibition, he was looked to as the president who would ensure its implementation. (Although Wilson's final year in office overlapped with the policy, he was tepid on its enforcement, since he believed it to be an unwarranted infringement on state sovereignty.) As the Eighteenth Amendment was silent on how the manufacture, sale, and transportation of liquor would be prohibited, the Volstead Act had been passed in January 1920, providing for a Bureau of Prohibition that would be provided funding to hire agents to enforce the ban. State enabling laws supporting and supplementing the Volstead Act were also passed. But enforcement proved to be the destructive flaw of Prohibition. The bureau was run inefficiently and in some instances even corruptly, and there was a great deal of federal and state rivalry over enforcement powers. But it is questionable whether any force of federal and state agents could have adequately implemented this policy. The banned activities were simply too broad, and the nation too large, to effectively control.

Despite these difficulties, however, Harding was an unwavering advocate of the policy. Although he was a drinker (at least until early 1923, when he took a pledge of abstention), he took the "dry" position in his 1920 campaign against a "wet" opponent, Democrat James Cox, the governor of Ohio, and was supported by the most powerful temperance group of the times, the Anti-Saloon League. When the New York state legislature revoked its own enforcement statute in May 1923, Harding warned Governor Alfred E. Smith, "It is difficult to believe that public approval will ever be given to any other than a policy of fully and literally discharging this duty."[1] In his speech given in Denver on the western speaking tour just two months before his death, the president acknowledged some of the difficulties but continued his dogged support of this policy that he felt was every American's duty to obey.

But Harding seemed increasingly out of touch on this issue. Public opinion in support of Prohibition was rapidly declining. Enforcement appeared to be causing more problems than it solved, and people could see that the criminalization of liquor did not end its influence—it simply turned the industry over to criminals. A *Literary Digest* poll taken in September 1922 reported that only 38.6 percent of Americans supported enforcement through the Volstead Act, while 40.8 percent supported some sort of modification (e.g., exempting beer and wine) and 20.6 percent supported outright repeal.

Just as women's organizations had been an important component of the temperance movement, women were also involved in the fight to end Prohibition. One of the more active groups was the Women's Organization for National Prohibition Reform, founded by Pauline Morton Sabin. Sabin (the Morton Salt heiress, granddaughter of the governor of Nebraska, and daughter of Roosevelt's secretary of the navy) was prominent in American society and the Republican Party. Although initially a supporter of Prohibition, she, like many other Americans, changed her mind. For Sabin, the great danger of Prohibition was that enforcement had come to be treated as joke by many citizens, thus threatening the very legitimacy of government. Since, in addition, the policy had failed to eliminate most of the evils associated with drinking, and indeed had exacerbated many of them, she advocated repeal.

The debate continued through the Harding and Coolidge administrations but reached new heights during the 1928 presidential campaign. Although the winner, Hoover, was a "dry," his opponent, Governor Smith of New York, was able to attract great support through his repeal position. In the campaign of 1932, Franklin D. Roosevelt also pledged to end Prohibition (even the Republicans promised to modify it), and the Eighteenth Amendment was officially repealed through passage of the Twenty-first Amendment in 1933.

NOTE

1. Mark Sullivan, *Our Times, 1900–1925*, vol. 6 (New York: Scribner's, 1939), 214.

HARDING—REMARKS ON PROHIBITION (JUNE 25, 1923)

The prohibition amendment to the Constitution is the basic law of the land. The Volstead Act, providing a code of enforcement, has been passed. I am convinced that they are a small, and a greatly mistaken, minority who believe the eighteenth amendment will ever be repealed. Details of enforcement policy doubtless will be changed as experience dictates. Further, I am convinced that whatever changes may be made will represent the sincere purpose of effective enforcement, rather than moderation of the general policy. It will be the part of wisdom to recognize the facts as they stand.

The general policy of the States to support the prohibition program, and to cooperate with the Federal government regarding it, is attested by the fact that almost unanimously the States have passed enforcement laws of their own. A difficulty, however, arises at this point. Considerable testimony comes to Washington that some States are disposed to abdicate their own police authority in this matter, and to turn over the burden of prohibition enforcement to the Federal authorities. It is a singular fact that some States which successfully enforced their own prohibition statutes before the eighteenth amendment was adopted have latterly gone backwards in this regard.

. . .

. . . The National policy ought to be supported by the public opinion and the administrative machinery of the whole country. For myself, I am confident that we are passing now through the most difficult stage of this matter, and that as time passes there will be a more and more willing acceptance by authorities everywhere of the unalterable obligation of law enforcement. The country and the Nation will not permit the law of the land to be made a byword.

This issue is fast coming to be recognized, not as one between wets and drys, not as a question between those who believe in prohibition and those who do not, not as a contention between those who want to drink and those who do not—it is fast being raised above all that—but as one involving the great question whether the laws of this country can be and will be enforced. So far as the Federal government is concerned, and, I am very sure, also so far as concerns the very great majority of the State governments and the local governments, it will be enforced. A gratifying, indeed it may fairly be said an amazing, progress has been made in the last few years toward better enforcement.

. . .

It was very generally believed that the adoption of the constitutional amendment would take the question out of our politics. Thus far it has not done so, though I venture to predict that neither of the great parties will see the time, within the lives of any who are now voting citizens, when it will declare openly for the repeal of the eighteenth amendment. But, despite all that, the question is kept in politics because of the almost fanatical urgency of the minority of extremists on both sides. Unless, through the recognition and acceptance of the situation in its true light, through the effective enforcement of the law by all the constituted authorities, and with the acquiescence of the clearly dominant public opinion of the country, the question is definitely removed from the domain of political action, it will continue a demoralizing element in our whole public life. It will be a permanent bar to the wise determination of many issues utterly unrelated to the liquor question. It will be the means of encouraging disrespect for many laws. It will bring disrepute upon our community, and be pointed to as justifying the charge that we are a Nation of hypocrites. There can be no issue in this land paramount to that of enforcement of the law.

Speeches and Addresses of Warren G. Harding. Washington, D.C.: U.S. Government Printing Office, 1923, 105–109.

PAULINE MORTON SABIN—"I CHANGE MY MIND ON PROHIBITION" (JUNE 13, 1928)

We have a Prohibition Law. It is embedded in the Constitution. We have had it for eight years. If it means anything and is to be taken seriously, it means that no person in the United States shall be able to obtain anything to drink that may be intoxicating. Millions of people are discussing it. It is the prevailing topic of conversation in every walk of life. Every one is analyzing and estimating the effect of this effort to compel all Americans to be total abstainers. I have watched its workings during the years, commencing in a sympathetic frame of mind. I have reached certain conclusions and am willing to set them down here, conscious of my fallibility but anxious to contribute my little bit toward a wise solution.

It is true that we no longer see the corner saloon; but in many cases has it not merely moved to the back of a store or up one flight under the name of a "speak-easy"?

It is true that in our universities groups of boys can no longer go together to a *Rathskeller* and drink their beer genially and in the open. Is it not true that they are making their own gin and drinking it furtively in their rooms? Indeed, the authorities of certain colleges have instituted the practice of searching the students' rooms, without their consent and during their absence.

It is against the law to sell alcoholic beverages, but hundreds of thousands of respected citizens are daily conniving at the breaking of that law by buying it. And most of them realize that the beverage reaches them through channels extending through a long line of law violation and corruption down to the consumer.

In my opinion, the majority of women with young children favored prohibition because they felt that when the Eighteenth Amendment was enacted drinking to excess would never be a problem in their children's lives, that temptation would be completely eliminated. But now they are wondering and troubled about the result. They have found that their children are growing up with a total lack of respect for the Constitution and for the law.

We must admit that many of the parents are responsible for this attitude among the young, owing to the example they set in breaking this particular law. In connection with the attitude of the youth of the Nation today towards the Constitution, I want to cite two incidents which have been brought to my attention recently.

The first is the case of six boys between the ages of fifteen and eighteen, who were students at one of the oldest and most respected private schools in the country. An older person asked these boys a few questions regarding the Constitution of the United States. Not one of them had any knowledge of the Constitution nor its Amendments, with the exception of the Eighteenth, and in chorus they shouted they knew about that. The manner in which they said it proved that they held that Amendment in great derision.

To my mind, this was a shocking revelation. I do not deny that this situation was largely the fault of both the school and the parents of the boys for not having taught them about the most sacred of our political documents. How unfortunate that the Eighteenth Amendment should typify the Constitution to our children—the one Amendment which they are conscious is not being upheld, and the one Amendment which many of us feel is contrary to the spirit of the rest of the Constitution, as it is the only Amendment which curtails personal liberty, the only one which attempts to control the habits of a human being.

The other incident I have in mind occurred at the conference which was called last year by one of the colleges, and to which the various preparatory schools were asked to send a representative boy, to discuss the "transition period between school and college." A boy I know was selected to represent his school. He has since told me that one of the subjects discussed was the pros and cons of drinking at college. The discussion lasted for over an hour, each boy having something to contribute to the subject. It was approached from various angles—the effect of drinking on athletics, on scholastic standing, and on a boy's reputation as a good fellow. Not once during the discussion did any boy mention the fact that prohibition was the law of the land. In other words, that phase of the situation was completely ignored, just as though the Eighteenth Amendment had never been enacted. In my opinion, this is an eloquent commentary on the status of prohibition among the younger generation.

I was one of the women who favored prohibition when I heard it discussed in the abstract, but I am now convinced that it has been proved a failure. Its effect upon the coming generation is so grave and so serious that all women who have come to this conclusion (and I believe there are many thousands of them) should organize and work for a repeal of the Eighteenth Amendment and in its place a substitution of some law that will bring about true temperance and respect for law.

The adoption of the Eighteenth Amendment was due, to a great extent, to the influence and efforts of women. They conscientiously believed that the result would be beneficial, but I think there has been a tremendous change in the sentiment of women during recent years.

The Outlook. June 13, 1928, 254.

RECOMMENDED READINGS

Bagby, Wesley M. *The Road to Normalcy: The Presidential Campaign and Election of 1920*. Baltimore, Md.: Johns Hopkins University Press, 1962.

Ferrell, Robert H. *The Strange Deaths of President Harding*. Columbia: University of Missouri Press, 1996.

Grieb, Kenneth J. *The Latin American Policy of Warren G. Harding*. Fort Worth: Texas Christian University Press, 1976.

Hicks, John D. *Republican Ascendancy, 1921–1933*. New York: Harper, 1960.

Kaufman, Robert Gordon. *Arms Control in the Pre-Nuclear Era: The United States and Naval Limitation Between the Wars.* Columbia: University of Missouri Press, 1990.

Murray, Robert K. *The Harding Era.* Minneapolis: University of Minnesota Press, 1969.

Sherman, Richard B. "The Harding Administration and the Negro: An Opportunity Lost." *Journal of Negro History* 49 (1964): 151–168.

Sinclair, Andrew. *The Available Man.* New York: Macmillan, 1965.

5

CALVIN COOLIDGE

(1923–1929)

INTRODUCTION

Given the common portrayal of Calvin Coolidge as a terse and taciturn man virtually antithetical to active predecessors such as Theodore Roosevelt and Woodrow Wilson, it is easy to dismiss his administration as fairly devoid of content. But this would not be an accurate assessment. In comparison with his predecessor Warren G. Harding, who, for the most part, *reacted* to the nation's issues, Coolidge offered a more decisive agenda. Because it involved a reduced federal presence, however, it is somewhat invisible in retrospect. Yet, in the economic realm in particular, Coolidge, while continuing Harding's attempt to shrink expenditures and restore the economy to prewar status, provided more of a vision of budgetary and taxation theory, expressly advocating tax relief for wealthier Americans as a means to jumpstart the entire economy. In the social and foreign policy realms, while generally favoring a reduction in government activities, Coolidge was obliged to decisively advance particular policies in regard to international stability, some of which represent key transitions between this period and the subsequent era of the Great Depression and the New Deal.

Ironically, the Republican Coolidge, like Roosevelt, can best be understood as a career politician driven by a duty to public service. However, unlike Roosevelt, he did not bask in the role, treating it more with grim determination. Coolidge, the descendant of Vermont dairy farmers and shopkeepers, and an attorney by profession, duly worked his way up through elected offices from the local to state level in Massachusetts and eventually to the vice presidency, the presidency upon Harding's death in 1923, and then election in his own right in 1924. On the one hand, he was an able politician—winning praise, for example, as the governor of Massachusetts when he refused to give in to the 1919 Boston police strike, at a time when Americans where not particularly sympathetic to labor agitation. On the other hand, he did not seem to have been particularly likeable. In comparison to Harding's relaxed and congenial demeanor, Coolidge was perceived as unpleasant and tense, leading Roosevelt's daughter Alice Roosevelt Longworth to remark, "I do wish [Coolidge] did not look as if he had been weaned on a pickle."[1] But Coolidge was also viewed as unfailingly honest and incorruptible, a quality that served him well as several scandals of the Harding administration came to light after Harding's death.

Given his rather noncharismatic approach to politics in general, it is not surprising that, as president, Coolidge threw himself into consequential, but fairly dull, fiscal issues. His driving ambition was to scale back both spending and taxation and thus reduce the national budget on all levels. Coolidge had an uncomplicated view of the economy—just as families should live within their means, so too should the federal government. For good or bad, he was not a practitioner of emerging theories that took a more strategic view of the economy, in which debts, deficits, and foreign loans could sometimes lead to long-term gains. One example of this is his reaction to the continued difficulties Allies were experiencing in war debt repayments to the United States. Some economists and government officials believed that a reduction of the Allied debt burden (although slowing America's own debt repayments) would help to stabilize the entire European political situation, including the dire effects of reparation payments in Germany. But Coolidge's response was simply, "They hired the money, didn't they? Let them pay it!"[2]

Although the movement toward fiscal economy had begun in the Harding administration, Coolidge was more energetic in his personal pursuit of this goal. His basic philosophy was that lessening the tax burden on businesses and corporations would bring prosperity to the entire nation, an approach that was to reappear again strongly some fifty years after his administration. President Ronald Reagan was also an adherent of these views and, upon moving into the White House, requested that a portrait of President Harry S Truman be taken down and replaced with one of Coolidge.

Coolidge's focus was not completely on such "supply-side" economics designed to provide tax relief for businesses and wealthy citizens. Together with Treasury Secretary Andrew Mellon, Coolidge forged and pushed through Congress a tax plan that granted relief to lower income Americans as well. And because Coolidge wanted to pay off the national debt at the same time he was lowering taxes, he also focused on decreasing government expenditures. He once proved himself the perfect advocate for federal fiscal responsibility, and further underscored his lack of charisma when he informed a group of reporters of the cost of pencils to the federal government.

Overall, the Coolidge economic agenda did appear to work. Taxes were lowered in conjunction with a reduction of the national debt. Additionally, the budget even allowed for the financing of several new programs, including a nationwide road building effort and the construction of several major federal buildings. At the time, these results seemed to provide the perfect retort to critics who had questioned the possibility of lowering taxes and paying debts concurrently. Yet despite the prosperity, there were also signs of danger. For example, unemployment was growing, the nation's natural resources were overexploited, stock speculation was rampant, and the system of buying on credit was on the increase while overall consumption was down. Although these trends were probably not triggered by administration policies, the president failed to ever acknowledge them as potentially worrisome economic symptoms that needed to be addressed.

Many of these negative developments were registering first and most detrimentally in the agricultural sector, and the question of how the federal government might help the American farmer was one of the main issues of the Coolidge administration. The president, in his typical conservative manner, refused to sanction government aid to one particular sector of the economy. He vetoed two attempts by Congress to aid farmers through federally controlled crop distribution programs, drawing a great deal of opposition for what was characterized as a shortsighted and dangerous attitude.

In the social realm, again driven by his philosophy of limited government, Coolidge provided no vision for America on social issues—never speaking out, for example, on women's or civil rights. While a supporter of Prohibition, and a true abstainer, he made no effort to enhance enforcement of the policy. In fact, the only real energy Coolidge expended in the social realm was in a negative direction by supporting and signing into law the strictest limits yet proposed on immigration. His advocacy of attempts to reduce immigration to 1890 levels (through quotas aimed at restricting eastern and southern European arrivals in particular) is one example of his heeding the growing power of socially conservative elements of American society, and contrasts sharply with Wilson's refusal to approve even more moderate restrictions.

In the foreign policy realm as well, Coolidge's record is clearly transitional. His decision to send two thousand U.S. Marines to help restore stability in Nicaragua in January 1927 is in some ways reminiscent of Roosevelt's and Wilson's activism in this part of the world. However, Coolidge's insistence that the action was taken only to secure American interests in Nicaragua and the Panama Canal presaged Franklin D. Roosevelt's noninterventionist Good Neighbor policies to follow.

Another Coolidge initiative—advocacy of the Kellogg-Briand Pact (eventually ratified in 1929)—is also indicative of an interregnum in American attitudes. The years between the two world wars were marked by an intense desire to retain peace—even to the extent of widespread (but largely unrealistic) faith in proposals designed to preclude war. The Kellogg-Briand Pact's attempt to outlaw war was, as recognized by some critics, largely meaningless but served as an effective public tonic at the time.

Although superficially perhaps the most uneventful and unexciting administration of this era, the Coolidge presidency in retrospect provides an illustrative window onto America in a key transitional time. The most important initiatives of this administration, generally focused on scaling back the federal government, represented the rejection of earlier ideas. Progressivism was significantly weakened. The old guard conservatives had regained control of the Republican Party, but with a new twist—an acceptance of an ascendant rural-based conservatism (with its hints of nativism and white supremacy) in the American populace. The hardships of the war years seemed to be a thing of the past, but long-term optimism for continued economic prosperity and freedom from global conflict was, in retrospect, hopelessly naive.

TAX RELIEF

One major war issue remaining on the domestic agenda during the Coolidge administration was the high tax rates held over from the war years. Coolidge attempted to convince Congress to reduce these rates, while at the same time working to lower the national debt. He finally succeeded in getting a policy at least close to what he wanted with the Revenue Act of 1926. Although the tax relief it brought was generally welcomed, some legislators objected to it as fiscally irresponsible and an example of favoritism toward the wealthy.

After the Great War, although the United States had moved from a debtor to a creditor nation overall, there were still high war debts to pay. As a result of war expenses, the debt of the United States had exploded from $1.3 billion in early 1917 to $26.6 billion in 1919. In 1917, laws had been passed to expand the tax base to help pay for these outlays and, by the time Coolidge took office, the debt was slowly being reduced. But Coolidge did not believe in *any* national debt and wanted to increase the paydown rate. However, he somewhat surprisingly proposed to do this in combination with lowered taxes, believing that sharp cuts in government expenditures could be dedicated to paying down the debt, without the burden being borne by American taxpayers. (He even seemed willing to make personal sacrifice in this regard, opposing expenditures for repairs to the White House roof, which was in danger of collapsing.)

Coolidge's like-minded partner in these economic plans was Secretary of the Treasury (and America's third richest man) Andrew Mellon, who had been appointed to the position by Harding and asked by Coolidge to remain in the job. Mellon's basic philosophy was to tax enough to provide sufficient revenue for vital government functions, but to lessen the burden on lower income groups as well as on business and industry. Mellon and Coolidge ascribed to the theory that the people of America were best served by freeing up businesses to invest as much as possible in the economy. As noted in what is perhaps Coolidge's most quoted comment, "the chief business of the American people is business."[3] The president explained in his 1924 speech to the National Republican Club that while proportionately higher tax rates on larger incomes are justifiable to a degree, "there is no escaping the fact that when the taxation of large incomes is excessive, they tend to disappear."[4] The reduction of tax *rates* would lead to increased prosperity and thus increases in total tax *revenue*.

The Coolidge-Mellon tax plan called for across-the-board decreases in income, corporate, and inheritance tax rates. In 1924 (as in 1921, during the Harding administration), Congress responded with some reductions but not at the levels the plan called for. The Revenue Act of 1926 was in keeping with administration preferences, with the highest income tax and inheritance tax rates reduced to 20 percent. This act also abolished open public access to every citizens' income tax information, as had been mandated two years earlier. However, the 1926 law was not a complete victory for the president, as it included a small increase on corporate incomes.

There was some criticism of the 1926 act as a representation of Coolidge's favoritism to the wealthy. This is at least somewhat unwarranted. Whether an accurate assessment or not, Coolidge did seem to genuinely believe that tax cuts for the wealthiest segments of society would trickle down to all citizens eventually. Additionally, these tax reductions were largely geared toward the lowest economic brackets. Proportionately, tax rates were decreased the most for this group, and one-third of those who had paid income tax in 1925 did not have to pay in 1926.

Other objections to Coolidge's tax policy were of greater merit. In his comments in Congress, the progressive Senator George W. Norris (R–Neb.) reasoned that while the reduction of government expenditures would help to reduce war debts, tax cuts could only slow that process, thereby adding to the interest burden. Furthermore, Norris argued that it is best to err on the side of caution. If Coolidge was correct, and the nation could enjoy both lower taxes and an increased payoff of war debts, the "worst" that could happen as a result of keeping rates relatively high is that government would have an unexpected surplus of funds.

Overall, Coolidge was able to deliver on his promises. Cuts in government expenditures in combination with tax reductions led to an increased rate of payoff on the debt, which dropped from $22.3 billion in 1923 to $16.9 billion in 1929. The ultimate impact of these policies is still controversial. While some historians assert that the reduction of tax rates to the wealthiest Americans indirectly helped to fuel the Great Depression, others believe the policies represented sound economic principles that had no connection to the later downturn.

NOTES

1. Dick Schaap, "Why We Are Laughing at Bush and Gore," *George* (July 2000): 75.

2. William Allen White, *A Puritan in Babylon* (New York: Macmillan, 1938), 324.

3. Calvin Coolidge, *Foundations of the Republic: Speeches and Addresses* (Freeport, N.Y.: Books for Libraries Press, 1968), 187.

4. Andrew W. Mellon, *Taxation: The People's Business* (New York: Macmillan, 1924), 220.

COOLIDGE—REMARKS ON TAXATION
(FEBRUARY 12, 1924)

Out of an income of about $60,000,000,000 a year the people of this country pay nearly $7,500,000,000 in taxes, which is over $68 for every inhabitant of the land. Of this amount the National Government collects about $3,200,000,000, and the State and local governments about $4,300,000,000. As a direct burden this is a stupendous sum, but when it is realized that in the course of our economic life it is greatly augmented when it reaches the consumer in the form of the high cost of living, its real significance begins to be appreciated. The national and local governments ought to be unremitting in their efforts to reduce expenditures and pay their debts. This the National Government is earnestly seeking to do. . . .

. . . In time of war finances, like all else, must yield to national defense and preservation. In time of peace finances, like all else, should minister to the general welfare. Immediately upon my taking office it was determined after conference with Secretary Mellon that the Treasury Department should study the possibility of tax reduction for the purpose of securing relief to all taxpayers of the country and emancipating business from unreasonable and hampering exactions. . . .

The proposed bill maintains the fixed policy of rates graduated in proportion to ability to pay. That policy has received almost universal sanction. It is sustained by sound arguments based on economic, social, and moral grounds. But in taxation, like everything else, it is necessary to test a theory by practical results. The first object of taxation is to secure revenue. When the taxation of large incomes is approached with that in view, the problem is to find a rate which will produce the largest returns. Experience does not show that the higher rate produces the larger revenue. Experience is all in the other way. . . .

I agree perfectly with those who wish to relieve the small taxpayer by getting the largest possible contribution from the people with large incomes. But if the rates on large incomes are so high that they disappear, the small taxpayer will be left to bear the entire burden. If, on the other hand, the rates are placed where they will produce the most revenue from large incomes, then the small tax-payer will be relieved. The experience of the Treasury Department and the opinion of the best experts place the rate which will collect most from the people of great wealth, thus giving the largest relief to people of moderate wealth, at not over 25 per cent.

A very important social and economic question is also involved in high rates. That is the result taxation has upon national development. Our progress in that direction depends upon two factors—personal ability and surplus income. An expanding prosperity requires that the largest possible amount of surplus income should be invested in productive enterprise under the direction of the best personal ability. This will not be done if the rewards of such action are very largely taken away by taxation. . . .

. . . It is entirely possible to have a first-class bill. I want the country to have the best there is. I am for it because it will reduce taxes on all classes of income. I am for it because it will encourage business. I am for it because it will decrease the cost of living. I am for it because it is economically, socially, and morally sound.

But the people of the Nation must understand that this is their fight. They alone can win it. Unless they make their wishes known to the Congress without regard to party this bill will not pass. I urge them to renewed efforts.

Mellon, Andrew W. *Taxation: The People's Business*. New York: Macmillan, 1924, 216, 219–222, 227.

SENATOR GEORGE W. NORRIS—REMARKS ON THE REVENUE ACT (FEBRUARY 2, 1926)

Everybody, of course, wants his taxes reduced. I should be glad if we could reduce everybody's taxes to a minimum and eliminate them entirely if it were possible. It is not an agreeable task to be charged with the responsibility of levying a tax upon your fellow men.

It is always burdensome, and I confess that I do not enjoy it. I hate to feel that it is my duty to vote for a high tax upon anybody or upon anything, because it is always hard and mean. Except in the case of those taxes that come from very large incomes or very large estates, it is always a burden. It is disagreeable. Everybody would like to relieve his fellow men from it if he could. But, we have the debt to pay. We have gone through the war and piled up an enormous debt. Somebody must pay it. The longer we postpone it, the more interest we will have to pay on it.

I am not afraid of a surplus. I do not think we ought to be frightened with the phantom idea that we may have in surplus of a few million dollars at the end of a fiscal year. The ordinary business man in business life who has a large debt to pay and who works year after year to pay it is delighted if he has been able by his toil and his labor to make a little more than he calculated he would make, in order to lessen the debt that some time he must pay. We can not escape this debt. Our people can not escape this burden. It is going to fall upon the shoulders of coming generations. It will be many, many years before it is paid off; and I think it is a mistake to run any risk of shaving too closely. Let the doubt always be in favor of getting too much money by taxation, as long as we have this debt to pay.

If we did not have the debt, it would be an entirely different proposition. Remember, also, Senators, that if we pay this debt now, especially if we levy a high percentage rate upon large incomes, we shall be getting a large proportion of it from those who made their money out of the war itself. Unless we do that now or soon, those who made money in that way will escape forever. I am not finding fault with anybody who made his money under the law. I am not complaining of it in any sense but, as a matter of common, ordinary justice and business, the men who made the most money on account of the difficulties that brought on the debt can not complain if we levy more heavily upon them to help pay the debt.

In addition to that, the more we pay each year the less interest we will have to pay, and it is just as hard for our people to raise the money to pay the interest as it is to raise money to pay on the principal. Every year that we postpone it, every time we defer the payment of part of our debt, we are only increasing the interest burden.

I know it is a disputed question as to how much we should pay now, how much we should set aside each year. Men will disagree on that, and we have to decide on it. I am not finding fault with that. But I am, in a very friendly spirit, finding fault with those who, with the very best of motives, are trying to see how close they can hew to the line in order not to have a surplus.

It may be if we hew too closely to the line that we shall get a deficit. No man can positively tell what will be in store for us a year from now, but it seems to me we should act as good business men would act, we should take no chance of hewing too close to the line. There is danger on the other side. There is no danger if we have a surplus, because we can take that surplus and buy bonds, cancel them, and thus eliminate not only so much of the debt but avoid the payment of interest not only for ourselves but for our children. So I will not be worried if we get too much money. I would be glad if we could. I would be glad if the expectations of those who have been making estimates were erroneous, and we would get more money than any of them have admitted we are going to get. It would be a good thing for us and would be a good thing for those to follow, and it seems to me it would be good business.

Congressional Record. 69th Congress, 1st sess., 1926. Vol. 67, 3161.

NATIONAL ORIGINS ACT

The immigration issue returned quite forcefully in the Harding and Coolidge administrations. Both presidents signed bills advancing the most restrictive immigration mechanism yet considered—nation of origin quotas that discriminated against southern and eastern Europeans and Asians. The issue was much more heated and divisive for Coolidge as it was prominent during his attempt to win election in his own right in 1924.

Although the literacy provision of 1917 represented the first major limitation to free immigration, the quota acts took restriction to a new level. While there had been some sincere arguments that the literacy provision was an unbiased measure meant to slow immigration in general, the quotas were clearly designed to keep out the more undesirable, newer wave of immigrants. The temporary quota act supported by Harding in 1921 limited yearly immigration from each European nation to 3 percent of the total immigrants from that nation residing in the United States in 1910. But the permanent 1924 legislation changed the formula to 2 percent of the totals in 1890. Since 1890 was approximately the year in which the great southern and eastern European wave had begun, the act's discriminatory effects on those groups was undeniable. Additionally, the act barred virtually all immigration of Japanese and most other Asians.

It is illustrative to view passage of the 1924 National Origins Act in light of the concurrent election year politics. Nationwide, anti-immigrant sentiment and the push for "Americanization" (i.e., rapid assimilation for immigrants already in the United States) had reached an apex. Blatant hostilities against southern and eastern European nationalities were beginning to be more freely spoken as when Representative Jasper Napoleon Tincher (R–Kan.) stated in the House of Representatives, "If you thrust open the gates the districts we have examples of here will keep increasing until finally when you get up and say 'Mr. Speaker' you will have to speak in Italian or some other language."[1]

This trend was largely coincident to the rise of the Ku Klux Klan, which had been reorganized in Atlanta in 1915. The Klan, stressing "100% Americanism" and immediate, severe immigration restrictions, was gaining prominence outside of the South and was not easily ignored by political parties or candidates. This political and social movement (which is what it amounted to at that time) was largely responsible for fostering a Democratic Party split into a conservative, rural wing largely sympathetic to Klan ideology (if not necessarily their violent practices of intimidation), and a liberal, urban faction opposed to these nativistic and prejudicial views. While the Democratic compromise nominee John W. Davis excoriated the Klan in his campaign speeches, Coolidge refused to speak out against the group and its positions. His vice presidential running mate Charles Dawes did make some anti-Klan speeches but was soon ordered by the party to stop. Thus, although initially linked to the Democratic Party, the Klan endorsed Coolidge in this election, favoring tactics such as the distribution of not-so-subtle pamphlets advocating "Kandidate Kalvin Koolidge."

Although it is difficult to assess whether it was a deliberate campaign ploy, the proquota position helped Coolidge to attract some traditionally Democratic votes. However, since he did not want to alienate more moderate Americans, Coolidge defended his position in far less extreme terms than the Klan did. As articulated in his 1923, 1924, and 1925 messages to Congress as well as in the remarks to a group of foreign-born Americans visiting the White House in 1924, Coolidge justified quotas as a way to maintain the quality of life and economic opportunities for native-born Americans as well as recent and established immigrants. Predictably, the president's softest comments, his concerns that the quotas could divide immigrant families, came one year after the election.

Louis Marshall, chairman of the American Jewish Relief Committee, attempted to convince Coolidge to veto the 1924 bill. In his letter to the president, he focused on the clearly discriminatory nature of the proposed law, stating that any attempts to portray this policy as an even-handed attempt to lower immigration in general were misguided or deliberately misleading, and outlined the potential dangers of institutionalizing prejudice.

The National Origins Act did lower immigration levels from southern and eastern Europe. However, the effects were not as dramatic as intended. Because the 1890 census was discovered to have largely failed to identify residents by nation of origin, the quotas were instead based on the 1920 census, with the result of increasing allowable numbers of immigrants. The provision of the law relating to Japanese immigration had more ominous consequences, as many historians view this act as the beginning of the decline of U.S.–Japanese relations. The quota system was renewed and in some ways made even more restrictive in the Immigration and Nationality Act of 1952 (passed over President Truman's veto) but was dismantled in 1965 during Lyndon B. Johnson's administration. Although limitations remained in effect, national quotas were largely reconfigured and made more globally equitable.

NOTE

1. Robert H. Ferrell, *The Presidency of Calvin Coolidge* (Lawrence: University Press of Kansas, 1998), 114.

COOLIDGE—REMARKS TO CONGRESS ON IMMIGRATION (1923, 1924, 1925)

(December 6, 1923) American institutions rest solely on good citizenship. They were created by people who had a background of self-government. New arrivals should be limited to our capacity to absorb them into the ranks of good citizenship. America must be kept American. For this purpose, it is necessary to continue a policy of restricted immigration. It would be well to make such immigration of a selective nature with some inspection at the source, and based either on a prior census or upon the record of naturalization. Either method would insure the admission of those with the largest capacity and best intention of becoming citizens. I am convinced that our present economic and social conditions warrant a limitation of those to be admitted. We should find additional safety in a law requiring the immediate registration of all aliens. Those who do not want to be partakers of the American spirit ought not to settle in America.

(December 3, 1924) Two very important policies have been adopted by this country which, while extending their benefits also in other directions, have been of the utmost importance to the wage earners. One of these is the protective tariff. . . . The other is a policy of more recent origin and seeks to shield our wage earners from the disastrous competition of a great influx of foreign peoples. This has been done by the restrictive immigration law. This saves the American job for the American workmen. I should like to see the administrative features of this law rendered a little more humane for the purpose of permitting those already here a greater latitude in securing admission of members of their own families. But I believe this law in principle is necessary and sound, and destined to increase greatly the public welfare. We must maintain our own economic position, we must defend our own national integrity.

(December 8, 1925) While not enough time has elapsed to afford a conclusive demonstration, such results as have been secured indicate that our immigration law is on the whole beneficial. It is undoubtedly a protection to the wage earners of the country. The situation should, however, be carefully surveyed, in order to ascertain whether it is working a needless hardship upon our own inhabitants. If it deprives them of the comfort and society of those bound to them by close family ties, such modifications should be adopted as will afford relief, always in accordance with the principle that our Government owes its first duty to our own people and that no alien, inhabitant of another country, has any legal rights whatever under our Constitution and laws. It is only through treaty, or through residence here, that such rights accrue. But we should not, however, be forgetful of the obligations of a common humanity.

While our country numbers among its best citizens many of those of foreign birth, yet those who now enter in violation of our laws by that very act thereby place themselves in a class of undesirables. If investigation reveals that any considerable number are coming here in defiance of our immigration restrictions, it will undoubtedly create the necessity for the registration of all aliens. We ought to have no prejudice against an alien because he is an alien. The standard which we apply to our inhabitants is that of manhood, not place of birth. Restrictive immigration is to a large degree for economic purposes. It is applied in order that we may not have a larger annual increment of good people within our borders than we can weave into our economic fabric in such a way as to supply their needs without undue injury to ourselves.

Israel, Fred L., ed. *The State of the Union Messages of the Presidents.* Vol. 3. New York: Chelsea House, 1967, 2651, 2663–2664, 2678–2679.

COOLIDGE—"REMARKS TO DELEGATION OF FOREIGN-BORN CITIZENS AT THE WHITE HOUSE" (OCTOBER 16, 1924)

The members of this delegation, whom I have much pleasure in receiving, are all American citizens who chance to have been born in other countries than our own. You have called upon me to testify for yourselves and the millions of others who, though not natives to our soil, are in every other respect thorough-going, loyal and devoted Americans. I am glad to welcome you, not only to this place, but to the full privileges and opportunities, and especially to the full responsibilities and duties, of American citizens. It is not very long, as history views matters, since all of us were alien to this soil. . . .

It is a truism, of course, but it is none the less a fact which we must never forget, that this continent and this American community have been blessed with an unparalleled capacity for assimilating peoples of varying races and nations. . . .

But with the passing of the day of lands so cheap as to be well-nigh free, we are coming to confront a new set of conditions. It has been found necessary to inquire whether under these new conditions we can be sure of finding employment for the diverse elements and enormous numbers of new immigrants that are offered to us. We are all agreed, whether we be Americans of the first or of the seventh generation on this soil, that it is not desirable to receive more immigrants than can reasonably be assured of bettering their condition by coming here. For the sake both of those who would come and more especially of those already here, it has been thought wise to avoid the danger of increasing our numbers too fast. It is not a reflection on any race or creed. We might not be able to support them if their numbers were too great. In such event, the first sufferers would be the most recent immigrants, unaccustomed to our life and language and industrial methods. We want to keep wages and living conditions good for everyone who is now here or who may come here.

Coolidge, Calvin. *Foundations of the Republic: Speeches and Addresses*. Freeport, N.Y.: Books for Libraries Press, 1926, 159, 162.

LOUIS MARSHALL—LETTER TO COOLIDGE ON IMMIGRATION RESTRICTIONS (MAY 22, 1924)

On behalf of many hundred thousands of citizens of the United States, both native-born and naturalized, who feel slighted by the terms of the Immigration Bill now before you for Executive action, and availing ourselves of your permission, we venture to state reasons justifying your disapproval of the measure.

. . .

The present quota law is based on the census of 1910 and fixes a rate of three per cent. That idea was fathered by the late Senator Dillingham, who had given the subject careful study as the Chairman of the Immigration Commission appointed during President Roosevelt's Administration. He proposed a rate of five per cent, but it was reduced while the bill was on its passage. The census of 1910 was chosen because that of 1920 was not then available. The idea was that the proper test was the number of foreign-born individuals of the various nationalities in the country at the time the quota was to become effective. Even that bill gave rise to great hardships. It was, however, fair, in that it did not discriminate among the foreign-born individuals of various nationalities.

The present bill, however, is avowedly discriminatory, as is apparent from the Majority and Minority Reports of the House Committee on Immigration which reported this bill. While under the present law the number of immigrants who come from Northern and Western Europe and of those who come from Southern and Eastern Europe are equal, under this bill the number of immigrants who may come from Northern and Western Europe is largely increased, even on the reduced basis of two per cent, over the number admitted from those countries under the present law; whereas those coming from Southern and Eastern Europe will not exceed one-fifth of those now admitted from that portion of Europe. . . .

This is the first time in the history of American legislation that there has been an attempt to discriminate in respect to European immigration between those who come from different parts of the continent. It is not only a differentiation as to countries of origin, but also of racial stocks and of religious beliefs. Those coming from Northern and Western Europe are supposed to be Anglo-Saxon or mythical Nordics, and to a large extent Protestant. Those coming from Southern and Eastern Europe are of different racial stocks and of a different faith. There are today in this country millions of citizens, both native-born and naturalized, descended from those racial stocks and entertaining those religious beliefs against which this bill deliberately discriminates. There is no mincing of the matter.

To add insult to injury, the effort has been made to justify this class legislation by charging that those who are sought to be excluded are inferior types and not assimilable. There is no justification in fact for such a contention. In common with all other immigrants, those who have come from the countries sought to be tabooed have been industrious and law-abiding and have made valuable contributions to our industrial, commercial and social development. They have done the hard, manual work which is indispensable to normal economic growth. Their children, educated in our public schools, are as American in their outlook as are those of the immigrants of earlier periods. Some of the intellectual leaders of the nation have sprung from this decried origin. During the World War some of these very immigrants and their children fought for the country, thousands of them waiving the exemption to which they would have been entitled. To say that they are not assimilable argues ignorance. The facts show that they adopt American standards of living and that they are permeated with the spirit of our institutions. It is said that they speak foreign languages, but in those languages they are taught to love our Government, and to a very great extent they are acquiring the use of the English language as completely as most Americans would acquire foreign languages were they to migrate to other countries.

. . .

What we regard as the danger lurking in this legislation is, that it stimulates racial, national and religious hatreds and jealousies, that it encourages one part of our population to arrogate to itself a sense of superiority, and to classify another as one of inferiority. At a time when the welfare of the human race as an entirety depends upon the creation of a brotherly spirit, the restoration of peace, harmony and unity, and the termination of past animosities engendered by the insanity and brutality of war, it should be our purpose, as a nation which has demonstrated that those of diverse racial, national and religious origins can live together and prosper as a united people, to serve as the world's conciliator. Instead of that this bill, if it becomes a law, is destined to become the very Apple of Discord.

. . .

[W]e most respectfully and earnestly submit that if this bill shall become a law it will be a positive misfortune to the country and will mark a sharp departure from those policies which have proven a blessing to mankind as well as to our beloved land.

Reznikoff, Charles, ed. *Louis Marshall, Champion of Liberty*. Philadelphia: Jewish Publication Society of America, 1957, 208–212, 214.

U.S. INTERVENTION IN NICARAGUA

Coolidge's policy toward the independent Central American nation of Nicaragua is most clearly understood as a transition between the activist Roosevelt Corollary/Dollar Diplomacy of an earlier era, and the noninterventionist Good Neighbor policy of Franklin D. Roosevelt's administration of the 1930s and 1940s. In trying to chart a course somewhere between intervention and noninterference in this nation troubled by continual political upheaval, Coolidge faced frustrating and seemingly unsolvable conditions. The decisions he made in favor of limited intervention were generally approved of, but were criticized by some who believed they represented an out-of-date and unethical American imperialism.

American intervention in Nicaragua had actually begun during the Taft administration in response to a series of civil wars. Military forces were sent to help restore order in 1909 and 1912, and a small group of Marines stayed until 1925, when a stable truce between the liberal and conservative Nicaraguan Forces appeared to have been established. In their place remained a U.S. trained constabulary led by an American military officer hired by the Nicaraguans. However, stability lasted just over three weeks. The previous president, conservative Emiliano Chamorro, began a disruption of the recently elected liberal government with a raid on a dinner party in which several guests were taken hostage. The liberal president and vice president fled, and Chamorro regained control. Almost immediately the liberals began to plan their coup against *him*. Additionally, the United States refused to recognize his legitimacy. Eventually, another former president of Nicaragua, Adolfo Díaz, was brought in as a compromise leader, but he was also opposed by various factions, including one led by the increasingly popular rebel leader Augusto Sandino. Díaz was, however, supported by the United States and in response to the threat to the Díaz administration, Coolidge ordered two thousand marines to Nicaragua in January 1927.

Coolidge was not the sort of president to actively assert himself formulating foreign policy. However, he was compelled here to consider the U.S. position in regard to unstable Latin American nations. There were several reasons why, according to Coolidge, the United States was forced to intervene on behalf of Díaz. American citizens residing in Nicaragua, as well as business investments, were potentially in danger. Additionally, instability and revolution in this region potentially threatened the vital Panama Canal. And, in fact, the United States had still not given up the idea of constructing a second canal in Nicaragua itself (the U.S. Senate ratified a treaty in 1916 that established sole rights of construction). There were also fears that the Mexican government, which backed Juan Bautista Sacasa, the conservative former vice president, as the rightful leader, would potentially play too great a role in the power struggle. Finally, the United States had, in 1923, encouraged the five Central American nations to sign a joint treaty stating that governments attained by force would not be recognized, thus arguably accepting an implicit obligation to discourage revolutionary actions.

But, by its rather defensive tone and narrow focus on the clear threats to U.S. interests, Coolidge's statement suggests that the conduct of foreign policy had indeed changed. No longer could a president attempt to justify Latin American intervention solely on the basis of a weaker nation needing U.S. protection. In constructing an argument resting on the defense of American concerns, Coolidge was foreshadowing the move to a basic policy of nonintervention except under extraordinary conditions.

However, the guarded tone of Coolidge's message was not enough for many critics who saw the situation as unwarranted meddling in the affairs of an independent nation. Some members of Congress and State Department employees felt that Coolidge greatly exaggerated the perceived threat to American interests. Many Nicaraguans also resented the continued U.S. presence. Sandino, interviewed in his mountain hideout, spoke out against the "yanqui" role and the invasion. In the domestic press, *The Nation* in particular was a constant critic of administration policy. As expressed in the editorial from July 1926 (written even before Díaz returned to power and the marines were sent back), there is no difference in kind in regard to intervention, and the United States simply had no justification for interfering in the affairs of other nations. Additionally, the sponsorship of the 1923 treaty, as well as the rejection of Chamorro because he attained the presidency via violent means, was portrayed as hypocritical since America itself gained independence only through revolution.

In 1933, the inauguration of Sacasa as president and Sandino's truce with the new government led to the final withdrawal of the marines. Although the situation became volatile again with the assassination of Sandino, the deposition of Sacasa, and the emergence of the Somoza family regime in 1934, the United States adhered to the noninterventionist Good Neighbor doctrine of the Roosevelt era and remained neutral. It was not until the 1980s, during the Reagan administration, that American involvement (albeit of a covert nature) in Nicaraguan power struggles recurred.

COOLIDGE—MESSAGE TO CONGRESS ON NICARAGUA (JANUARY 10, 1927)

While conditions in Nicaragua and the action of this government pertaining thereto have in general been made public, I think the time has arrived for me officially to inform the Congress more in detail of the events leading up to the present disturbances and conditions which seriously threaten American lives and property, endanger the stability of all Central America, and put in jeopardy the rights granted by Nicaragua to the United States for the construction of a canal.

It is well known that in 1912 the United States intervened in Nicaragua with a large force and put down a revolution, and that from that time to 1925 a legation guard of American Marines was, with the consent of the Nicaragua government, kept in Managua to protect American lives and property. In 1923 representatives of the five Central American countries, namely, Costa Rica, Guatemala, Honduras, Nicaragua, and Salvador, at the invitation of the United States, met in Washington and entered into a series of treaties.

These treaties dealt with limitation of armament, a Central American tribunal for arbitration, and the general subject of peace and amity. . . .

The United States was not a party to this treaty, but it was made in Washington under the auspices of the secretary of state, and this government has felt a moral obligation to apply its principles in order to encourage the Central American states in their efforts to prevent revolution and disorder. The treaty, it may be noted in passing, was signed on behalf of Nicaragua by Emiliano Chamorro himself, who afterwards assumed the presidency in violation thereof and thereby contributed to the creation of the present difficulty.

· · ·

Immediately following the inauguration of President Díaz, and frequently since that date, he has appealed to the United States for support, has informed this government of the aid which Mexico is giving to the revolutionists, and has stated that he is unable solely because of the aid given by Mexico to the revolutionists to protect the lives and property of American citizens and other foreigners.

· · ·

For many years numerous Americans have been living in Nicaragua, developing its industries and carrying on business. At the present time there are large investments in lumbering, mining, coffee growing, banana culture, shipping, and also in general mercantile and other collateral business. All these people and these industries have been encouraged by the Nicaraguan government. That government has at all times owed them protection, but the United States has occasionally been obliged to send naval forces for their proper protection. In the present crisis such forces are requested by the Nicaraguan government, which protests to the United States its inability to protect these interests and states that any measures which the United States deems appropriate for their protection will be satisfactory to the Nicaraguan government.

In addition to these industries now in existence, the government of Nicaragua . . . granted in perpetuity to the United States the exclusive proprietary rights necessary and convenient for the construction, operation, and maintenance of an oceanic canal. . . .

There is no question that if the revolution continues, American investments and business interests in Nicaragua will be very seriously affected, if not destroyed. . . .

... The proprietary rights of the United States in the Nicaraguan canal route, with the necessary implications growing out of it affecting the Panama Canal, together with the obligations flowing from the investments of all classes of our citizens in Nicaragua, place us in a position of peculiar responsibility. I am sure it is not the desire of the United States to intervene in the internal affairs of Nicaragua or of any other Central American republic. Nevertheless, it must be said that we have a very definite and special interest in the maintenance of order and good government in Nicaragua at the present time, and that the stability, prosperity, and independence of all Central American countries can never be a matter of indifference to us.

The United States cannot, therefore, fail to view with deep concern any serious threat to stability and constitutional government in Nicaragua tending toward anarchy and jeopardizing American interests, especially if such state of affairs is contributed to or brought about by outside influences or by any foreign power. It has always been and remains the policy of the United States in such circumstances to take the steps that may be necessary for the preservation and protection of the lives, the property, and the interest of its citizens and of this government itself. In this respect I propose to follow the path of my predecessors.

Consequently, I have deemed it my duty to use the powers committed to me to ensure the adequate protection of all American interests in Nicaragua, whether they be endangered by internal strife or by outside interference in the affairs of that republic.

Congressional Record. 69th Congress, 2nd sess., 1927. Vol. 68, 1324–1326.

THE NATION—"BIG BROTHER OR BIG BULLY" (JULY 14, 1926)

What are we up to in Nicaragua now? With the withdrawal of our marines from that republic last year, and the resumption of control by Nicaragua of its bank and railways, there appeared to be hope that the long period of interference on the part of the United States had ended. Vain expectation! When we are not interfering for the selfish advantage of big business, we seem destined to be meddling for what defenders of such a policy would doubtless call "Nicaragua's own good." We are playing either the big bully or the big brother. And a policy that permits us to play the big brother allows us also to play the big bully.

It will be recalled that the present President of Nicaragua, General Chamorro, obtained office last year by forcing out his predecessor. General Chamorro belongs to a party and a family that have long been serviceable to the commercial interest of the United States, but we have refused to recognize him because of the treaty signed in 1923 with Central American republics in which it was mutually agreed that recognition would be refused to governments set up by force. Commenting on this action in our issue of June 23 we observed that the Department of State was deserving of credit for logically standing by its announced policy in an instance where it worked against our interests. But we added: "whether the policy itself is a sound one is another matter. *The Nation* believes that the old practice of international law, by which any established government is recognized regardless of origin, is wiser and less provocative of meddling in other people's affairs."

Recent news from Nicaragua seems designed expressly to bear out the last sentence. Advices received by Nicaraguans in this country, if accurate, indicate that our charge d'affaires at Managua has been conducting what amount to a deliberate and organized attempt to drive General Chamorro out of office. A telegram from President Chamorro himself, dated June 10, says, when translated:

> The American charge d'affaires, Mr. Dennis came today to see me and notified me that he was going to undertake a campaign to enlighten the Nicaraguan people about the necessity of forcing me to retire from power, and that in case I did not retire voluntarily the United States would compel me by force, because it was going to accomplish its purpose whether I was willing or not . . . He has already had the first handbill distributed.

Another telegram says that on June 15 Mr. Dennis called a meeting at the legation of various members of the Conservative Party (that of General Chamorro) to discuss the situation and had previously made public a statement in which he said that "my Government cherishes the hope that the Nicaraguan people by a return to a constitutional form of government will make it possible for the United States Government to extend recognition to such a government and to enter into formal diplomatic relations therewith."

All this, it must be obvious, is an entirely different thing from merely refusing to recognize an existing regime because it was set up by force. It is a practical invitation to the friends of General Chamorro to desert him as they would a sinking ship—and to his opponents to overthrow him by any means at their command. When one recalls that President Cleveland sent a British ambassador packing because he indicated a preference in a pending presidential election, one realizes the extent of the breach of diplomatic etiquette and practice of which we are guilty in Nicaragua.

But the Department of State and the sponsors of the treaty of 1923 will reply that the intrigue is for "Nicaragua's own good." We don't doubt for a minute that in their opinion it is. And that's precisely the point we would make against a treaty that prevents the recognition in Central

America of a government that is set up by force. Our own republic could not have been recognized in 1776 under such a rule. To decide if a country has what Mr. Dennis piously calls "a constitutional form of government" involves a judgment upon its domestic affairs which cannot well be neutral. It is none of our business to play either the big brother or the big bully in Latin America or elsewhere. We are rapidly becoming the world's worst meddler both at home and abroad. And we won't get back to legitimate international practices until we cancel the Central American treaty of 1923.

The Nation. July 14, 1926, 25.

McNARY-HAUGEN BILL

One of the most pressing quandaries and greatest controversies of the Coolidge administration was the farm crisis. Agricultural surpluses depressed prices and profits for farmers while other economic sectors prospered for the most part during the "roaring twenties." In response, Congress passed two McNary-Haugen bills in the late 1920s, which attempted to involve the federal government in surplus distribution schemes. Coolidge vetoed both of them. While supported by some conservatives, the president's actions were strongly criticized by others including Rexford G. Tugwell, a Columbia University professor who would later become the undersecretary of agriculture in Franklin D. Roosevelt's administration.

The Great War had represented a boom period for American farmers, as foreign nations purchased large quantities of U.S. crops. But after the war, production levels remained high while demand from foreign markets tapered off. As a result, crop prices dropped. Although farmers benefitted from a protective tariff that kept the price of agricultural imports artificially high, this did not address the domestic surplus. To make matters worse, the rest of the economy was inflationary, so prices of other necessary goods were relatively expensive. Farmers simply were not making enough money to live on.

Coolidge was not blind to the problems of the farmers. However, his insistence on sometimes treating farming as just another business made him appear insensitive to their needs, and his occasional comments that Americans who could not make a living farming should find another profession certainly did not help the situation. The president did propose his own solution to the crisis. He reasoned that since production was so high, the answer lay in the distribution of goods. Again applying basic business principles, he concluded that the "middle men" (i.e., processors and distributors of farm products) were taking up too much profit, and suggested that farmers voluntarily form distributive cooperatives in order to retain a greater share of sales proceeds. No one but Coolidge appears to have thought this would have any real impact.

In a speech he made to a large crowd at an American Farm Bureau Federation convention in Chicago in December 1925, the president attempted to articulate his sympathy for the farmers, stating that "the strength and character and greatness of America has been furnished by the strength and character and greatness of its agriculture,"[1] and reminding them of his own family's farming background. But he also stressed his opposition to any government involvement in agriculture, suggesting that it would destroy the independence of American farmers. His speech was met with weak applause, and the disappointed crowd quickly dispersed.

By that time, many farmers had become supportive of the emerging notion of a governmental mechanism for surplus distribution. This plan was originated by George N. Peek, the president of the Moline Tractor Company, whose sales had dropped with the farmers' profits. The concept became known as McNary-Haugenism, after being first introduced in Congress in 1924 by Senator Charles L. McNary (R–Oreg.) and Representative Gilbert N. Haugen (R–Iowa), both from farming areas. Basically, this called for the federal government to purchase surplus goods from local and regional farming cooperatives. These goods would then be "dumped" overseas at the lower world prices. Although there would be some loss involved in this export strategy (which would be charged to the farming cooperatives through an "equalization fee") it would be offset by the resulting rise in domestic prices as the national surplus disappeared.

The U.S. Congress, in 1927 and 1928, passed two versions of the McNary-Haugen bill (differing in detail, but not in general theme) and both were vetoed by President Coolidge. In the second veto message, he clearly states his objections were based on his belief that the bill represented government price-fixing, an unjust attempt to use government resources to help a select group, and a potentially unworkable bureaucratic muddle.

Conservative Republicans were pleased with the vetoes, but many members of Congress found them maddening, although a 1928 Senate veto override attempt failed. Given his history, some accused Coolidge of simply being far too concerned with business interests and completely unsympathetic to the farmer's needs. But, to be fair, there were some rather shaky assumptions involved in the McNary-Haugen policy. First, even if the plan did result in higher prices, there was the danger that farmers would then produce even more, thus leading to a vicious cycle of overseas dumping and continued overproduction. Second, there was no guarantee that other nations (facing their own agricultural crises) would accept underpriced American goods.

Tugwell, while acknowledging the potential problems with the bill, and the fact that not even all farmers supported it, still sharply criticized

Coolidge for the veto, viewing the president's actions as shortsighted and unsophisticated. In particular, he portrayed Coolidge's views that government should play a very limited role in agriculture as out-of-step with the times. For Tugwell and other agricultural policy experts, the situation was so bad that McNary-Haugenism was worth taking a chance on.

It is impossible to assess whether McNary-Haugenism would have had an impact on the 1920s farm crisis. By the early 1930s, after the Great Depression had begun, a more activist government response was deemed necessary—one (hinted at by Tugwell) in which actual production controls were instituted through crop-yield ceilings and subsidy programs. These controls formed the basis of the 1933 Agricultural Adjustment Act and remained the core of U.S. agriculture policy until the controls began to be phased out in 1995.

NOTE

1. Calvin Coolidge, *Foundations of the Republic: Speeches and Addresses* (Freeport, N.Y.: Books for Libraries Press, 1968), 338.

COOLIDGE—McNARY–HAUGEN VETO MESSAGE
(MAY 23, 1928)

The recurring problem of surpluses in farm products has long been a subject of deep concern to the entire nation, and any economically sound, workable solution of it would command not only the approval but the profound gratitude of our people. The present measure, however, falls far short of that most desirable objective; indeed, although it purports to provide farm relief by lessening the cares of our greatest industry, it not only fails to accomplish that purpose but actually heaps even higher its burdens of political control, of distribution costs, and of foreign competition.

It embodies a formidable array of perils for agriculture which are all the more menacing because of their being obscured in a maze of ponderously futile bureaucratic paraphernalia. . . .

A detailed analysis of all of the objections to the measure would involve a document of truly formidable proportions. However, its major weaknesses and perils may be summarized under six headings:

1. *Price fixing.* This measure is as cruelly deceptive in its disguise as governmental price-fixing legislation and involves quite as unmistakably the impossible scheme of attempted governmental control of buying and selling of agricultural products through political agencies as any of the

other so-called surplus control bills. In fact, in certain respects, it is much broader and more flagrant in its scope.

. . .

These provisions would disappoint the farmer by naïvely implying that the law of supply and demand can thus be legislatively distorted in his favor. Economic history is filled with the evidences of the ghastly futility of such attempts. Fiat prices match the folly of fiat money. . . .

2. *The equalization fee*, which is the kernel of this legislation, is a sales tax upon the entire community. It is in no sense a mere contribution to be made by the producers themselves, as has been represented by supporters of the measure. It can be assessed upon the commodities in transit to the consumer and its burdens can often unmistakably be passed on to him.

. . .

Incidentally, this taxation or fee would not be for purposes of revenue in the accepted sense but would simply yield a subsidy for the special benefit of particular groups of processors and exporters. It would be a consumption or sales tax on the vital necessities of life, regulated not by the ability of the people to pay but only by the requirements and export losses of various trading intermediaries. It would be difficult indeed to conceive of a more flagrant case of the employment of all of the coercive powers of the government for the profit of a small number of specially privileged groups. . . .

3. *Widespread bureaucracy.* A bureaucratic tyranny of unprecedented proportions would be let down upon the backs of the farm industry and its distributors throughout the nation in connection with the enforcement of this measure. Thousands of contracts involving scores of different grades, quantities, and varieties of products would have to be signed by the board with the 4,400 millers, the 1,200 meat-packing plants, the 3,000 or more cotton and woolen mills, and the 2,700 canners. If this bill had been in operation in 1925, it would have involved collections upon an aggregate of over 16 billion units of wheat, corn, and cotton.

. . .

4. *Encouragement to profiteering and wasteful distribution by middlemen.* As was pointed out in the veto last year, it seems almost incredible that the farmers of this country are being offered this scheme of legislative relief in which the only persons who are guaranteed to benefit are the exporters, packers, millers, canners, spinners, and other processors. Their

profits are definitely assured. They have, in other words, no particular incentive toward careful operation, since each of them holding a contract, no matter how unscrupulous, wasteful, or inefficient his operations may have been, would be fully reimbursed for all of his losses.

. . .

5. *Stimulation of overproduction.* The bill runs counter to an economic law as well settled as the law of gravitation. Increased prices decrease consumption; they also increase production. These two conditions are the very ones that spell disaster to the whole program. . . .

6. *Aid to our foreign agricultural competitors.* This measure continues, as did its predecessor, to give substantial aid to the foreign competitors of American agriculture and industry. It continues the amazing proposal to supply foreign workers with cheaper food than those of the United States, and this at the expense of the American farm industry, thereby encouraging both the foreign peasant, whose produce is not burdened with the costs of any equalization fees, and also affording through reduced food prices the means of cutting the wage rates paid by foreign manufacturers. . . .

This is indeed an extraordinary process of economic reasoning, if such it could be called. Certainly it is a flagrant case of direct, insidious attack upon our whole agricultural and industrial strength.

By the inevitable stimulation of production the bill can only mean an increase of exportable surplus to be dumped in the world market. This in turn will bring about a constantly decreasing world price, which will soon reach so low a figure that a wholesale curtailment of production in this country with its attendant demoralization and heavy losses would be certain. Where is the advantage of dragging our farmers into such folly?

Furthermore, as the board undertakes to dump the steadily mounting surplus into foreign countries at the low-cost figures, it will come into direct conflict with the dumping and similar trade laws of many foreign lands which are interested in the maintenance of their own agricultural industries. We might, therefore, expect immediately a series of drastic, retaliatory discriminations on the part of these consumer countries. This will drive our surplus into narrower market channels and force even further price reductions, with consequent increases in the burdens of the equalization tax.

Congressional Record. 70th Congress, 1st sess., 1928. Vol. 69, 9524–9526.

REXFORD G. TUGWELL—"REFLECTIONS ON FARM RELIEF" (DECEMBER 1928)

Eight years of gradually liquidating depression have incalculably injured the nation's agricultural plant. Fertility has been depleted, equipment has run down, man-power has deteriorated. Not only farmers themselves, but all thoughtful social observers are seriously concerned that some ingenuity and some public action should be enlisted and at once. At best farming suffers needless handicaps. Back to 1913 is not good enough. For, strictly speaking, what happened between 1920 and 1928 is nothing new in our history. Indeed a more or less organized agrarian revolt is nothing new. If we were to look backward we should see that each of those phenomena we call the business cycle and which, in Europe, they call the economic rhythm, has had similar consequences for rural folks....

. . . The disadvantage of farmers is measured roughly by the fact that they lose more in depression than they gain in prosperity, and that this continues to be true, with a periodical exploitation of those engaged in this activity for the benefit of those engaged in other pursuits.

. . .

The McNary-Haugen idea was that this price disparity, recurrently so disastrous, might be traced to the economic rule that small surpluses have disproportionate effects on prices and that this situation might be relieved by the segregation of this small percentage which has such great consequences. It might then be disposed of safely in either of two ways: storage or export. Coöperative storage, assisted by government financing, might enable farmers to wait for favorable markets. At least marketing could be spread throughout the year. Dumping abroad, with proper management of import duties, could be done at any price, provided the elimination of the surplus was complete; for then domestic prices could be kept at a level which would yield a profit on the whole of any crop. This device, it was argued, would at least admit farmers to the American protective system on an equality with other industries.

. . .

All this was objected to by Mr. Coolidge as unconstitutional and as administratively impossible. There is doubt as to constitutionality, but it is only doubt; and that decision belongs to the courts. As to the complexity of administration, this is a charge which might be brought against almost any governmental device. Simplicity is desirable, but lack of it ought not to prevent the adoption of a desirable policy. Besides, the scheme, if complex, was necessarily so. It may be better to do something difficult than to do nothing at all. His real objection was a stubborn determination to do nothing. New England minds revolt against any economic proposal which is more socially oriented than Vermont shop-keeping. But the veto stood.

The scheme seemed workable enough, and administratively possible, provided only that foreign governments made no retaliatory moves to protect their own farmers, and that the surpluses in question did not grow so big, with profit insurance, as to prove unwieldy. But obviously it applied mostly to exportable (or easily stored) products; and, quite as obviously it depended upon a huge coöperative organization among farmers of which only the barest beginnings were to be discerned.

. . .

Mr. Coolidge inherited the puzzle of farmers penalized for productivity. But puzzles do not worry him. Besides he held it certain that prosperity would recur in his time to justify inaction. The obstinate persistence of the farm leaders in pointing out the remarkable duration of the depression and the certainty of its recurrence has annoyed him, but not unbearably. His last McNary-Haugen veto lacked something of aplomb; it was even sharp. But it may be doubted whether it satisfied everyone that the economics of New England shop-keeping is adequate to the solution of the difficulty.

. . .

. . . Indeed the more I study the Bill of 1928 the deeper my admiration becomes. As a piece of social legislation it surpasses anything an American Congress ever framed. The remaining troublesome consideration is its dependence on a non-existent coöperative structure. Perhaps, however, ways around this difficulty may be found.

Political Science Quarterly 43 (1929): 481–497.

KELLOGG-BRIAND PEACE PACT

Just months before leaving office, President Coolidge signed the document approving Senate ratification of the Kellogg-Briand Peace Pact. Also known as the Multilateral Peace Treaty, this attempt to outlaw war was more of an outgrowth of the American peace movement and post-war diplomatic maneuvering than a vigorous presidential initiative.

However, Coolidge did ultimately lend his support and advocacy despite widespread doubt as to the potential efficacy of such an ambitious document.

In the years following the Great War, a great many solutions were offered to avoid future wars. In America and other nations, a strong peace movement emerged, designed to foster discussion and adoption of potential antiwar polices. Although the U.S. Senate had rejected entry into the League of Nations, the idea of some sort of peaceful union of nations still had its adherents. Coolidge himself strongly supported U.S. participation in the league-sponsored Permanent Court of International Justice (or World Court), which was designed to facilitate peaceful resolutions of international disputes. Other propositions centered on arms reduction agreements, such as those set by the Washington Conference on the Limitation of Armament of the Harding administration, or more extreme proposals for total disarmament. Another idea gaining credence was the concept of simple, signed agreements promising the rejection of warfare as a means of settling conflict. A limited peace pact along these lines had been drafted by several European nations in the form of the Locarno Agreements of 1925, which were a series of pledges to seek peaceful resolutions to disagreements.

Thus, in the late 1920s, the time was ripe for a proposal to outlaw all wars. However, the Kellogg-Briand Pact had more complicated origins. Although the treaty was suggested to Foreign Minister Aristide Briand of France (who had won the Nobel Peace Prize for his role in the Locarno Agreements) by American peace activists, it was strongly suspected at the time that Briand's advocacy of a Franco-American agreement to avoid war was a ploy to keep the United States from participating in future acts of aggression against France. When the proposal was communicated to Secretary of State Frank B. Kellogg in 1927, he was infuriated at the suggestion yet was powerless to simply refuse the offer since it was gaining broad public accolades.

Kellogg decided that the only way to satisfy public demand and at the same time avoid the negative implications of a pact of nonaggression with a single nation was to transform the document into a multilateral agreement. After some initial recalcitrance from Briand, Kellogg convinced him to accept the treaty under these new terms, in which virtually all nations would be invited to sign. The agreement had two main provisions. The first worked to "renounce [war] as an instrument of national policy," and the second declared that the solution of disputes "shall never be sought except by pacific means."[1]

After making this alteration, Kellogg pursued the treaty energetically and convinced Coolidge to join in its advocacy. Coolidge had previously been only moderately supportive of such an agreement, noting in his first message to Congress that while proposals designed to limit war were promising, a lasting end to aggressions would not occur until two milestones were achieved—global economic stability and a true desire for peace in the hearts of mankind. However, his position did evolve somewhat. In the speech given in Kansas City late in 1926 (actually in support of U.S. participation in the World Court), Coolidge commented in near religious terms on the vital need for a strenuous effort to achieve world peace. And in his final message to Congress in December 1928, he stressed the value and necessity of ratification of the Kellogg-Briand Pact. According to Kellogg at least, Coolidge ultimately considered this the most important contribution of his administration.

The pact was ratified by the Senate on January 15, 1929, by a vote of eighty-five to one. The only holdout was the progressive Senator John J. Blaine (R–Wisc.). Its most ardent supporter was the staunchly isolationist Senator William E. Borah (R–Idaho), who saw this as a way for the United States to avoid any future entangling alliances. But while there was little opposition to the treaty, there was a great deal of doubt as to its effectiveness. Senator Hiram W. Johnson (R–Calif.) stated, "It's only a hope that peace on earth may come."[2] And, in his remarks during the Senate debate, Senator William C. Bruce (D–Md.), who had recently lost his bid for reelection, pointed out the complete lack of practical value in the pact. As noted by many international law experts at the time, questions such as the binding nature of the agreement, the actual definition of "war," and the propriety of actions taken in self-defense were left unanswered, probably making the treaty unenforceable. Tellingly, nine senators were absent for the vote. Even some delegates to the Conference on the Cause and Cure of War, a meeting of peace activists held in Washington, D.C., at the time of the ratification vote, expressed doubt as to its import.

Somewhat portentously, the signing ceremony at the White House two days later seemed to reflect the powerlessness of the treaty. After the proceedings were interrupted by the president's barking dog, Tiny Tim, Coolidge snapped at an aid for getting in his way, Kellogg's pen ran dry while he was signing the document, and a heavy inkwell that was subsequently passed to him was fumbled. True to his nickname, "Silent Cal" Coolidge made no public comment upon signing.

Despite (or perhaps because of) its weaknesses, sixty nations ultimately agreed to the terms of this treaty, and Kellogg received the Nobel Peace Prize for his part in it. Additionally, the American people welcomed its passage. After the shock of the Great War, it is understandable that they allowed themselves the luxury of this optimism. Although the events of the 1930s leading up to the previously unthinkable World War II highlight the irrelevance of the pact, it remains a symbolic vestige of the last remaining days and years of this more innocent time.

NOTES

1. "Full Text of the Kellogg Treaty Renouncing War," *New York Times*, January 16, 1929, 2.
2. "Senate Ratifies Anti-War Pact," *New York Times*, January 16, 1929, 1.

COOLIDGE—ARMISTICE DAY ADDRESS
(NOVEMBER 11, 1926)

It is often said that we profited from the World War. We did not profit from it, but lost from it in common with all countries engaged in it. Some individuals made gains, but the nation suffered great losses. . . .

In time this damage can be repaired, but there are irreparable losses which will go on forever. We see them in the vacant home, in the orphaned children, in the widowed women, in the bereaved parents. To the thousands of the youth who are gone forever must be added other thousands of maimed and disabled. It is these things that bring to us more emphatically than anything else the bitterness, the suffering, and the devastation of armed conflict.

It is not only because of these enormous losses suffered alike by ourselves and the rest of the world that we desire peace, but because we look to the arts of peace rather than war as the means by which mankind will finally develop its greatest spiritual power. We know that discipline comes only from effort and sacrifice. We know that character can result only from toil and suffering. We recognize the courage, the loyalty, and the devotion that are displayed in war, and we realize that we must hold many things more precious than life itself.

> 'Tis man's perdition to be safe
> When for the truth he ought to die.

But it can not be that the final development of all these fine qualities is dependent upon slaughter and carnage and death. There must be a better, purer, process within the realm of peace where humanity can discipline itself, develop its courage, replenish its faith, and perfect its character. In the true service of that ideal, which is even more difficult to maintain than our present standards, it can not be that there would be any lack of opportunity for the revelation of the highest form of spiritual life.

American Journal of International Law (Supplement: Official Documents) 21 (1926): 16–17.

COOLIDGE—REMARKS TO CONGRESS ON THE KELLOGG-BRIAND PACT (DECEMBER 4, 1928)

One of the most important treaties ever laid before the Senate of the United States will be that which the 15 nations recently signed at Paris, and to which 44 other nations have declared their intention to adhere, renouncing war as a national policy and agreeing to resort only to peaceful means for the adjustment of international differences. It is the most solemn declaration against war, the most positive adherence to peace, that it is possible for sovereign nations to make. It does not supersede our inalienable sovereign rights and duty of national defense or undertake to commit us before the event to any mode of action which the Congress might decide to be wise if ever the treaty should be broken. But it is a new standard in the world around which can rally the informed and enlightened opinion of nations to prevent their governments from being forced into hostile action by the temporary outbreak of international animosities. The observance of this covenant, so simple and so straightforward, promises more for the peace of the world than any other agreement ever negotiated among the nations.

Israel, Fred L., ed. *The State of the Union Messages of the Presidents.* Vol. 3. New York: Chelsea House, 1967, 2730–2731.

SENATOR WILLIAM C. BRUCE—REMARKS ON THE KELLOGG-BRIAND PACT (DECEMBER 15, 1928)

If the face of grim-visaged war ever relaxes into a smile, it is, I am sure, when he reads some empty, grandiose declaration as the Kellogg peace pact. As I see it, it is only in the great number of its signatories that it differs from the many treaties in which His Christian Majesty, His Most Catholic Majesty, or some other royal potentate has, in the past, plighted his solemn troth that he would never, so long as water ran or grass grew, wage war on some country with which his own country had lately been at war, and was soon to be at war again. To show how untrustworthy such engagements have ever been, we need go no further back than a few years ago, when one of the most powerful and enlightened countries on the globe—Germany—did not scruple, despite its explicit treaty obligation to respect the neutrality of Belgium, to open up with fire and sword, a pathway to France, across the violated soil of the former country. Then, as in a vast number of other similar instances, when a puissant and aggressive nation has found itself restrained by nothing stronger than treaty covenants from gratifying its lusts, the pact that was supposed to exempt Belgium from invasion was derisively tossed aside by Germany as a mere "scrap of paper."

If there is anything with which it would seem that the public conscience of the people of the United States should be sated, it is foolscap guarantees of peace between them and other nations. The benevolent instincts of the late William Jennings Bryan, when Secretary of State, fairly revelled in things of this sort, as we all know. Just as he fondly imagined that all that was necessary to keep men from drinking was to pass a law forbidding them to drink, so he appears to have thought that all that was necessary to keep nations from fighting was to induce them to enter into a little conciliation treaty with each other. . . .

The Kellogg peace pact contains no provisions designed to give practical effect to its condemnation of recourse to war for the solution of international controversies, its renunciation of war as an instrument of national policy, and its abjuration of all settlement or solution of international disputes or conflicts except by pacific means. It creates no court, arbitral commission, or conciliation agency. It contains no sanctions. It suggests no means by which its pacific intentions can be made good. It is a mere brutum fulmen, a stab in the air, a futile gesture, one of those things that begin and end in smooth words. . . .

A covenant renouncing war as an instrument of national policy may not be a bad thing but a covenant between the parties to the Kellogg pact reducing, to some reasonable extent, instruments of war, such as ships, warplanes, rifles, ordnance, caterpillar tanks, and the like, would be a far better thing. The only way really to renounce war is to renounce the instruments of war. There is nothing, however, to evidence the fact that national disarmament is keeping pace with the millennial yearning for unweaponed peace, of which the Kellogg pact is the most grandiloquent expression. On the contrary, all the unceasing palaver that has gone on about national disarmament since the end of the World War has accomplished practically nothing. . . .

I reach the conclusion, therefore, that as a direct, immediate agency for the repression of war the Kellogg pact has no practical value whatever. It is, as a weapon for such a purpose, imbelle telum sine ictu—that is to say, roughly a weapon without a punch. Moreover, all such sanctionless resolves are open to the objection that they tend to foster the idea that peace is attainable by merely willing it, or by simply donning white robes and repeating over and over again in plaintive accents, "Peace! Peace! Peace!" Such an idea, if honestly carried to its logical consequences, could have no result except that of giving additional point to the old saying that it makes no difference to the wolf how many the sheep are. . . .

When Thales once said that death and life were the same, some one asked, "Why, then, do you not kill yourself?" "Because," said Thales, "it is all one." Convinced that many thousands of kindly, worthy men and women in the United States earnestly wish for the ratification of the Kellogg peace pact, but that it will never prevent a single war, I feel that it is really all one whether I vote in favor of its ratification or not. However, it seems to me that the joint participation in it of the United States and the other great civilized powers of the earth might, in at least some appreciable degree, tend to hasten the entry of the United States into the World Court and the League of Nations: and I shall, therefore, under the determining influence of this thought, vote in favor of ratifying the mighty, multilateral Kellogg peace pact, which may the prayers of the pious induce heaven to prosper far beyond my present expectations!

Congressional Record. 70th Congress, 2nd sess., 1928. Vol. 70, 678–681.

RECOMMENDED READINGS

Coolidge, Calvin. *Foundations of the Republic: Speeches and Addresses.* Freeport, N.Y.: Books for Libraries Press, 1968.

Ferrell, Robert H. *The Presidency of Calvin Coolidge.* Lawrence: University Press of Kansas, 1998.

Fite, Gilbert C. *George N. Peek and the Fight for Farm Parity.* Norman: University of Oklahoma Press, 1954.

Haynes, John Earl, ed. *Calvin Coolidge and the Coolidge Era.* Washington, D.C.: Library of Congress, 1998.

Johnson, Robert David. *The Peace Progressives and American Foreign Relations, 1913–1935.* Cambridge: Harvard University Press, 1995.

Kamman, William. *A Search for Stability: United States Diplomacy toward Nicaragua 1925–1933.* South Bend, Ind.: University of Notre Dame Press, 1968.

Macaulay, Neill. *The Sandino Affair.* 2nd ed. Durham: Duke University Press, 1985.

Silver, Thomas B. *Coolidge and the Historians.* Durham: Carolina Academic Press, 1982.

Sobel, Robert. *Coolidge: An American Enigma.* Washington, D.C.: Regnery Publishing, 1998.

White, William Allen. *A Puritan in Babylon.* New York: Macmillan, 1938.

BIBLIOGRAPHY

Allen, Robert L. *Reluctant Reformers: Racism and Social Reform Movements in the United States*. Garden City, N.Y.: Doubleday, 1975.

American Memory, Library of Congress. "American Leaders Speak: Recordings from World War I and the 1920 Election." http://memory.loc.gov/ammem/nfhome.html (accessed 27 October 2000).

Barbeau, Arthur E., and Henri Florette. *The Unknown Soldiers: Black American Troops in World War I*. Philadelphia: Temple University Press, 1974.

Boller, Paul, Jr. *Presidential Campaigns*. New York: Oxford University Press, 1984.

Burton, David Henry. *The Learned Presidency: Theodore Roosevelt, William Howard Taft, Woodrow Wilson*. Rutherford, N.J.: Farleigh Dickinson University Press, 1988.

Chambers, John Whiteclay, II. *To Raise an Army: The Draft Comes to Modern America*. New York: Free Press, 1987.

Coletta, Paolo E. *William Jennings Bryan*. 3 vols. Lincoln: University of Nebraska Press, 1964–1969.

Croly, Herbert. *The Promise of American Life*. New York: DaCapo, 1914.

Diner, Steven J. *A Very Different Age: Americans of the Progressive Era*. New York: Hill and Wang, 1998.

Dos Passos, John. *Three Soldiers*. New York: Doran, 1921.

Douglas, Ann. *Terrible Honesty: Mongrel Manhattan in the 1920s*. New York: Farrar, Straus and Giroux, 1995.

Eksteins, Modris. *Rites of Spring: The Great War and the Birth of the Modern Age*. New York: Houghton Mifflin, 1989.

Fass, Paula. *The Damned and the Beautiful: American Youth in the 1920s*. New York: Oxford University Press, 1977.

Filene, Peter. "An Obituary for 'The Progressive Movement.' " *American Quarterly* 22 (1970): 20–34.

Fussell, Paul. *The Great War and Modern Memory*. New York: Oxford University Press, 1975.

Gould, Lewis L. *The Progressive Era*. Syracuse, N.Y.: Syracuse University Press, 1974.

Grantham, Dewey. *Southern Progressivism: The Reconciliation of Progress and Tradition*. Knoxville: University of Tennessee Press, 1983.

Handlin, Oscar. *The Uprooted: The Epic Story of the Great Migrations That Made the American People*. New York: Little, Brown, 1951.

Harries, Meirion, and Sue Harries. *The End of Innocence: America at War, 1917–1918*. New York: Random House, 1997.

Higham, John. *Strangers in the Land: Patterns of American Nativism, 1860–1925*. 2nd ed. New Brunswick, N.J.: Rutgers University Press, 1990.

Hofstadter, Richard. *The Age of Reform*. New York: Knopf, 1972.

Huthmacher, J. Joseph. "Urban Liberalism and the Age of Reform." *Mississippi Valley Historical Review* 49 (1962): 231–241.

Influenza, 1918 (video recording). The American Experience Series, 1998.

Kennedy, David M. *Over Here: The First World War and American Society*. New York: Oxford University Press, 1980.

Kobler, John. *Ardent Spirits: The Rise and Fall of Prohibition*. New York: Putnam, 1973.

Kolko, Gabriel. *The Triumph of Conservatism: A Reinterpretation of American History, 1900–1916*. New York: The Free Press, 1990.

Kraditor, Aileen S. *The Ideas of the Woman Suffrage Movement, 1890–1920*. New York: Norton, 1981.

Kyvig, David E. "Women against Prohibition." *American Quarterly* 28 (1976): 465–482.

La Follette, Robert M. *A Personal Narrative of Political Experiences*. Madison, Wisc.: La Follette, 1911.

Leuchtenberg, William E. "Progressivism and Imperialism: The Progressive Movement and American Foreign Policy, 1898–1916." *Mississippi Valley Historical Review* 39 (1952): 483–504.

Lewis, Sinclair. *Main Street*. New York: The Modern Library, 1999.

Link, Arthur, and Richard L. McCormick. *Progressivism*. Arlington Heights, Ill.: Harlan Davidson, 1983.

Marks, Carole. *Farewell—We're Good and Gone: The Great Black Migration*. Bloomington: Indiana University Press, 1989.

Milkis, Sidney M., and Jerome M. Mileur, eds. *Progressivism and the New Democracy*. Amherst: University of Massachusetts Press, 1999.

Ogren, Kathy J. *The Jazz Revolution: Twenties America and the Meaning of Jazz*. New York: Oxford University Press, 1989.

Porter, Glenn. *The Rise of Big Business, 1860–1920*. 2nd ed. Arlington Heights, Ill.: Harlan Davidson, 1992.

Rothman, Sheila. *Women's Proper Place: A History of Changing Ideals and Practices, 1870 to the Present*. New York: Basic Books, 1978.

Sanders, Francine. "The Changing Nature of Progressive Reform Coalitions in the United States: An Analysis of the Seventeenth and Eighteenth Amendments in the House of Representatives." *Southeastern Political Review* 24 (1996): 469–484.

Schneider, Dorothy, and Carl Schneider. *Into the Breach: American Women Overseas in World War I.* New York: Viking Penguin, 1991.

Sinclair, Upton. *The Jungle.* New York: New American Library, 1906.

Skocpol, Theda. *Protecting Soldiers and Mothers.* Cambridge: Belknap Press of Harvard University Press, 1992.

Stallings, Laurence, and Maxwell Anderson. "What Price Glory." *Three American Plays.* New York: Harcourt Brace, 1926.

Sullivan, Mark. *Our Times, 1900–1925.* 6 vols. New York: Scribner's, 1939.

Tentler, Leslie Woodcock. *Wage Earning Women: Industrial Work and Family Life in the United States, 1900–1930.* New York: Oxford University Press, 1979.

Terraine, John. *White Heat: The New Warfare 1914–1918.* London: Sidgwick & Jackson, 1982.

Timberlake, James H. *Prohibition and the Progressive Movement, 1900–1920.* New York: Atheneum, 1970.

Toland, John. *No Man's Land: 1918, The Last Year of the Great War.* Garden City, N.Y.: Doubleday, 1980.

Vincent Voice Library. "U.S. Presidents of the Twentieth Century." http://www.lib.msu.edu/vincent/presidents/index.htm (accessed on 27 September 2000).

The White House. "The Presidents of the United States." http://www.whitehouse.gov/president/ (accessed on 2 April 2001).

Woodward, C. Vann. *The Strange Career of Jim Crow.* New York: Oxford University Press, 1974.

———. *Tom Watson, Agrarian Rebel.* New York: Oxford University Press, 1963.

INDEX

About the Author

FRANCINE SANDERS ROMERO is Assistant Professor of Public Administration at the University of Texas at San Antonio. Her main research agenda involves the politics of policy making. In addition to a scholarly interest in the Progressive Era, her work has focused on the impact of institutional level and structure on civil rights and land use policy outputs.